"This compendium puts Host Leadership at the forefront of leadership development approaches, where it deservedly belongs. More than a collection of well-crafted papers from a diverse global cadre, this Field Book represents a solid record of phronesis – wisdom gathered from practice. A wonderful addition to McKergow and Bailey's excellent introduction of *Host* that can help you effectively embody and apply new skills as a host leader."

Paul R. Scheele, PhD. in Leadership & Change, CEO, Scheele Learning Systems, co-founder, Learning Strategies Corporation

"Accomplishes what we all want – real life examples: a compilation of experiences, developments, learnings, applications and further enquiry into Host Leadership around the world. The gentle art of hosting is one of the only tools you will need in becoming a collaborative and successful human being."

Andrew Paine, Learning & Development, Lush Cosmetics

"Mark and Helen have spent years diligently documenting and understanding the key leadership capacities needed to host in the world. Whether it is working in management or leadership, facilitating meetings, or organizing to improve our communities, the six roles they have identified are crystal clear distillations of a key leadership practice suited for our times. This book takes that knowledge to the field with stories and insights from all over to inspire and encourage your own practice of Host Leadership. Take it on your journey with you. It may just be the map you need."

Chris Corrigan, global steward, Art of Hosting community of practice

"Bringing people together is important, and doing it well makes all the difference. In this wonderfully varied book you will find all kinds of ways to put in place the key principles of hosting that will help you effectively and quickly build cooperation, trust and results."

Dr Ivan Misner, Founder of BNI and NY Times Bestselling Author

"Host Leadership is inspiring metaphor. Like all generalizations, it becomes useful only insofar as one's knowledge of the particulars will take you. Because this book so thoroughly fills in the particulars, it will take you a long way, indeed."

Stephen Josephs, Ed.D. Santa Barbara, CA, USA

"A sharing platter of insights, stories and wisdom, crammed with guidance and experience and a vital companion to anyone in a leadership role. I thoroughly recommend it!"

Dr Andrew Bastawrous, Founder & CEO Peek Vision, Associate Professor in International Eye Health

"A tremendous and inspiring resource for anyone involved in leadership, coaching, or change. The Field Book is a veritable smorgasbord of practical ideas for working with others in organisations – whether they be multinational companies, small family firms, charities or community projects. This book proves the worth of Host Leadership as a practical and relevant tool in our VUCA world."

Mike Brent, Member of Faculty & Professor of Practice at Ashridge Executive Education @Hult International Business School, co-author of the Leader's Guide to Influence and the Leader's Guide to Coaching (FT Publishing)

"A brilliant gem of a book! Perfect to inspire and engage readers into the art and practice of Host Leadership. Whether you're a beginner or advanced, there are wonderful stories of ways of engaging people, stimulating curiosity and giving lots of fascinating ideas for us to play with. The stories and ideas range from the hard-hitting practical to the deeply human."

Professor Alex Steele, Director, Improwise

"A true testament to the power of hosting – a movement that became a meeting that became a manual. Host Leadership comes of age with game-changing insights from community activation to agile management and tools you can apply tomorrow to unlock resourcefulness."

Paul Wicks, TED Fellow and CEO, Wicks Digital Health

The Host Leadership Field Book

Building engagement for performance and results

Edited by Mark McKergow PhD and Pierluigi Pugliese

Foreword by Helen Bailey

First published in Great Britain in 2019 by
Solutions Books
20 Atholl Crescent
Edinburgh
EH3 8HQ
Scotland
United Kingdom

No part of this publication may be reproduced, stored in a retrieval system, or transmitted in any form, or by any means, electronic, mechanical, photocopying, recording, or otherwise, without the written permission of the publisher

Copyright © Mark McKergow and Pierluigi Pugliese 2019, shared with the chapter authors

The moral right of the contributors to be identified as the authors of this work has been asserted in accordance with the Copyright, Designs and Patents Act, 1988

Rights enquiries should be addressed to Solutions Books via info@sfwork.com or by post to the address above.

ISBN 978-0-9933463-3-0

Cover design by Cathi Stevenson
Design, typesetting and production by The Choir Press, Gloucester

Contents

Foreword by Helen Bailey, co-author of *Host* — viii
Acknowledgements — x

1. Introducing the Host Leadership Field Book
   Mark McKergow and Pierluigi Pugliese — 1

Part One: Host Leadership in action

2. Co-creating housing strategies: Hosting five families with housing challenges   *Bjørn Z Ekelund, Ellen S Andvig and Lars U Kobro (Norway)* — 11
3. Anyone for dinner? Celebrating your goals with Host Leadership *Maria Serafim (Australia)* — 21
4. 'Host' as an attitude in rural development management *Petra Wähning (Germany)* — 28
5. Courage and humility: A Maasai view of Host Leadership *Emmanuel Mankura (Kenya)* — 34
6. Host Leadership in outdoor, bush, wilderness, and adventure therapy *Stephan Natynczuk (UK)* — 42
7. Apprenticing students into Host Leadership in global virtual teams *Rachel Lindner (Germany)* — 53
8. How Host Leadership handles conflicts *Sieds Rienks and Leo Blokland (Netherlands)* — 64
9. Host Leadership as a basis for leadership in a hybrid organisation: Roskilde Festival *Jonas Hedegaard and Hans Christian Nielsen (Denmark)* — 74

Part Two: Host Leadership in Agile settings

10. How to host a successful stand-up meeting
    Rod Sherwin (Australia) — 83

11. Host your team in a relationship retro
    Olga Kiss and Gabriella Peuker (Hungary) — 97

12. Creating a self sustaining community with rotating hosts in a high stakes situation   *Michael de la Maza (USA)* — 103

13. The trainer as a host leader   *Pierluigi Pugliese and Markus Reinhold (Germany)* — 107

14. Can it be that simple?   *Géry Derbier (France)* — 113

Part Three: Host Leadership in organisational change

15. Hosting stakeholders for engagement in generative change   *Gervase Bushe (Canada)* — 121

16. Hosting company-wide process improvements
    Jessika Jake (USA) — 128

17. Helping engagement with messy experience: Organisational transformation at Assimoco Group
    Gian Carlo Manzoni (Italy) — 132

Part Four: Introducing Host Leadership in organisations

18. Attracting people to the host metaphor
    Veronika Kotrba and Ralph Miarka (Austria) — 141

19. Introducing Host Leadership to your organisation
    The Host Leadership Gathering Collective — 145

20. Pick your poster: Getting started on a learning journey with Host Leadership   *Leah Davcheva (Bulgaria)* — 150

21. Hosting new beginnings: Bringing together a 'cellular company'   *Paul Hookham (UK)* — 168

Part Five: Developing as a host leader

22. Hearing what is being called for: What's next in your team, organisation and life?
    Mark McKergow (UK)   183

23. Shapeshifting, beaming and the chameleon shuffle
    Rolf F Katzenberger (Germany)   189

24. The role of guests/followers: Risk and permission
    Roddy Millar (UK)   200

25. Coaching with the user's guide to the future
    Peter Röhrig and Mark McKergow (Germany/UK)   205

26. The elegant art of noticing: Utilising what happens to improve the quality of interaction   *Wim Sucaet (Belgium)*   212

27. Introducing the Inviter
    Veronika Kotrba and Ralph Miarka (Austria)   219

Part Six: Next steps for Host Leadership

28. 'Its simplicity belies its depth': Picking up where we left off and deepening into the essence of host   *Helen Bailey (UK)*   225

29. Combining Host Leadership and coaching: Towards a new 'Agile humanware'   *Laurent Sarrazin (France)*   236

30. Why were you born? *Martin Rutte (Canada)*   252

Index   256

Foreword by Helen Bailey

'Be our guest'

It is my pleasure and privilege to write the foreword to this Host Leadership Field Book. Huge thanks to Pierluigi Pugliese whose idea for this book was seeded at the 2019 Host Leadership Gathering. From that original idea, Mark McKergow (my co-author of *Host: Six new roles of engagement*) and Pierluigi have done a superb job in hosting this book into being.

And hosting it into being is exactly what they have done. The book you have in your hands is a wonderful example of hosting in action: Pierluigi had a sense of something being called for from the 2019 Host Leadership Gathering. He initiated the idea for a Field Book and invited people to get involved, created a space where people stepped forward with their contributions and connected on ideas *and* co-participated. It seems to me that throughout the process Mark acted as gatekeeper for the contributions, helping shape them into this superb collection.

The power of hosting is further illustrated for me in the fact that the contributions have not only come from people who attended the Gathering. The invitation also went out to the whole Host Leadership community and a great response was received – including from me as I wasn't able to be at the gathering this year! So there must have something attractive in the invitation.

There is such joy in my heart as I read the contributions and contemplate the threshold they represent. These chapters are literally from around the world: from five continents (if I include reference to work in Asia from Emmanuel Mankura our African contributor in chapter 5!). Furthermore, the range of applications and sectors is heart-warming: Education, Housing, IT/Agile, Global Virtual Teams, Music Festival, Rural Development, Project Management, Trainers, Coaches, Consultants, Organisational Development and Start-ups.

The geographical reach *and* the broad range of applications truly reflects the versatility and flexibility of the host metaphor as well as the wide-ranging appeal of a new approach to leadership. This book literally illustrates what is happening in the field and how the ideas are spreading. The full title of the original book authored by Mark McKergow and me is: *Host: Six new roles of engagement for teams, organisations, communities and movements* and I sense we are on the threshold of our community becoming a movement. It is thanks to all the contributors for sharing how they are moving out with the ideas of Host.

I'm also mindful of all the people who have been touched by the book and the ideas through all the work represented here.

Pausing here and taking a step back makes me think about the other part of the host relationship: the guests. Reading and reflecting on the chapters to write this Foreword made me think of myself as a guest, being hosted by the metaphor and each contributor.

I invite you to do the same as you read. As we do that, we can be open to what we might hear or learn, be open to what calls to us. There are always new possibilities as I yet again experienced in engaging with the ideas presented here. Even though I am very familiar with the metaphor and regularly share the ideas with others, it always amazes me that more emerges. The richness of the metaphor invites us to continue exploring its many layers.

We are all both hosts and guests. We know about good hosting and we know about being good guests. From our own experiences, we know what works for us as guests, what encourages and supports us to step forward and bring our gifts. We are also aware of the environment that does exactly the opposite. One of the things I'm passionate about is the need to bring about a shift from a focus on what I want as a leader to what they might want from me as a leader and being involved in what we're creating together. In my experience this paradigm shift is transformational. And it is hard to do; it's hard to really put oneself in another's shoes and consider what they might want, from their perspective rather than from my own perspective.

I believe there is something offered by Host, in seeing the other as 'guests', that opens a doorway into the paradigm shift that is so needed in our world. Thinking first about the other. Putting others' needs first.

> "Guests are carrying precious gifts with them, which they are eager to reveal to a receptive host"
>
> Henri Nouwen

Imagine the possibilities inherent in a world where hosting is the norm? How might it be as a guest in such a world? Imagine what might open up and how different things might be.

Helen Bailey
Cartmel, Cumbria, United Kingdom
October 2019

Acknowledgements

This book came into being thanks to the encouragement of Pierluigi Pugliese and his team at Connexxo GmbH, who not only organised our 2019 Host Leadership gathering in Oberschleissheim, Germany but also proposed the idea of making the production of a Field Book the central purpose of the event. Pierluigi and his colleagues Cecilia Maria Zannini and Katrin Seger organised the event and kept things moving when it mattered. The Open Space day supporting the initial writings for the book was hosted by Cecilia Maria Zannini.

The participants in the Open Space day all contributed in one way or another to the work presented here. Some of them went on to be chapter authors, and all of them deserve a mention and a round of applause for coming and playing their part: Fabio Asnicar, Dario Campagna, Leah Davcheva, Bjørn Z Ekelund, Dave Hogan, Rolf F Katzenberger, Jessika Jake, Olga Kiss, Veronika Kotrba, Claudia Luca, Jannie Lund-Nielsen, Mark McKergow, Ralph Miarka, Nicola Moretto, Dave Nicolette, Gabriella Peuker, Bruna Teresa Pietracci, Pierluigi Pugliese, Markus Reinhold, Katrin Seger, Luca Sturaro, Athena Valdovinos and Cecilia Maria Zannini.

After the event other people got in touch to offer chapters. Thank you to everyone! You will see all the authors' names in the text.

Mark McKergow would like to thank Jenny Clarke, always his first and sternest editor, for her support over nearly thirty years to togetherness in work and life. Thanks also to Helen Bailey, who provided not only a chapter but also the Foreword, for her participation in the joint journey of Host Leadership from concept to model to book to international movement. Thanks as always to Miles Bailey and his team at The Choir Press for their usual immaculate work in preparing the book for publication.

1
Introducing the Host Leadership Field Book

Mark McKergow and Pierluigi Pugliese

The publication of the book *Host: Six new roles of engagement for teams, organisations, communities and movements* (McKergow & Bailey, 2014) has led to a growing community engaging in practising and exploring Host Leadership. Gatherings in London (2016) and Paris (2018) helped to develop links and connections within this community. When plans for the next gathering in Oberschleissheim near Munich, Germany began to emerge, Pierluigi Pugliese and his team at Connexxo GmbH proposed that the purpose of the gathering should be to write a Field Book: a compilation of experiences, developments, learnings and applications of Host Leadership around the world.

The gathering itself comprised three days: an introductory workshop led by Pierluigi, a conference day with workshops and presentations, and finally an Open Space day to start writing the Field Book. Pierluigi was keen to adapt 'mob programming' methods from the Agile world into 'mob writing'; many different conversations were convened and work commenced! We are delighted to say that eleven of the chapters here result directly from work commenced on that day.

What we were not really prepared for was the response from people who could not, for one reason or another, join us in Germany. We received proposals, ideas and even draft chapters from around the world, many of which have subsequently been developed into full chapters for this book. The resulting collection is 30 chapters of international experience and inspiration including contributors from Australia, the Pacific shores of Canada, the Great Lakes region of Africa, Bulgaria, the German alps and Scandinavia. The book has been produced to preserve something of the original voices of the authors, so you may find different ways of writing and expressing ideas here – it's all part of the worldwide movement of Host Leadership.

The settings described in the book are equally diverse. We have contributions from organisational leadership, education, social services, agile project management, coaching, support groups, virtual teams and community leadership. There are sections on how to introduce Host Leadership into organisations and how to develop yourself and your colleagues and clients as host leaders. There are also some provocative thoughts about where the Host Leadership movement might develop in the years to come.

Mark McKergow and Helen Bailey's original book *Host* presented for the first time their models of six roles and four positions for a host leader. While their book is not the first to look at hosting as a key aspect of being with people, it was the first to explore in depth and in detail, through history and in different cultures, what great hosts actually do, and how this can transfer directly into leading. The metaphor of a host is instantly apparent to almost everyone. These roles and positions add a wealth of detail and possibility. It's worth briefly outlining the roles and positions here, as many of the following chapters draw on and expand them in different contexts.

Step forward or step back?

The key question for leaders: are you going to step forward or step back next? Both of these moves, and combining them into a dance, are at the heart of Host Leadership. Are you going to step forward to make something happen, or step back and allow others space and time to respond and make their own contributions?

Six roles for a host leader

These six roles are different ways for a host leader to step forward when they need to. They are ways to bring people together in a useful fashion, to create engagement which in turn leads to performance and results.

Initiator

We rarely initiate entirely on our own, from nothing or out of thin air. There is usually a call to action of some kind. This may take the form of an interest, dissatisfaction, a passion, a rage, or just wanting to see something done better or differently; it may be big, for example, ending child exploitation, or it may be smaller, for example, organising the team's documents so people can find what they need more quickly. Whatever, leaders step forward and make the first move.

Inviter

Thinking invitationally is at the heart of Host Leadership. When we invite, and people accept, they show up being involved, open, engaged, part of the process. When we invite, and people don't accept, well, that's a message that what we're offering isn't exactly what is wanted. Thinking invitationally is about reaching out and engaging with those around us in a way which invites – rather than insists – that they join us in working on some project, purpose or endeavour. It's about seeing the participation of others as a valuable gift, rather than the result of a contract of employment.

Space Creator

The role of host involves creating a suitable space – physical and interactional/psychological – for events to emerge and unfold. Much of the new literature on leadership speaks of the importance of the space and of allowing and nurturing emergence within the space. The host plays a vital role upfront in deciding on the space and how it is to be decorated, laid out and used. This is another example of the flexibility of the host role – one minute making brave and influential decisions and the next clearing up a spilled drink to keep the space refreshed and useful.

Gatekeeper

A host leader knows the importance (and the creative possibilities) of defining boundaries. A boundary can serve the host header well by making clear what expectations and norms apply. In the same way as a host can have a "leave your shoes in the hall" norm, the host leader will take care to choose boundaries that can help people understand where they are and what they are committing to do in a certain place or role.

Connector

Host leaders build connections between people, link people and ideas AND know when to leave them to get on with it. The connector joins people together and creates the possibility of something emerging. If we've initiated something, invited people and created a space, we clearly want to create something that wouldn't happen without people getting together. As connectors, we understand that, having brought people together, at some point we need to get out of the way, let the magic work and allow possibilities to emerge.

Co-participator

Co-participators initiate, provide AND join in along with everyone else. It is no surprise: for example, when we are invited for dinner, we expect the host not to only serve us with food, but eat the same food with us. Not only that: hosting etiquette the world over demands that the host serve their guests first. In hosting terms, this is a clear expectation. In leadership terms, it's not so clear. When the news is full of stories about bank CEOs who appear to have eaten heartily in terms of massive bonuses, we might think that the ancient values of relationship and hospitality have well and truly been abandoned.

Four positions for a host leader

It's good to think about how we spend our valuable time at work. When was the last time, however, you thought about *where* you spend your time? The answer to this is not just 'in the office', 'in the car' or whatever – it's about the kind of positions we take up in relation to others. It turns out that host leaders are very good at moving from one position to another, alternating close contact with their 'guests' and more detached and reflective standpoints. We can all use these lessons to spread our attention and build relationships quickly and effectively.

In the spotlight

Being in the spotlight is very much the public-facing part of the leader's role. It is where the action is, in full view of everyone – and everything about you gives off messages. Being comfortable taking the spotlight from time to time is a key part of everyone's job these days.

Spotlight moments are the times when everyone's eyes are on you – the team briefing, the pitch meeting, the presentation to potential customers. These are of course key times. However, there is much more to building successful engagement than simply being a confident presenter.

With the guests

Taking the metaphor of hosting, a good host knows the value of spending time with their guests. This is also time spent in public, although the focus will be different. Rather than being in the spotlight, with all eyes on you, you can take time to go around and meet people individually.

This is a much less formal process, and often involves spending time with people individually or in very small groups. It's time for catching up, asking how the person is getting on, and connecting with others. This is time for discovering and remembering people's strengths, interests, particular concerns and so on. Lots of key information can be discovered and stored away for future use. Think of how good it is when someone takes enough interest to remember your football team, children's names or dream holiday plans.

In the gallery

The gallery is a place high above the action. From there, the room can be surveyed from a position above the hubbub and interaction down where the party is happening. From a spot such as this, it's possible to take an overview, to see what's happening without (for a moment) the distraction of being in the hubbub.

Time in the gallery is time observing from above. In our normal work life, this might include:

- Taking a break from everyday business and distraction
- Taking a pause to look at the big picture
- Taking a 'helicopter view' – looking from above at wider issues, progress and challenges ahead

In the kitchen

As a host, we will invariably sometimes retreat to the kitchen. This is a more private place – where preparation is done, where family members may come and go, but which the guests are normally steered away from. The kitchen will be the place in which we work in private, out of view of most of the guests.

This can be the most challenging place to find time – after all, life is so busy getting out there! Effective leaders and managers know the value of private time in the kitchen – to reflect and review, to discuss things with trusted colleagues and confidants, to take time to learn with a coach. Even a focused and scheduled hour per week in the kitchen can make a huge difference.

Using this Field Book

As you embark on this international tour of experience and wisdom, here are a few tips to help you get the most from the rich mixture of resources, ideas and possibilities presented here.

Have a question in mind

If you have an idea about what you are looking for, it will help you to find it. This is true in many fields, and in particular in reading and observing. As the 19th century French scientist Louis Pasteur observed, "in the field of observation, chance favours only the prepared mind". So if you are facing a particular challenge or are in search of inspiration on a certain topic, take a moment to focus on it. Write it down. Maybe even give it a name, to help you bring it back to mind quickly. Think about the benefits of moving forward to you and others. Is it worth proceeding? Yes – then dive in.

Of course you can also read the book without a question in mind and have a very interesting time. Having a question in mind will help different parts of the book jump out at you.

Look at the contents and the index

Mark always used to start reading books in the middle, by opening them and seeing what happened. While this is a fun and intuitive way to start engaging with a book, he has now found that many people actually prefer the more logical approach of starting by looking at the Contents page, to see what's actually in the book and going from there.

A less usual, but still highly effective, way to approach a book is via the Index. We have taken a lot of trouble to ensure that the Index for this book is comprehensive and useful. Why not open the book at the back and take a skim through it? If you have a question in mind you might find your attention grabbed by a particular term – and there will be an immediate page number for you to follow up.

Dip into the book

This is a collection of 30 chapters written by different people in different places describing different situations. It is not intended to be read cover-to-cover as a piece, but rather as a rich buffet of field-tested ideas. Just as you won't want to eat everything at the buffet in one sitting, so you probably won't want to just plough through the book in detail. See what draws your attention and then follow up on that. Then come back another time for something else – a sneaky top-up, or something complementary (a dessert to follow your main course). The book will still be there tomorrow, when you want another meal!

Try things out

One of the great advantages of the Host Leadership metaphor and model is that you don't have to commit very much at first. Think of yourself as a host. Who are your guests? What do you hope to encourage them to do? How can you support them in that? Now take a small step to try it out and see what happens. Organisation Development champion Gervase Bushe mentions in his chapter the value of 'probes', small experiments to get feedback from the real world (rather than toying endlessly with an idea in your mind and wondering whether it will work). It's a great way to make progress, particularly when things are confusing or stuck.

Connect with other host leaders

There is no better way to expand your world of possibilities and know-how than to connect with others with shared interests. There are currently several ways to do this: we have Linkedin and Facebook groups (search 'Host Leadership') where you can connect with others, get news of updates and so on. The Host Leadership website (hostleadership.com) hosts new blogs and news updates, and you can sign up there for occasional emails. Rolf Katzenberger has started a German language site at hostleadership.de. We hope there will soon be more portals, connecting points and other places to share news, successes, learnings and developments.

Now ... it's time to get into the book. Guten appetit, as they say in Germany.

Reference

McKergow, M., & Bailey, H. (2014). *Host: Six new roles of engagement for teams, organisations, communities and movements.* London: Solutions Books.

Part One
Host Leadership in action

2
Co-creating housing strategies: Hosting five families with housing challenges

Bjørn Z Ekelund, Ellen Andvig and Lars U Kobro (Norway)

It has long been a part of the public sector tradition to offer shelter to people in need. What happens when it's no longer "we" are helping "you", but "let's do this together"? Is it possible to collaborate with vulnerable people, developing a new housing policy? In this chapter, we hear about a project from a local context in Norway, using Host Leadership ideas to work with families in poverty to develop a new way of working for housing, across sectors.

Introduction

The welfare state in Norway and similar countries has challenges to continue serving the people in the municipality with the equivalent organisation and service level we see today, given the growing number of elderly people in relation to the number of tax-payers. For this reason there has been a request for new practices in different service areas including social housing, especially in relation to low-income families with children. Involving the public sector and families in co-creating solutions has been identified as an innovative approach in changing the interaction between public services and citizens. This case is a part of an action research study of a project that aimed to develop and pilot co-creating new housing strategies for families in poverty.

This project took place in Larvik city, a municipality in Norway with 45,000 inhabitants. The city was chosen since it is the home-city of the project leaders and we found possibilities to establish a relatively innovative idea inside trustful relations with representatives of different local institutions. We saw the opportunity and chose the city for this reason. Five families were involved in a six month joint group process. The families were invited to join a process which aimed to increase their psychological quality of life. Another aim was to inform and challenge the public systems to deliver solutions across sectors better fitting the target group's needs. In this case we will focus on the processes and meetings with the five families. We will apply central elements mentioned in the seminal *Host* book by McKergow and Bailey (2014). We will present our practice in relation to the six roles of Host Leadership and conclude with some learning points about co-participation and stepping forward.

Theoretical background

This project's ambition was to apply three theoretical models in our meetings with the families. The time elements were organised with Otto Scharmer's U-turn (Scharmer & Kaufer, 2013). The Diversity Icebreaker concept (Ekelund & Pluta, 2015; Ekelund, 2019) was used to create a shared language of diversified preferences and perspectives. The method was integrated within a Theory U perspective to generate self-appraisals through from mind, heart and will. Subsequently the Diversity Icebreaker concept of Red, Green and Blue was applied to elicit various perspectives, thought processes and action plans associated with desired housing outcomes. This is the left side and right side of Scharmer's U-curve (see Figure 1 below).

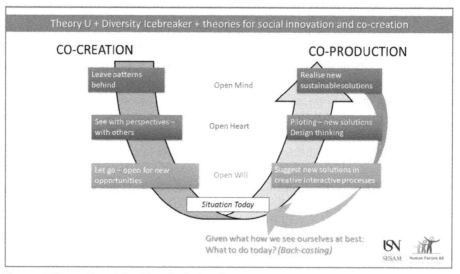

Figure 1 Theory U and the Diversity Icebreaker

Voorberg, Bekkers and Tummers (2015) define Social innovation as the creation of long-lasting outcomes that aim to address societal needs by fundamentally changing the relationships, positions and rules between the involved stakeholders, through an open process of participation, exchange and collaboration with relevant stakeholders, including end-users, thereby crossing organisational boundaries and jurisdictions. According to the European Commission (European Commission, 2011, p. 30), "social innovation mobilises each citizen to become an active part of the innovation process".

The terms co-creation and co-production refer to the active involvement of end-users in various stages of the production process (Voorberg, et al, 2015). These authors reserve the term 'co-creation' for involvement of citizens in the (co)-initiator or co-design level. Co-production is considered to be the involvement of citizens in the (co-)implementation of public services. Co-creation is considered to be a cornerstone for social innovation in the public sector. Co-creation with citizens is a necessary condition to create innovative public services that actually meet the needs of citizens.

The co-creation perspective in this project happens in multiple settings. The co-creation of 'how to understand ourselves in relation to housing' was the main focus in this case.

In practice

The families met monthly with two researchers at a local charity. In the meetings, the families were involved in a six-month development process to generate solutions to their housing-related challenges. A primary aim was to strengthen participants' influence on and autonomy in relation to the process, focusing on their resources over their limitations. Other foci included exploring values, developing pragmatic housing solutions and building relationships with the other families participating in the project.

Host Leadership (McKergow & Bailey, 2014) defines six roles:

1. Initiator
2. Inviter
3. Space creator
4. Gatekeeper
5. Connector
6. Co-participation

We will now describe how we worked and share our most important experiences and learnings, organised through the structure of these six roles.

Initiator

Recruitment of participants to the project was effectuated by the person that was most central in the Larvik municipality's social housing office function. The inclusion criteria were low-income families with children having a difficult dwelling situation. Six families wanted to participate. She obtained acceptance from the families to give their names and contact information to me (Bjørn Z. Ekelund), the lead author.

Inviter

I then visited each of the families and informed them about the plans: six meetings, some elements of the theories that would be applied, the ambition also to include learning for public institutions plus our research ambitions. The sixth family did not want to take part because they were afraid that the confidentiality from the families to others in the society would not be respected by everyone in the group of families. I underlined that the project had no connection to future decision-making concerning future housing issues for the families. They signed an agreement of participation in line with this scope.

Space Creator

As a meeting space we used the large kitchen of a voluntary organisation that distributed cheap secondhand accessories and furniture. The meetings took place from 6pm to 9pm. This created an informal atmosphere, and at the same time had a context relevant to smart living, given the little money available – how to get more out of less.

We started all meetings with setting the table together with soups or sandwiches. Then different topics were introduced. Getting to the meeting space was not that easy for everyone. I contacted each of them before every meeting to offer to bring them with my car if needed. Some of the single mothers needed baby care, and we paid for this expense. We did not want to add to the economic burdens on their shoulders through this project.

Gatekeeper

The gatekeeping role consisted here of two functions: one is to introduce the elements of our theories into practice, naming U-curve and Diversity Icebreaker, and the other is to create a psychological safe climate for participation and sharing. The first one is the formative elements of stepping forward that implies taking control by giving the participants tools and language for understanding themselves, others and the challenges of housing. The second one is the practice of acknowledging what each of the participants share. The host leader's acknowledgement might function as a non-directive promotion of change. The acknowledgement and comments from the other participants in equal position leads to more relevant self-validation and shared information relevant for solving problems.

At the first meeting we stepped forward with setting the norms for confidentiality. Then each person was invited to talk about themselves and their family in a way that could help the others to understand them. No structure was set on the content except time. The research interview identified the positive effect of not being alone. Participants consistently identified being with others in the same boat as one of the most important contributions of the project. Being able to discuss their housing situation with their peers was experienced positively. Peter summarises this as follows:

"It's important to realise that you're not alone, to meet other people who are struggling. Helps you get perspective on your situation".

Vigdis refers to the support he felt from others in the group:

"It's about motivating each other. Helping each other understand you are not alone. When we meet like this, you get so see that everyone is struggling with the same things, and we can help each other out. We get some respite, a breather."

The second meeting was about recognising themselves in the Diversity Icebreaker concepts of Red, Blue and Green through questionnaires and other material. This is a short version of the main qualities of the three colours.

The categories in Diversity Icebreaker

RED	BLUE	GREEN
Feelings	Concrete	Big picture
People-oriented	Practical	Possibilities
Interaction	Facts	Future
Easy-going	Details	Ambitious
Patient	Logical	New ideas
Heart	Mind	*Will/Body/Hand*
Feeling	Thinking	*Behaviour*
Pathos	Logos	*Ethos*

Figure 2 The categories in the Diversity Icebreaker

Then they draw their housing history non-verbally in the downward slope of the left side of the U-curve (Figure 1). Afterwards they interviewed each other, and the dialogue partners had different colour preference within the Diversity Icebreaker categories. Shahila similarly described the process as a voyage of self-discovery:

"I learned a lot about myself when we were drawing the various places we'd lived in. I drew the family I was born into, and my travels to a different country. I lived alone, looked after myself, and started trusting myself. And I drew the first time I slept without my mother or my brother nearby. Then I became a mother myself. Things like that. I learned who I was, got to know myself."

The third meeting was centred around the economic situation and challenges for each of the families. Some of the families volunteered to be a case for creative input for improvement. Interesting ideas emerged about how to make good economic solutions by renting parts of the house – these ideas helped one of the families to buy a house six months later.

The fourth meeting was about how the housing situation could look if it was as good as possible. We explored Red, Blue and Green perspectives on what a best possible housing situation could look like. We asked the participants to write a letter to themselves that could be sent in about three years, on how things could look at their best. They refused this exercise by saying that this was too unrealistic. They found it more relevant to focus on today's and tomorrow's situation. As a facilitator I found it important to respect the ideas voiced by the participants. I realised that my idea was not right at this time, in this context, and decided to bring this forward as an important learning about participants' openness for moving position mentally along the U-curve, into the future.

Being content emerged as a topic. Tonje describes this as follows:

"I'm past a lot of the shame. I've learned to accept my situation and make the most of it. Appreciate what I have. It's been a kind of epiphany. I was so stuck in my way of thinking before. Trapped. I've learned I don't have to be ashamed of being 'poor'. And I use the scare quotes because I don't feel that I'm deprived."

The fifth meeting was on a Saturday with all the children in a trampoline park and pizza as a lunch meal. We informed the participants about this at the outset in order to create some positive event in the future that also could be shared with the children. It was also identified as meaningful in terms of getting to know the other families, getting to know people from other generations, with different cultural backgrounds. And most importantly, they had fun.

The sixth meeting was a wrap-up for each family and some sharings of what they planned to do next. Given the time spent and topics shared during these six months, what implications did it have for their actions in the near future? They also reflected upon the learning points of being content with the positive sides of life. Tonje also emphasised the importance of focusing on the positives, of living in the moment. For her family, this represented a survival strategy:

"Why sit around yearning for things that aren't achievable. There's something to be said for living in the moment. If we're constantly waiting, constantly deferring, things start to get on top of you. Sometimes it's good to compartmentalise. Push things into a corner. To say you know what, we'll do the things we HAVE to do. Then things are pretty much fine."

She said she'd spoken to her children about being happy with what they had, not focusing on what they didn't have.

Connector

This was the first time ever in Norway where multiple families who are in poverty met and developed a joint confidentiality, breaking the tradition of confidentiality between the service provider and the individual family. The consequence of this was both validation as well as empowerment. Practical help was given among family members from day one, without being an intention from our side. The effect seen was very similar to what we see in successful group therapy when people at last meet someone who has shared similar experiences. Some of the members still keep contact in order to solve problems for each other. It became for some of them a unique network, different to what they already had from before.

In this process participants identified being with others 'in the same boat', validated and normalised their own life circumstances, and narrowed the cultural distance between participants. They focused on finding the positives in their situations, and began to meet welfare service providers in a new and more constructive way. As such, they re-formulated strategies for how to improve communication with the representatives from the municipality.

The way participants spoke in these contexts suggests they were starting to see themselves as autonomous agents in their dealings with these services. Tonje felt she had increased her consciousness of how she interacted with others through the project. This also gave her insights into the dilemmas facing providers:

> "Something's changed in me in relation to meeting other people, like we've learned on the course. Like how we are, and how others are. There are people working in these places, they're snowed under with work. It's easy just to think about yourself in these situations, but when we understand what life is like for them it's easier to approach them differently. This may lead to them approaching you differently as well."

This is an illustration of how the participants themselves developed new connector strategies with important others outside the family group.

Co-participating

A central element in Host Leadership is that we as leaders take part in some of the processes. We, Ellen and I, were eating together with the participants. We tidied up the room together afterwards. When there were not enough people for group processes, we stepped in. When economic challenges and solutions were discussed in the third meeting, we shared our best knowledge and experience. We took part in the mapping of colour preferences. It even led to an act where one of the participants voiced a meta-perspective, sharing with the others but knowing that we also heard:

> "You know that Bjørn Z. and Ellen, they are both very Green. It implies that if we talk with big words, in a very enthusiastic way, share ideas of what potentially could happen – then they will be happy."

The co-participating role seemed to make it easier for the participants to take an agency role based upon their learning. In the follow-up of the project we also involved the participants to validate our research. They became our research assistants.

Conclusion

This project has some unique qualities. First and most important is the act of bringing together families who normally are treated individually with confidentiality by representatives of the municipality. Second, in the host function we did not act as teachers or experts, but as people that hosted the meetings in a very informal context, where the host function of sitting together around a table and eating was the starting point. The space created is easily recognisable from the hosting literature and metaphors. Third, in the gatekeeping function we imposed concepts where the U-curve created a sequence of goals for each meeting and with Diversity Categories of Red, Blue and Green language that created a new language that participants enjoyed practising.

The qualitative research (in progress; Andvig, Kobro and Ekelund) shows that the participants seems to have experienced a personal growth of dignity and empowerment through the dialogues and the group processes described above. The citations above illustrate this. We believe that the friendly hosting function combined with a simple and trust-creating structure made it possible for participants to experience unique learning processes.

References

Ekelund, B. Z., & Pluta, P. (2015). *Diversity Icebreaker II – Further Perspectives.* Oslo: Human-Factors AS.
Ekelund, B. Z. (2019). *Unleashing the Power of Diversity. How to Open Minds for Good.* Oxen, UK: Routledge.
European Commission. (2011). *Empowering People, Driving Change: Social Innovation in the European Union.* Luxembourg: Publications of the European Union.
Kobro, L. U., Andvig, E. S., & Ekelund, B.Z. (2019). En u-sving til bedre bolig. Et prosjekt for boligsosial innovasjon i kommunal kontekst. Skriftserie nr 14. Universitet Sørøst Norge: To be downloaded: https://brage.bibsys.no/xmlui/bitstream/handle/11250/2581081/2019_14_Kobro.pdf?sequence=1&isAllowed=y
McKergow, M., & Bailey, H. (2014). *Host: Six new roles of engagement.* London: Solution Books.

Scharmer, O., & Kaufer, K. (2013). *Leading from the Emerging Future: From Ego-System to Eco-System Economies*. Berrett-Koehler; San Francisco.

Voorberg, W. H., Bekkers, V. J., & Tummers, L. G. (2015). A systematic review of co-creation and coproduction. *Public Management Review, 17*(9), 1333–1357.

Authors

Bjørn Z Ekelund *is a psychologist, MBA, and chairman of Human Factors AS, Norway. Contact information: Bjørn Z Ekelund; bze@human-factors.no*

Ellen Andvig *is a professor at University of South-Eastern Norway, Faculty of Health and Social Sciences.*

Lars U Kobro *is an associate professor and CEO of Centre for Social Entrepreneurship and Social Innovation at University of South-Eastern Norway, Faculty of Health and Social Sciences.*

3
Anyone for dinner? Celebrating your goals with Host Leadership

Maria Serafim (Australia)

In this chapter Maria Serafim, Director, Educational Leadership with the New South Wales Department of Education in Australia, shows how she uses a Host Leadership twist to 'turn the tables' in her review meetings with school leaders. The strategy outlined below is a solution focused approach for leaders who want to foster genuine relationships, strengthen professional connections and enhance feedback conversations.

The what

Imagine being invited to host a 'dinner' with your choice of guests to celebrate and highlight what you have achieved in your leadership over a specified period. The idea for hosting a 'dinner party' came from the metaphor of leading as a host (McKergow & Bailey, 2014). As a metaphor, the leader as host provides an entry into building quality, trusting relationships. It sparked the idea of sitting amongst people, being invitational, being a co-participant. This requires moving from being the hero or the servant as leader to the host. It means learning to 'dance' as a leader – knowing when to step forward and when to step back, how to keep the conversation flowing and how to create the right atmosphere for celebration and growth.

From this emerged the idea of hosting a 'dinner party' and all that entails for it to be a memorable, reflective and psychologically safe experience. The setting of an environment so that conversation allows others to connect and share their growth and learning, and where people leave feeling and thinking "what a great and authentic experience".

The how

Since 2017 groups of school leaders in New South Wales have engaged in this approach to reflect and receive feedback on their professional goals. The invitation to participate was co-designed by the school leaders so that they were empowered to 'host' in the way that suited them best. Here is the resulting invitation:

Invitation

Host Leadership is a leadership style developed by Mark McKergow and Helen Bailey, where the leader behaves as a host would where they receive and entertain guests.

In keeping with our co-designed approach to working together, I am writing to invite you to engage in an innovative approach to our discussion about your goals.

I invite you to apply the notion of Host Leadership as a way of creating a purposeful space for us to share successes and reflections of your goals for 2017.

Consider the leader as host in the context of hosting a dinner party. As a dinner host we put thought into who to invite, how to cater, topics of conversation and setting the scene for everyone to enjoy themselves. This is your opportunity to host, or for me to host you, to celebrate and share the end of year reflection of your leadership. The dinner party is a metaphor for a leadership style so you certainly aren't expected to cook up a storm ... in fact, you are not expected to cater, rather create the space and atmosphere for us to talk in a purposeful, refreshing and supportive way. Like all great dinner parties, let's create a space that is relaxed, can allow for plenty of conversation and an opportunity for your invited guests to share stories and/or artefacts that affirm their reflection of your goals. The duration of our time together is **90 minutes.**

So, what could this look like? In keeping with the 'dinner party' metaphor you could, or request that I, host:

A 'dinner party' for two – you and me meeting to discuss your goals.

A 'dinner party' with invited guests – you may choose to invite staff, students or community members to support and reflect your perceptions and evidence towards your learning goals. For instance you may involve administrative staff if you had a goal around finance, members of your leadership team if you were building capacity in others, students for your focus on enhanced student voice.

Consider what type of 'meal' this will be – another metaphor for the approach you want to take. For instance you may want guests to join us at different 'courses'. It could be a degustation meal with many different 'tastings' and so it goes. You can be as innovative as you choose.

The impact

When leaders are trusted to share how they want to reflect on their achievements and progress, the results can impress and amaze. The Host Leadership 'dinners' allowed leaders to demonstrate their individual 'hosting' reflections on their leadership. For some this meant inviting a range of guests from within and beyond their setting. Others chose a more 'intimate' approach with one or two guests.

To illustrate the creative approach taken by leaders, some produced menus to reflect their goals. Examples include degustation menus that had tastings of achievements and highlights, a buffet meal with a 'smorgasbord' of feedback and reflection from students, community members and staff, a Hollywood Star Highlights meal, Mad Hatter's Tea Party, Chinese Banquet complete with giving guests the name of Gods and a Thanksgiving dinner that included students, staff and a neighbouring colleague.

Many meals included a menu that guided the conversation. During our Thanksgiving 'meal' the host principal was our guide, stepping forward and

asking "What are we thankful for in our school?", and stepping back to hear the reflections from her guests. When it came to 'The Stuffing and the Gravy' our host asked what was hidden and what the school showcased well. What was experienced was an atmosphere that set the scene for honest reflections with suggestions for future and ongoing improvement. This was true for every 'dinner party'.

One reflection received via text from a colleague after the 'dinner' that had been hosted at a nearby café illustrated the way we can use our influence as leaders to harness new and even more valued ways to connect with colleagues:

> "My 'dinner' meeting with you today touched me on a real and personal level that I have never before experienced. You inspire the people you support to reach higher through your personal connection, encouragement, trust and positivity. Thank you for being my inspiration."

This reflection shows that more meaningful and honest conversations occur when leaders are respected to express themselves in a way that works best for them.

Being a host leader creates empowerment. To see yourself through the lens of a host and apply this in the way that you interact leads to positive, respectful and valued conversations. Unlike a conventional line management approach to feedback on goals, the unique position of the host leader is invitational as one would experience in a dinner party context. The various positions of the host support the success of this experience – at the table to keep the conversation flowing, as a co-participant and part of the conversation, in the kitchen or in the gallery where the 'host' supports the success of the 'party' and stepping forward and back to allow others to feel included and valued for their contributions. All the while the leader is receiving feedback on their achievements and progress and this is often outlined in the 'menu' experience.

The 'dinner party' experience is non-threatening, inclusive and fun. It leads to permission to affirm and say, "I'm really impressed with what you're doing". This in turn builds positivity and trust. This collaboratively developed way of

working with leaders has been shown to enable change in the way that leaders connect with each other.

The leader as host of a dinner party is an opportunity to model and have guests experience what it feels like to be respected and valued as an individual. From this experience leaders can be assured that people will leave their 'party' empowered, included and inspired. Consider the following quotes that leaders shared when they hosted their party:

"It's not what's on the table that matters, it's who's in the chairs."

"Lend an ear, give a hand, provide assistance to the weary, generosity makes a gracious host."

Through this solutions focused approach to leadership, host leaders have been supported to share their progress towards improvement goals. The approach has identified a creative and innovative way to enhance authentic professional conversations, embed solution focused strategies and build collective efficacy.

Reference

McKergow, M., & Bailey, H. (2014). *Host: Six new roles of engagement for teams, organisations, communities and movements*. London: Solutions Books.

Author

Maria Serafim is currently Director, Educational Leadership with the NSW Department of Education. Her work involves collaborating with colleagues at a local, community and system level to ensure that school leaders are positioned and supported to successfully lead their school communities. A primary focus of her role is to harness the potential of collective efficacy and a solution-focused approach to acknowledge, and to share and celebrate leadership and actions that positively impact on success for students.

4

'Host' as an attitude in rural development management

Petra Wähning (Germany)

Host Leadership can be particularly effective when the leader has little or no positional power, authority, resources or leverage. In this chapter rural development consultant Petra Wähning describes how she used Host Leadership to engage farmers, hotels and tourism authorities in Bavaria, Germany in looking to the future.

Rural or local development often does not happen within an organisation. As an example, the Bavarian Ministry of Agriculture started several initiatives with different conditions and goals to direct development in the more rural regions towards a defined direction. One of these directions is to enhance organic agriculture, organic production and goods sales, while another is to enhance social entrepreneurs at site. Rural communities can apply to these initiatives and – if accepted – they get financial support to hire a manager. They usually apply with a set of goals that has been defined by experts and maybe some locals. The manager starts on their own with this rather theoretical set of goals.

Having goals but no organisation, no company and mostly only very few resources in terms of money and power brings some challenges. At the same time these local managers have a lot of connection to the local community, officials and community, foundations and entrepreneurs. Some of these parties have a strong interest or expectation defined by the organisation they work for. Some of them have concerns or, even worse, blockages. This special context needs to be mentioned as it explains the usefulness and charm of the host approach in that context. Being a host is indispensable in this profession.

For example, in Bavaria alone there are 27 regions to enhance organic agriculture and organic food production. Financed by the government and the local community, they start in very different environments – geographically as well as regarding their office location. Some sit within the local community, others sit with an agriculture official, others being in an office with a foundation, others in an association that already deals with organic issues.

Starting at point zero without resources, the only way to get people and organisations involved is to inspire and attract them. This happens because the manager finds a way to successfully translate their goal into a useful benefit for the agenda of a decision-maker, a group of people or entrepreneur.

Knowing the concept of host as leader is a charming yet necessary toolkit to get started and to be effective in rural development.

Initiator

The initiator is an essential role. Thankfully the new approach to rural development in Bavaria is looking for new ways to create real effects. That is why managers (in regions to enhance organic agriculture) may modify the goals which are set by experts, if they find a different approach more useful. So, observing and talking in order to notice what is needed is an appropriate starting point. Listening to stakeholders and others, considering trends and the potential of the area as well as the people and enterprises you get an idea about what is needed that both fits into the conditions set by the government and the potential of the region. This is the initiator being 'with the guests' taking the temperature in small conversations.

For example, a district south of Munich close to the border with Salzburg has a reasonable number of tourists across the year. They also have a lot of agricultural goods produced by rather small organic farms. Recently the tourists have become more interested in organic and high quality, personalised food, and this might be a win/win situation for many in the area; the restaurants get a unique selling position, the farmers get long term partnerships and can sell their products at a reasonable price, and the guests get a unique travel experience where they enjoy the landscape and know that their organic food is produced on site. Taken all together this could create a new image for the area.

Once you have an idea the next step is to get started: who needs to be involved? Who might be open and interested? Who might benefit rather quickly? What could be different? Why should it be different? What could be the benefits? Who wants to take the first/next steps?

Meeting relevant players, talking to them, listening and learning builds crucial momentum in that process: who will be your guests and what are their expectations, needs, concerns? Whom do they want to meet? Then initiate, bring in an idea, a vision, your hope: step forward as a host.

Consider the benefit it might have for all (in the case above, the unique selling point of Alpine tourism in combination with local organic food in gastronomy). Bring in the idea, but do not stick to it – be ready to adapt your first approach, whenever players get involved and contribute their own ideas without losing yours completely. As soon as players talk and get involved – step back and use the power of not knowing. This means be curious, open, interested in their ways of dealing with the issue you brought to the table. Find out the interest and the questions, the concerns and the hopes – which lead to the next steps. This starts a process of steps followed by steps, a mutual learning as Nora Bateson (2016) states it– where every involved person gets the chance to find their own motivation, get support, find (business) partners. When this starts moving that way in a useful direction, the host has to step back and watch in the gallery or amongst the people, to see what kind of additional support might be needed.

Inviter

Once you have found the players you want to work with, you want to make your idea attractive to them. To be successful with the invitation, you need to respect and value the players you want to involve, and you need to bring a perspective that attracts them. As an inviter you know or want to know your guests, appreciate their unique perspective, and want to create a space of mutual learning. And you have to accept if people do not follow the invitation. If they do not see why they should join it is probably better if they don't. As you are in any case not in the position to force someone, a "no" is welcome.

Inviting also means an honest interest in the opinion of your guests – concerns are as valuable as tips. You are curious about their opinion, hopes, concerns, questions as they lead you to your next steps. Be rather open and ask than state your position – which might lead to resistance.

Space creator

At a certain point a meeting of the identified players is a compelling step towards reaching your goal. In the example mentioned it does make a difference, if you meet at a farm or at a restaurant to value the site and to give more power to the imagination of the people. Do you want people to listen to inspirational speeches? Do you want them to discuss their point of view? Do you want them to connect with each other? What space fulfils your needs best? Do you want to serve food? Who cares for drinks? What is the structure of the meeting? You could start with an inspiring speech, then have time for questions and input, and later a more interactive part. When will be the start and when will it end? (This is a very important question if you want to bring chefs and farmers together as they are busy people!)

After setting the theme and the scenery it is time for the inviter to trustfully let go and see what happens. This opens new possibilities where players already bring in their own ideas, find interesting business partners and talk about terms and conditions. Stepping back means finding yourself in the gallery or with the guests.

Gatekeeper

You want to have the right people together. Governmental initiatives in particular can attract concerns and expectations that have nothing to do with the issue you want to address. So it is very important to ensure that the meeting or event has the benefits you are looking for.

For example a bigger, inspiring event around the potential of organic food in gastronomy that is announced in the local media might be a good starting point. There, you ensure that grumblers and doubters will not get enough space to impair your event. But you might need this bigger event to find your partners by self-selection. You want to continue in a more confidential meeting with the keen ones. There you build trust and a safe space. If you cannot design an event that deals constructively with doubters it might be better to wait or find different ways. Or perhaps an article in the local media might bring you into contact with the right people. By taking these routes you still cannot guarantee a helpful response but it can assist you in making sure that you can have a constructive meeting.

Once you have built this group, a certain policy as well as a strengths finder (perhaps the diversity icebreaker from Björn Z. Ekelund, mentioned elsewhere in this book) will help to work in a constructive way with people who have different backgrounds, interests and communication skills. As a host you should be permanently alert to note if someone needs explanation, if important questions come up or if important steps are close to happening and need support. Players who do not fit will not be invited next time. This sounds hard, yet it is necessary to keep the motivation high. In the example an organic farmer did not stop complaining about the restaurant managers. By doing that, the motivation of everyone else was suffering and the complaints led to conflict rather than a solution. So he was not invited to the upcoming events where reasonable choices towards local-organic ingredients were made. Interestingly he is now selling his organic products to a hotel, so I think he came around in the end.

Connector

In this case, one aim is to connect farmers and chefs. So understanding their needs is more important then the manager's vision at that point – he has to step back, acknowledging the ideas and concepts that the players bring up. Their questions, concerns and ideas lead you to the next steps – such as which expert to bring in the next time, or which questions to answer in more detail. Connecting people at this point means clearly stepping back, listening and answering their needs. Connecting to the expertise that is needed right now, connecting to an idea or a proofed solution is part of the host as a connector. The role at this point – unless there is no critical turn – is constantly in the gallery, among the people or in the kitchen to reflect. People at this point need to make their own choices, to take responsibility and do their first step in engagement.

In the case mentioned above there were concerns about the organic certification. An expert could manage to dispel doubts and clarify how this could be done and at what cost. Having this useful information, one gastronome decided to run a test selling conventional and organic burgers at the same time. Bingo! 70% bought the organic burger, event though the organic one cost €3 more than the conventional one. Now the organic burger is an essential part of the menu. This is momentum: your goal as a rural developer has now transformed to boost in sales in a restaurant. This will cause others to seriously consider organic beef as well, it will cause the restaurant to consider organic vegetables and so on. In the best case, they see themselves as a group where all win and more momentum generates a dynamic of a small sustainable local production chain.

Now we have reached the end of the process. Being a host enabled those who were open to new ideas to experiment – with success. They 'took over' the host's ideas and created momentum.

In the context of rural development, I see leading as a host is crucial. There is no way to reach goals by hierarchy or power. You have to attract, you have to connect, you have to serve others' ideas, provide different perspectives and bring in what is needed to take the next steps. You win when your guests are attracted by your vision and translate it into their own action – and then you have to step back.

Reference

Bateson, N. (2016). *Small Arcs of Larger Circles: Framing through other patterns.* Charmouth: Triarchy Press.

Author

Petra Wähning is a sociologist and consultant for rural development and grass roots projects, small scale economies and community supported investments. After several years of experience in market research, marketing and media planning, Petra has worked as a self-employed consultant since 2009. Her main interests are new forms of project development and leadership: creating win\win situations in a non-hierarchical environment with multiple stakeholders, all bringing in their own perspective and wisdom. In doing that she creates solutions that cover necessities of all parties – nature, our environment, the producers along the production chain, commerce and consumers. Petra engages in the network of community supported agriculture, launched an association that looks for a new relation between farmers and consumers and was part of a documentary film dealing with a strong solution focus. http://www.utopia-revisited.com/

5

Courage and humility: A Maasai view of Host Leadership

Emmanuel Mankura (Kenya)

> *As a tribal elder of the Maasai tribe in Kenya, Emmanuel Mankura acts as a conduit to build connections between the traditional ways of his people and the latest developments in Western approaches to building progress and change. In this chapter, Emmanuel writes about how Host Leadership is indeed a new yet ancient art as he describes the Maasai ways of building leadership and engaging with newcomers and strangers.*

Introduction

I believe that every pastoralist and nomadic tribe knows very well about the topic of Host Leadership; many are the challenges that they face in their daily lives and there is power in interaction and proper communication. Our tribe the Maasai has been practising this for many years and we are still doing so.

For more than 15 years now I have been hosting both my community members and people from outside our community. After such an experience, many of them write to me telling me how we have opened their eyes and hearts. Some of the people that we have hosted in our community over the years are from different countries around the world, including England.

I am sometimes invited to other countries to join in with retreats and share our practices. In China and other parts of Asia we set up the village to look like a Maasai village and we hosted them the way we normally host people in our community, gave them gifts and engaged them in solving their problems – most of their problems were very personal. It has been so powerful!

Hosting and Leadership

HOSTING + LEADERSHIP are two very strong words when put together. As I have said earlier, our community is very good at hosting. As a community leader, I have personally experienced the power and effects of hosting. A leader who can host well can definitely achieve more.

In our community we have a set of values which are still very important to us. They bind us together and have really shaped the way we live. Below, I am going to explain briefly about the values demonstrated in Host Leadership as well as how they show up in practice and affect our ways of working.

Over the years, people around the world have become very busy in their work and personal lives. They have abandoned the rich community life, creating walls and barriers around themselves. They have become more selfish leading more lonely and miserable lives. Such people become solidified (like rocks). They start being suspicious, prejudiced and unsafe. In the end they become less happy and try to do many weird things in search of happiness. I have seen many people in Kenya who have lost community life and decided to engage in other activities but in the end they quest for community life.

In our community, we have a proverb that says "MEMUT ELUKUNYA NABO ENG'ENO" (one head cannot boast to know everything). We need other people in our lives. We learn from other people. Engagement is important. When we have a ceremony in the community we don't issue special invitations – people just come and join us, and they know they can do that. It's part of our community to join happily in these ceremonies.

As leaders we expect to deal with people in different ways: people who have problems who need to be given hope, people who need support (and perhaps the support they need is not available right now), people who need to solve conflicts. We also host people who are just coming for advice on different issues. All these situations require wisdom and understanding.

We also need to know the problems of the neighbouring communities, the challenges of our guests – that way we can understand them and help them in useful ways. The way we present ourselves is also very important – we are hosting ourselves in our own communities and we need to help people to concentrate on what they are doing.

We welcome people in different ways. If they are tourists, we of course welcome them, saying 'how are you', being open to them. However, if someone is coming to learn from us, someone who is really interested, that is a special case. We will take them as a special person, and we want them to feel part of us, to open up and share what we have, to make sure that other members of the community will accommodate them as they go around.

We have an important welcoming ceremony. We look for a host family to look after them. We wear our traditional clothes, we give gifts, we accompany them with traditional songs to make them feel at home, part of our community. We also give them a Maasai name – my colleague Anthony Willoughby is 'Lemayian', which means 'the one with blessings', which also helps community members to feel that yes, they are part of us.

The purpose of hosting our guests in the above way is to create room for them to feel that they are part and parcel of the community – a sense of belonging. We believe that no one is useless! Everyone in this world is important and special in a different way, has a role to play and creates a certain percentage in the success of the community. Accommodating them in our community creates freedom of association and from the freedom of association they get to know the challenges that we are facing as a community and from that they feel that they have a positive role to play (engagement and responsibility). After playing the role (no matter how small or big the role is), it creates satisfaction for them and success for the community. The community starts to recognise their input into the community and more trust is given to them; and if more trust is given to them they make more effort without being forced by anyone!

One of the reasons why many people feel less important where they are is because they have not been given a platform, a chance to be heard, a chance to contribute, a chance to grow. They have been inclined to believe that they cannot produce more; being limited/confined only to certain levels not only kills morale and self-confidence but also promotes stunted growth, lack of vision, lack of direction among others.

Over the years our community has benefited hugely through that system of host leadership. Therefore, personally, I have witnessed the benefits of Host Leadership. I have used Host Leadership to build our community and make it more sustainable.

It is also very important to note that in accommodating guests and strangers in our community we don't beg for their help BUT we create awareness. If there is any support that they want to give as a result of a feeling of responsibility, then it is their choice to do so. We induce a person to participate without any expected limits; that is how our community works.

Courage

In hosting, the first value we exercise is COURAGE. Once we take the first step of courage, we open doors (our hearts) to the guests – they get to know who we are. By welcoming a guest or stranger by stretching your arms wide open, giving a warm smile –it works like magic. It immediately changes the perception and attitude of the guest or stranger – they start to feel that they are welcome, loved, valued and part of that community.

This gives us an opportunity to break down the walls and barriers, and step by step we start entering into the inner chambers of their hearts. They willingly confide in us and it enables us to help them overcome their challenges and – if they are leaders – develop leadership in them.

I remember one white lady from England who visited my home and our community several years ago. When we gave her our community welcome, she broke down. She was so emotional. She had her personal challenges, and when she saw a materially poor community which had so much to give, she was touched and she realised that she was poor but we were rich!

Two years ago, we hosted a family from The Netherlands. The family was overwhelmed by how they were treated and the mother immediately became sick and we had to take her to a room to get rest. After inquiring what was the matter, we were told that the lady had high blood pressure and could not handle her feelings/emotions – she said that she had never seen anything like that in life.

In our community we totally need each other in order for our culture to thrive. Therefore, we must really engage other people to be part of us, in order for us to get the same mind set and improve performance.

Humility and Wisdom

The second and third values exercised when hosting are HUMILITY & WISDOM. Humility and wisdom MUST work together – in most cases people think that humility is a weakness, that some would like to take advantage of the leader's humility, and therefore tolerance has limits.

As a leader you may well be hosting different people, perhaps people you have never seen before, and perhaps their agendas or expectations are different to yours. Therefore, you have to be wise and also you have to have humour. When a topic is discussed, you have to change and adapt, to suit what is happening at that particular time and humour can be a good way to achieve this.

When you are hosting people as a leader, your feelings are very important. Some of the people you host can offend you in some way – talking about something that is offensive that evokes your ego, that doesn't please you. As a host you have to be very wise about how you handle these people – you cannot express in your face directly how you feel. If you cannot handle your personal feelings, then you will chase the people away immediately, which is not what is needed!

By controlling your own feelings, by humbling yourself as a wise person (as opposed to a fool), you can be strong and prevent people from undermining you and taking advantage of your humility. People can challenge you, and you need to be able to handle them by humbling yourself, to accommodate every type of person.

Responsibility

The fourth value we exercise while we host people is the value of RESPONSIBILITY. As a leader our calling is to serve and NOT only to be served. A good leader is a servant of the people and not a dictator! Directives are given and obeyed in leadership BUT as leaders, are we the people who can give an ear? Are we ready to learn new ideas? Culture is dynamic – are we ready to change and kill taboos? Are we ready to learn from our mistakes and change?

You have a responsibility to make people feel comfortable, to understand what the guests really need, to make sure they are entertained and engaged. And it's also important to have and show respect – respecting opinions, respecting how we live, respecting how we behave, and also respecting how YOU are. So we respect different cultures and beliefs. In order for us to accommodate, the value of respect is very important. When there are challenges affecting us and our neighbours, affecting our harmony and how we live together, then the territorial boundaries need to be checked and respected.

But in terms of Host Leadership, the most important parts are the invisible boundaries – where is this person coming from, what are their beliefs and values, we have to respect all that and they also need to respect us. We cannot say we are more special than anyone else, and we need to understand these people properly, where they come from, and you need to respect those boundaries. And then you can see how much further you can go with that person – sometimes they have personal issues which make them angry, and you don't want a problem, you just want to solve your problems in harmony.

Normally, a good leader is a problem-solver, not a problem-causer. They are there to pacify, ready to create solutions. So if a person comes who is very angry, we need to understand that person is under pressure and we need first to understand how to tackle that person and bring the pressure down. So, if people start quarrelling in a meeting, you as a leader can't be a problem-causer, it's your role to handle the people – and your success in this will determine the benefits of the whole meeting. It's very important for you as a leader to be able to handle people who are happy, who are angry, who have problems. If you counter-attack that person because they are angry, you answer with an angry word, you will not be a good leader.

Lemayian says that from his Western perspective what stands out when he comes to visit is the 'extraordinary' self confidence of the people in the nicest possible way. It's devoid of aggression, not a trace of "who the hell are you?" just immense respect: you are here, therefore you exist, therefore I respect you.

Trust

The fifth and most important value that we GIVE & SEEK while hosting is the value of TRUST (two way traffic). In our community where supervision is not there, every community member has a mandate to supervise themselves, and trust bestowed on us by other community members propels us to do as expected.

Trust is like a young plant which takes time to grow before it reaches maturity. It must be nurtured. Hosting enables people to be more relaxed, ready to give back and share what they have. Once a leader gives trust, they are most likely to win trust from the community members, and so their leadership becomes very easy. It is very hard to lead people who you do not trust or people who do not trust you. While hosting people, we are taking a bold step by first giving them our trust and, once we manage to win theirs, we improve performance, health and wealth.

In many cases, IF trust and responsibility are given to a wayward person it can transform them IF they just realise that they are valuable and they are given a second chance. It rehabilitates them. But this also needs keen observation and different levels of responsibility to be applied. This starts very early in life!

We want to create self-confidence in our young people, to help them believe in what they are doing. Now they are embarking on schooling, which is not the traditional Maasai way of learning, and we want them to bring knowledge and skills to the community. Therefore we teach them about confidence in meeting people, the importance of not losing our community values. If we do lose our values, then one day we will stop being who we are and lose our identity. Therefore, it is very important to invest more time in our youths because it is our responsibility to do so.

Conclusion

In this chapter, I have just discussed a few values demonstrated when hosting. There is so much more to talk about Host Leadership including how to be a good host leader in our community, how to apply Host Leadership in different fields, criticism of Host Leadership and so on. Personally I fully recommend Host Leadership to enhance and promote the following:

- Performance and production
- Education and the promotion of mental health
- Understanding and wisdom
- Peace and conflict resolution
- An environment where one can listen, be informed, be challenged in the mind, be awakened, be motivated.

Author

Emmanuel Milia Mankura is a tribal elder for the Maasai in southern Kenya, and has helped to solve many of his community's issues. Using his own life stories and powerful metaphors, he talks passionately about the challenges his community has faced. Many of these have direct relevance to the business challenges we face today, such as developing leadership, empowering others to take responsibility and creating a culture which is motivated, value based and embracing of change. Working with leading companies and institutes, Emmanuel has facilitated trainings and workshops across East Africa, and in the UK, Germany, Thailand, Japan, Malaysia and Hong Kong.

Acknowledgements

The editors would like to thank Anthony Willoughby (Lemayian) of the Nomadic School of Business for his help in connecting us with Emmanuel, and his own interest and support for Host Leadership.

6

Host Leadership in outdoor, bush, wilderness, and adventure therapy

Stephan Natynczuk (UK)

One of the original inspirations for our work in Host Leadership was Sir Chris Bonington, Everest mountaineer and expedition leader, who was interviewed and quoted in the original Host book. In this chapter Stephan Natynczuk describes how leading as a host can fit well with a variety of outdoor contexts based on his work in the field of adventure therapy.

Introduction

The idea of hosting an expedition to some far off, relatively unexplored place is nothing new. Typically, one has an idea for an expedition and invites people to join in. The expedition team, being selected on the basis of such things as a prospective member's personality, temperament, experience, knowledge and skills, all offered something to the collective effort by which the expedition will succeed. Sir Ernest Shackleton's poetic, yet possibly apocryphal, newspaper advert famously invited men to apply for a hazardous journey in the knowledge that they might not return (Morell & Capparell, 2003, p. 55). Shackleton, perhaps demonstrating aspects of Host Leadership, carefully invited extraordinary, exceptional men for his Antarctic expeditions; these people shared his vision, were hardy team players, and willing to do any necessary task.

However, there are more frequent contemporary expeditions where members self-select based on their own needs from the expedition, the number of places that are available, the amount of adventure on offer, the expedition's location, cost, duration and so on. Prospective members might choose at any time to take part or not. Occasionally membership is not voluntary (Tucker *et al*, 2015): expedition members being sent by a third party, their participation prescribed because it might be 'character building', therapeutic, or restorative in some way. Whatever the process by which expedition members are chosen, there remains a challenge to the leader about how the expedition meets its objectives and about how every member is maximally included to benefit both the collective effort and each individual's personal best interests.

Leading outdoor adventure activities

Outdoor adventure activities have traditionally been used for a wide range of personal development 'courses' from building character in challenging youth to developing leadership and teamwork in management – see Ogilvie (2013) for an extensive review. Leadership styles for outdoor adventure activities have been explored in many books over decades (for example Ogilvie, 1993) and the trend seems to have become more facilitative, adopting a softer approach (Bunyan, 2011) as coaching becomes a more significant aspect of leadership awards, certainly from U.K. national governing bodies. Host Leadership with its theoretical underpinning (McKergow, 2009) offers a new, humane, inclusive approach to providing people with a realisable chance to know themselves at their personal best, especially through adventure (Natynczuk, 2012).

While a Solution Focused practitioner working in a consulting room may seek exceptions (times when things go better) to whatever brought their client to therapy by asking carefully crafted questions, a Solution Focused practitioner (the host) in an adventure setting might also look for exceptions that occur within the adventure experience. Examples of exceptions to life as usual might include being cognitively and physically engaged, being happy all day, being considerate, caring and sharing, being conscientious about risk and safety, and taking responsibility for one's own actions as well as the group's safety. When debriefing, the host can, for example, ask for ways in which guests can continue to be their best versions of themselves, and what difference this will make to life beyond the adventure. Some of this concept is borrowed from Walsh and Golins' (1976) Outward Bound Process model and Sibthorp's (2003a) empirical overview, which described a motivated participant learning new skills and adapting to a new environment in search of satisfying success and mastery. Here, one role for the practitioner is to ensure this sense of mastery takes hold among participants and is transferable learning. The practitioner also takes on the role of a *co-adventurer* (Duncan, Miller, & Sparks, 2004), gently guiding participants to a state of success, perhaps aware of the Servant Leader model (Northhouse, 2013) yet acting as a host (McKergow & Bailey, 2014) in alignment with the initial invitation to take part in the adventure. In Host Leadership a participant is a guest, which is a significant relational shift. This contrasts strongly with the leader taking a position of power, deciding what is best for the participant, both holding progress away from individual participants and being the judge of that progress against norms that are not necessarily helpful to any single participant. Nyland and Corsiglia (1994) describe pressurising clients to form solutions before they are ready as solution forced, and suggest it is a novice's mistake. Clearly being solution forced does not sit well with Host Leadership, especially if it involves working for another's best interests and not those of the guest. Being solution forced risks harming the therapeutic alliance (Shennan, 2019, p. 123) and might be questionable both ethically and legally. These often complex considerations are dealt with in Mitchels and Bond (2010, 2011).

Host Leadership and Servant-Leadership – building relationships

I have previously been an advocate of the Servant-Leadership model though now regard Host Leadership as an evolution of Servant-Leadership within expedition and adventure leadership. Both of these approaches to leadership 'styles' place the leader in the role of a quiet facilitator, sometimes unseen, yet without whose facilitation the group achieves little. Servant-Leadership (Greenleaf, 1970) emphasises the development of agency in participants through applying seven leadership behaviours: conceptualising, emotional healing, putting followers first, helping followers grow and succeed, behaving ethically, empowering and creating value for the community.

Northhouse (2013) criticised Servant-Leadership for being the opposite of leadership, too utopian to be practical, and too much following to be leading. However, we can pragmatically adopt aspects that are useful to practitioners working therapeutically. McKergow and Bailey (2014) described leadership as a relationship with *leadership as engagement* in which the group is "engaged, aware, committed, involved, taking action, participating in an ever-changing landscape, everyone getting and giving more" (p. 5). McKergow and Bailey (2014) put the leader in a position similar to a host who has carefully and deliberately invited participants to an event with a common purpose, much like choosing participants for an expedition, yet here the host is also an initiator, inviter, connector, space creator, gatekeeper, and co-participator.

Being in a leadership role during a therapeutic adventure or expedition is a complex undertaking, as Harper (2009) found. One might be challenged by circumstance to be authoritarian for urgent reasons of safety, a guide, a coach, an instructor, a teacher, or a technician: any combination of these in a traditional leadership role (Brymer & Gray, 2006). Juggling these roles badly can put at significant risk the essential collaborative, or therapeutic alliance. Horvath et al (2011) are clear about the value of building an alliance in a therapeutic process.

Norcross (2010) defined collaboration as "the mutual involvement of the participants in the helping relationship" (p.122). That a helping relationship encompasses much more than the alliance goes without saying. Routinely monitoring the effect of one's therapeutic work and the quality of the alliance can have a significant impact on outcomes (Miller et al, 2015; Brattland et al, 2019). It is important to establish the alliance early in therapy (Joyce & Piper, 1998), which includes clarity about what to expect, agreement on what the practitioner and client are working towards, and the relational bond. Bachelor and Horvath (1999) suggest that the longer a client is engaged in therapy, without a positive or improving alliance, good outcomes are increasingly in jeopardy. Worse, Hannan et al (2005) found therapists struggle to predict how clients perceive the alliance. As hosts we have to privilege the client's experience in our care, and in our initial meetings, stress "the relational bond, the special sense of understanding, safety, and trust" (Norcross, 2010, p. 121) and actively facilitate the building of connections between expedition members.

When therapists were asked about what worked in their own personal experiences of therapy, over 80% said it was due to the relationship (Norcross & Lambert, 2011). When clients are asked, they do not emphasise particular techniques or theoretical assumptions made by their therapist. They, too, say it was the relationship. Both can be correct. The therapeutic alliance is simply the most robust finding we have for factors contributing to therapeutic outcomes (Wampold & Imel, 2015) and a good alliance is made up of a relational bond, agreement on what the client wants from therapy, and agreement on the tasks or method of the therapy (Bordin, 1979). Host Leadership is strong on intra-group relationships, the host connecting with their guests and connecting their guests to each other (McKergow & Bailey, 2014), and accepting guests' autonomy. The quality of inter-relationships and connections is everything.

The flexibility of the Host Leadership model is also pragmatic in encompassing a range of leadership styles and tasks, bridging leadership roles on the continuum between hero and servant (McKergow, 2009), allowing for flexibility in function with a pragmatic approach to achieving the objectives the host has in mind for the group. Managing adventures to keep the group safe sometimes requires the leader to step into a hero mode (especially during an emergency when an authoritative mode is perhaps most efficient and most effective), sometimes to be a servant, sometimes something in between. Within the host model there is also the 'space' for the leader to be authentic, working as Northouse (2013, p. 267) illustrates for the collective good, and as Harper and Dobud (2018) and Dobud (2017) argue, to work for the best outcomes for our guest.

Using Host Leadership in practice

To illustrate how the theory translates into practice I would like to draw from my own experience in adventure therapy. In this aspect of my work with adolescents I combine adventure activities such as caving, rock climbing, hill walking, canoeing, kayaking, off-road cycling and bush-craft, with Solution Focused practice and a broad, experiential curriculum of learning outdoors. This cohort generally does not engage with education for a variety of reasons and its members are at risk. For these young people I offer an alternative education package, commissioned by schools and local authorities. I will comment briefly on each of my main roles as a host leader.

Inviter

After receiving a referral, an introductory meeting with the young person follows. During this meeting I outline what is on offer in terms of activities, the broad objectives of the day-long sessions, and we agree on our expectations of each other. At this point the young person is invited to take part and to join me and my assistant in adventures of their own choice from the previous paragraph. Occasionally there might be up to three guests in our party for day long sessions and up to 12 guests for an expedition. It is explained that participation is a choice and our new guest is asked to take joint responsibility for our individual and collective safety. For example, if guests spot something "not right" or "a bit dodgy" there is an expectation that they point it out immediately.

Asking a young person to assume co-responsibility for the outcome of the adventure is possibly a very empowering step and is also a basic component of Solution Focused practice (O'Connell, 2005). Honouring the guest's choice of activity maximises engagement and potentially demonstrates that guests are taken seriously for their choices and are regarded positively as individuals. At this point we are living Rogerian core conditions of congruency, unconditional positive regard, empathy and Adler's Social Interest (Watts, 1998). Ideally our guest feels valued as a co-participant.

Initiator

Once we are underway with our adventures our guests are always expected to take an active part in dynamic risk assessments as we progress through the day. Trust is further developed through this type of meaningful collaboration and the therapeutic alliance takes hold. In my work, choice is always extended to the guest as to whether, when and how we complete our objectives or have a change of mind at any point, "Challenge by Choice" being a common component of adventure experiences (Hovelynck, 2003; Beames & Brown, 2016, p. 66; Harper, Rose & Segal 2019, p. 238). Within Host Leadership one cannot play 'lip-service' to challenge by choice. Guests are invited and participate by their own choice; disrespecting guests' choices would seem like holding them prisoner. Certainly the adventure would lose a vital sense of authenticity (Beames & Brown, 2016, pp. 50-51).

Space Creator

Careful and attentive use of the environment is vital to outdoor and adventure therapy, and is dealt with extensively by Harper, Rose and Segal (2019), and Gass, Gillis and Russell (2012), and Greenway (1995) provided accounts of the power of wilderness. It goes without saying that environment and habitat have to be respected and protected. The practice of Leave No Trace (Simon & Alagona, 2009) translates metaphorically both to therapy (Natynczuk, 2012) and Host Leadership as well as caring for the outdoor spaces we use. McKergow and Bailey (2014, pp. 120-137) described 'space' with several functions: a place for things to happen, as physical, interactional, headspace for planning and reflection. Additionally, space has a temporal component; it takes time and skillful pacing to allow for reflection to occur, and to ensure there is time for things to happen. The host has to be skilled at and mindful of "holding the space" (McKergow & Bailey, 2014, p. 130).

Gatekeeper

The role of gatekeeper is mostly about maintaining the integrity of the adventure experience or expedition for the whole group, perhaps helping to find solutions that do not draw heavily on limited resources (Ratner, George, & Iveson, 2012, pp. 86-88). It is not about controlling individual participant's experiences through preventing participants from leaving. In pragmatic terms, the role of gatekeeper includes our agreement about when we finish, medical considerations informing the appropriateness of the venture, and what happens if a guest's behaviour, cognitive ability, physical ability, and/or emotional condition change to make the adventure unsafe. These considerations are outlined in the joining instructions and form part of our contract, in turn informing the risk assessments for the venture, to which we have all agreed and consented.

Co-participator/ co-adventurer

It goes without saying that adventure and the day belong to the guests. I as a host might have visited the cave, rock face, river, or forest more times than I can remember, yet the experience and venue is most likely new and the adventure authentic for the guests. As host, the conversation and activity are managed so that nothing is taken away from the guest's experience by the familiarity of the venue and activity to the host. All that happens during the adventure is a new collective experience: the experiential learning is different for each guest and perhaps intangible (Hovelynck, 2003). Nonetheless, ideally with everyone at their best, perhaps discovering new meaning in their lives through adventure (Repp, 2004), the guests are living through exceptions to their usual experiences and reactions to challenge, and gaining transferable skills such as those discussed by Sibthorp (2003b). The shared physicality of the adventure is also a key factor in bringing about change in the way that the mixture of perceived risk and the sense of accomplishment at overcoming challenges blend to help construct a new appreciation of self (Russell & Farnum, 2004).

Connector

Connections between the guests, and between the guests and the host, develop from shared experiences, common endeavour, mutual dependency, respect, trust, and increased wellbeing that emerge from undertaking outdoor adventures as co-participants. Everything is agreed among the guests and with the host, and in this way agency and self-efficacy develop (Gass, Gillis & Russell 2012, p. 74) certainly within the group and on the day. The social aspects of the experience may be a greater contributor to change than the adventure experience, though cannot be wholly separated (Harper & Obee, 2019).

Conclusion

Host Leadership offers the expedition or adventure leader a model that draws on useful aspects of several approaches to leadership, whilst honouring the guests as valuable and important individuals and contributors to the group.

The host, in fulfilling McKergow and Bailey's (2104) six roles, gets the best for themselves, the guests and the organisation. Hill *et al* (2007) discuss the complexities of adolescent development and from their paper it is possible to regard this group as the hardest to work with. However, Sandu (2019) suggests good work can be done when alliances focus "On building a bond rather than dealing with risks or resolving conditions" and goes on to describe "Microprocesses characteristic of initiating, developing, and cementing these relationships".

Host Leadership would seem to be a most effective leadership model for working therapeutically with adolescents in outdoor, bush, wilderness and adventure therapy, and I have no doubt that this model translates well to working with adults in similar settings. It seems that Host Leadership, being a simple, pragmatic approach, especially in helping to build good alliances, facilitates the pursuit of happiness through adventure (Mortlock 1984, pp.120-127).

References

Bachelor, A., & Horvath, A. (1999). The therapeutic relationship. In M. A. Hubble, B. L. Duncan, & S. D. Miller (Eds.), *The heart and soul of change: What works in therapy* (pp. 133–178). Washington, DC: APA Press.

Beames, S., & Brown, M. (2016). *Adventurous Learning: A Pedagogy for a Changing World*. London: Routledge.

Bordin, E. S. (1979). The generalizability of the psychoanalytic concept of the working alliance. *Psychotherapy: Theory, Research and Practice, 16*, 252–260.

Brattland, H., Koksvik, J. M., Burkeland, O., Klöckner, C. A., Lara-Cabrera, M. L., Miller, S. D., ... Iversen, V. C. 2019. Does the working alliance mediate the effect of routine outcome monitoring (ROM) and alliance feedback on psychotherapy outcomes? A secondary analysis from a randomized clinical trial. *Journal of counseling psychology, 66*(2), 234.

Brymer, E., Gray, T. (2006). Effective Leadership: Transformational or Transactional? *Australian Journal of Outdoor Education, 10*(2), 13–19.

Bunyan, P. (2011). Models and Milestones in Adventure Education. In M. Berry, & C. Hodgson (Eds.), *Adventure Education: an Introduction* (pp. 5–23). Abingdon: Routledge.

Dobud, W. W. (2017). Towards an Evidence-Informed Adventure Therapy: Implementing Feedback-Informed Treatment in the Field. *Journal of Evidence Informed Social Work.* doi:10.1080/23761407.2017.1304310.

Duncan, B. L., Miller, S. D., & Sparks, J. A. (2004). *The heroic client: A revolutionary way to improve effectiveness through client-directed, outcome informed therapy.* San Francisco, CA: Jossey-Bass.

Gass, M. A., Gillis, H. L., & Russell, K. C. (2012). *Adventure Therapy: Theory, Research, and Practice.* New York: Routledge.

Greenleaf, R. K. (1970). *The Servant as Leader.* Atlanta: Greenleaf Publishing Center.

Greenway, R., (1995). The Wilderness Effect and Ecopsychology. In T. Roszak, M. E. Gomes & A. D. Kanner (Eds.), *Ecopsychology: Restoring the Earth, Healing the Mind.* San Francisco: Sierra Club Books.

Hannan, C., Lambert, M. J., Harmon, C., Nielsen, S. L., Smart, D.W., Shimokawa, K., & Sutton, S. W. (2005). A lab test and algorithms for identifying clients at risk for treatment failure. *Journal of Clinical Psychology, 61,* 155–163.

Harper, N. J. (2009). The relationship of therapeutic alliance to outcome in wilderness treatment. *Journal of Adventure Education and Outdoor Learning, 9*(1), 45–59.

Harper, N. J, & Dobud, W. W. (2018). Of Dodo birds and common factors: A scoping review of direct comparison trials in adventure therapy. *Complementary Therapies in Clinical Practice, 31,* 16–24.

Harper, N. J., & Obee, P. (2019). Client perspectives on wilderness therapy as a component of adolescent residential treatment for problematic substance use and mental health issues. *Children and Youth Services Review,* (105), October, 104450.

Harper, N., Rose, K., & Segal, D. (2019). *Nature-Based Therapy.* Gabriola Island: New Society Publishers.

Horvath, A. O., Del Re, A. C., Flückiger, C., & Symonds, D. (2011). Alliance in Individual Psychotherapy. *Psychotherapy, 48*(1), 9–16.

Hovelynck, J. (2003). Moving active learning forward. *The Journal of Experiential Education, 26*(1), 1–7.

Joyce, A. S., & Piper, W. E. (1998). Expectancy, the therapeutic alliance, and treatment outcome in short-term individual psychotherapy. *The Journal of psychotherapy practice and research, 7*(3), 236–248.

McKergow, M. (2009). Leader as Host, Host as Leader: Towards a new yet ancient metaphor. *International Journal for Leadership in Public Services, 5,*(1), 19-24.

McKergow, M., & Bailey, H. (2014). *Host: Six New Roles of Engagement for Teams, Organisations, Communities, Movements.* London: Solution Books.

Miller, S., Hubble, A., Chow, D., & Seidel, J. (2015) Beyond Measures and Monitoring: Realizing the Potential of Feedback-Informed Treatment. *Psychotherapy, 52*(4), 449-457.

Mitchels, B., & Bond, T. (2010). *Essential Law for Counsellors and Psychotherapists.* London: SAGE publications.

Mitchels, B., & Bond, T. (2011). *Legal Issues Across Counselling and Psychotherapy*

Settings: A guide for Practice. London: SAGE Publishing.
Morrell, M. and Capparell, S. (2003). *Shackleton's Way.* London: Nicholas Brealey Publishing.
Mortlock, C. (1984). *The Adventure Alternative.* Milnthorpe: Cicerone Press.
Natynczuk, S. (2014). Solution-Focused Practice as a Useful Addition to the Concept of Adventure Therapy. *InterAction – The Journal of Solution Focus in Organisations,* 6(1), 23–26.
Norcross, J. C. (2010). The therapeutic relationship. In *The heart and soul of change: Delivering what works in therapy* (2nd ed.). https://doi.org/10.1037/12075-004
Norcross, J. C., & Lambert, M. J. (2011). Psychotherapy relationships that work. *Psychotherapy (Chicago, Ill.),* 48, (August 2016), 4–8. https://doi.org/10.1037/a0022180
Northhouse, P. G. (2013). *Leadership: Theory and Practice* (6th ed.). Thousand Oaks, CA: SAGE Publications, Inc.
Nyland, D. & Corsiglia, V. (1994). Becoming Solution-~~Focused~~Forced in Brief Therapy: Remembering Something Important We Already Knew. *Journal of Systemic Therapies,* 13,(1), 5–12.
O'Connell, B. (2005). *Solution Focused Therapy,* (2nd ed.). London: Sage Publications Ltd.
Ogilvie, K. (1993). *Leading and Managing groups in the Outdoors.* Sheffield: NAOE Publications.
Ogilvie, K. (2013). *Roots and Wings: A History of Outdoor Education and Outdoor Learning in the UK.* Lyme Regis: Russell House Publishing.
Ratner, H., George, E., & Iveson, C. (2012). *Solution Focused Brief Therapy; 100 Key Points and Techniques.* London: Routledge.
Repp, G. (2004). *Friluftsliv* and Adventure: Models, Heroes and Idols in a Nansen Perspective. *Journal of Adventure Education and Outdoor Learning,* 4(2), 117–132.
Russell, K. C. & Farnum, J. (2004). A concurrent model of the wilderness therapy process. *Journal of Adventure Education and Outdoor Learning,* 4(1), 39–55.
Sandu, R. D. (2019). What aspects of the successful relationships with professional helpers enhance the lives of young people facing significant disadvantage? *Children and Youth Services Review,* (6), 104462.
Shennan, G. (2019). *Solution-Focused Practice: Effective Communication to Facilitate Change.* London: Red Globe Press.
Sibthorp, J. (2003a). An Empirical Look at Walsh and Golins' Adventure Education Process Model: Relationships between Antecedent Factors, Perceptions of Characteristics of Adventure Education Experience, and Changes in Self-Efficacy. *Journal of Leisure Research,* 35(1), 80-106.
Sibthorp. J. (2003b). Learning Transferable Skills through Adventure Education: The Role of the Authentic Process. *Journal of Adventure Education and Outdoor Learning,* 3(2), 145–157.

Simon, G. L. & Alagona, P. S. 2009. Beyond leave no trace. *Ethics Place and Environment (Ethics, Place and Environment (Merged with Philosophy and Geography)),12*(1), 17–34.

Tucker, A. R., Bettmann, J. E., Norton, C. L., & Comart, C. (2015). The Role of Transport Use in Adolescent Wilderness Treatment: Its Relationship to Readiness to Change and Outcomes. *Child Youth Care Forum.* doi 10.1007/s10566-015-9301-6

Walsh, V., & Golins, G. (1976). The Exploration of the Outward Bound Process. Eric. Denver, CO: *Outward Bound Publications.* Retrieved from http://www.wilderdom.com/theory/OutwardBoundProcessModel.html

Wampold, B. E., & Imel, Z. E. (2015). The great psychotherapy debate: The evidence for what makes psychotherapy work. (2nd ed.) https://doi.org/10.4324/9780203582015

Watts, R. E. (1998). The remarkable parallel between Roger's core conditions and Adler's social interest. *Journal of Individual Psychology, 54*(1), 4-9.

Author

Dr Stephan Natynczuk is an independent, solution focused, practitioner specialising in outdoor learning and adventure therapy as a practitioner, trainer, and supervisor. Stephan frequently works with adolescents referred by schools and local authorities. In working with adults his main interests are practitioner training, Host Leadership, and sustaining creativity, especially strategies for reducing burnout in key personnel. Stephan holds a good range of adventure leadership qualifications, is a Leading Practitioner of the Institute for Outdoor Learning, an accredited counsellor and supervisor, holds an executive MBA, and is an Honorary Senior Lecturer at the University of Worcester. He is best reached by emailing sparekrab@icloud.com or adventuretherapy@icloud.com

7
Apprenticing students into host leadership in global virtual teams

Rachel Lindner (Germany)

> *Rachel teaches English and communication skills for international business in a university context. In this chapter she considers how Host Leadership might be introduced into an online cross-cultural project and relates her experiences in doing precisely that within global virtual teams.*

Introduction

Many teachers of management in higher education would agree that the best way to learn about leadership is through experience – of leading as well as of following – and ongoing reflection on that experience, which may, in turn, inform future practice. At the faculty of business and economics at which I teach communication skills, a scenario in which my students can gain such experience is the Global Virtual Teams (GVTs) Project. I initiated this inter-university inter-disciplinary simulation exercise several years ago to provide students with an opportunity to develop competences – including leadership skills – for working in what Daim et al (2012) refer to as culturally diverse, geographically dispersed, electronically communicating teams.

A number of studies have been conducted on leadership in GVTs, since leadership naturally has a significant impact on team processes and project outcomes (see, for example, the studies by Kayworth and Leidner (2002), Misiolek and Heckman (2005), Murkherjee et al (2012), Nordbäck (2018), and Zigurs (2002)). GVT leaders tend to be emergent rather than designated. They may have one strong leader or multiple leaders, with leadership roles distributed throughout the team over time. Research also finds that the leadership role of building trust and maintaining positive group dynamics is particularly difficult in cross-cultural teams that rely on electronic platforms to communicate. I would like to suggest that an understanding of GVT leaders as hosts might go some way towards mitigating these difficulties. Furthermore, higher education is a good place to start apprenticing students, who may later find themselves leading a virtual team, into Host Leadership before they actually enter the workplace.

I had been hosting the GVTs Project among students in my own faculty and students at business schools in other countries for several years before I heard about Host Leadership. I say I host the project because that is the way I have always seen my role, despite my earlier lack of familiarity with the concept of the leader as host. On reflection, the way the project is set up as well as students' reports of their project experience resonate strongly with Host Leadership, without its being purposefully built into the project, as I shall show in the course of this chapter.

The project

In brief, this is how the project works: students from participating business schools in different countries are organised into mixed teams of 4-5 members. These teams are diverse not only in terms of their members' national and institutional culture, but also the representation of gender, language proficiency, academic maturity, age and work experience. In keeping with real GVTs, deadlines are purposefully tight. Teams have just eight weeks to conduct team-building and then negotiate, research and finally present the results of a project in which they compare a product, service or business procedure across at least two different cultures.

In the following I consider the project through the lens of Host Leadership. I firstly direct the spotlight at the project facilitators and their role(s) as host leaders in running the project. I then shift the focus to the students, who often intuitively take up both positions and roles of the host leader in their project teams. Finally I consider how Host Leadership might be better integrated into this and similar projects, so that students gain a better understanding of themselves as host leaders.

Project facilitators as host leaders

1. Initiating the project, inviting partners and gatekeeping

As a teacher of business communication, I originally conceived of the idea of the Global Virtual Teams Project as a subject-relevant learning scenario within which my students could enhance their language and intercultural communication skills in online exchange with students at other universities. I had a clear idea of what I wanted to achieve, but I needed to on-board project partners with similar interests to get the ball rolling. In the first iteration of the project, I therefore invited teachers in my networks to join me. I approached those who I believed I would like to work with, who had a compatible student cohort, and who I imagined would be equally keen to engage with the original idea. In the end I started small, with just one partner facilitator/developer and her student cohort.

Since then, I have run the project once a year, and the number of project partners and participant students has fluctuated. Some collaborations have worked better than others. Sometimes expectations, interests or needs have varied or they have changed over time. In one year, the participant numbers were so large that they were difficult to manage, and I found it necessary to downsize the project again. What is always important for me, however, is that colleagues not only bring their students to the project, but also their enthusiasm, input and, ideally, a shared vision of what we want to achieve.

A Host Leadership perspective

In setting up the project, I took on several host leader roles: I initiated it, invited teachers to join me in facilitating the project and also performed a gatekeeping role in setting boundaries for potential partners. For the project to work for our students, the teachers I invite need to become – or, by another facilitator, be apprenticed into being – host leaders in their own right. My best hopes are that partners feel welcome to take equal project ownership. At its best, the project has multiple host leaders working towards the same end.

---

2. Creating the project space

GVTs are geographically dispersed and communicate electronically. This is also the case in the GVTs Project. Although I meet my own students regularly in the physical classroom, neither facilitators nor students meet their co-facilitators or – for students – team members face-to-face. Since trust and positive dynamics are best fostered in a safe and welcoming environment, when initially setting up the project space, I considered the following aspects:

- Which virtual space or spaces are best suited to our project needs?
- Is it better to have a single central project hub or should facilitators and students be able to work in several dispersed spaces?
- How will the way the space is organised impact on open communication between facilitators, between students and between facilitators and students?
- What communication tools will be available in the space (forums, chat, video conferencing tools)?
- How much scaffolding is necessary to make the space both robust and flexible?
- How much scaffolding is necessary to make participants feel comfortable?

In the end I set up a central platform hub with different spaces for different aspects of the project. For example, invitations to join the project are sent out from the hub, and it is the place where we all initially 'meet' and introduce ourselves, asynchronously, on a dedicated welcome page. We invite students to upload pictures of themselves and where they live and study, so that everybody gets a feeling for the overall group.

The project hub is where students will find instructions, important project documents and links, a news forum, and where facilitators can contact students and vice versa. Students are allocated to project teams, each with its own team space – or room – on the hub. This team room is for teams to initially convene, and where they return to at the end of the project to upload project outputs, which are shared with all other teams.

For teamwork during most of the project, however, student teams are invited to create and work in their own space(s) beyond the hub, using communication tools of their choice. This is, we feel, an important part of the learning experience. In doing so, they find out, for example, whether there are personal or cultural preferences regarding communication tools, and they have the freedom to experience team dynamics within their own negotiated team space.

Finally we have video conferences at various points during the project, in which facilitators can hold tutorials with individual teams or across teams, and where students can report back and present on their progress or on project outcomes. Perhaps the most important aspect of video conferencing is that it creates synchronous visibility, which is known to build trust in teams, and has a completely different dynamic from the central project hub.

A Host Leadership perspective

As a house-proud host, I like to have a project hub which is well-organised and tidy and believe in having rules and cultivating common understandings about how the space is used. It is important, if the project is to run smoothly, for all facilitators to agree on these boundaries, to become co-gatekeepers of the space, and to set and model the tone of communication. In this way, we hope students will experience the hub as a safe environment in which everybody can engage equally. At the same time, I appreciate the buzz and clutter of having many people interacting in a virtual space. Just like a physical space, if the house rules are clear enough, there's rarely chaos, although there is occasional messiness!

3. Facilitator positions, connectors and co-participators

So far, I have referred to myself and my partners as project facilitators. As such, we need to perform different functions during the various project phases. I have adapted Tuckman and Jensen's (1977) five-stage model of team formation here to describe the phases of the GVTs Project and outline facilitator roles in them.

Phase 1 – Forming: After joining the project, participants have a week to familiarise themselves with the project hub, the other participants, their teams, important documents and instructions. This is the phase for making connections and building teams. It takes place on the project hub so that we, the facilitators, can mingle with students, make sure that everybody is in, and that teams are up and running.

Phase 2 – Storming: This phase of two weeks in total starts on the project hub while teams negotiate communication tools. They then move on to their own chosen spaces to brainstorm their project topic, organise team processes, write a team proposal and submit it to the hub. During this phase, facilitators mentor the teams in developing their project idea, and guide them when asked for help.

Phase 3 – Norming: Over the next four weeks, in the norming stage, two things happen. Firstly, student teams work autonomously on their projects. Parallel to this, at various points, facilitators offer video tutorials on themes relevant to the GVTs Project, such as agile team management, building trust in teams or intercultural communication. Facilitators take a step back from the individual teams (although they continue to monitor them from a distance), but they connect with students and maintain their presence more generally through the tutorials.

Phase 4 – Performing: In the last week of the project, students deliver project outputs, submitting a team report to the project hub and, in a video conference, presenting their results to one or two of the facilitators. Team and individual efforts are assessed. Opportunities are provided to share results across teams on the hub.

Phase 5 – Adjourning: In this final phase at the end of the project, there is a focus on goal achievement before teams disperse. Finally facilitators evaluate the project before winding it up.

A Host Leadership perspective

Throughout the project, facilitators assume further Host Leadership roles and take up different positions. They act as connectors, very much amongst the guests, when students are new to the project, getting to know one another and teams are forming. While facilitators mentor brainstorming teams in phase 2, they are still amongst the guests, though focused on specific teams, more of a guide on the side, and increasingly retreating to the gallery to monitor from a distance. During the norming phase, facilitators spend more time observing teams from the gallery, and exchanging observations with other facilitators in the kitchen. In the video seminars, on the other hand, they step forward into the spotlight as the sage on the stage. When teams present their results, the spotlight shifts to the students, and facilitators take a step back to the gallery again as they watch, monitor, assess and evaluate. Finally, as the project finishes and the gate is shut behind the last guest, facilitators reconvene in the kitchen to reflect on the project and celebrate its conclusion.

So far in this chapter, I have repositioned the GVTs Project to view it from a Host Leadership angle. In doing so, I have reviewed my own role in it – and that of the other facilitators – as a host leader. I am now going to shift the focus to the student participants to consider the ways in which they might perform host leader roles.

Students as host leaders

During the project I ask my students to archive communications in the media channels they use and keep a diary of the project from their insider perspective. After the project, they analyse the data they have collected, and compare their own experience with research from the field. Each of these analyses represents an insider case study of a student GVT and provides fascinating insights into the workings of teams. In the following, I retell the story of one of my students. Katja was not familiar with Host Leadership. Her narrative, however, is rich in examples of Host Leadership being played out in different ways.

1. Responding to the call to action

The challenge for Katja's GVT began once the five members had found their way to their team space on the project hub. They knew what their task was (remember they were to decide on a product, service or business procedure and compare it across at least two different cultures), but how were five students from different institutions and different countries without face-to-face communication going to organise themselves? Someone had to kick off.

Katja writes how, on the project hub, she started the ball rolling. She firstly greeted the team members when they announced their arrival in the team space and put them in touch with the others. When all were in, she introduced herself again, briefly repeated what the team task was, expressed her hopes for the team, and then scheduled a Skype call. Through this action, Katja notes in retrospect that she automatically, though unintentionally, became the team manager, a role she maintained throughout the project.

> **A Host Leadership perspective**
>
> In their book on Host Leadership (McKergow & Bailey, 2014), Mark McKergow and Helen Bailey note that the act of initiating something is usually in response to a call to action of some kind (p. 81). For Katja's team, this call came from the project facilitators, who were never far away, monitoring from the gallery. Katja responded to the call by taking the first step forward. In doing so, she demonstrates several traits of Host Leadership. Firstly, she is the first in and acts as a very welcoming gatekeeper as her teammates arrive. She assumes a connector role by introducing team members to one another. Katja also invites everybody to join her in a Skype call, and creates that first shared team space beyond the project hub. In fact, Katja took several small steps forward that were all instrumental in setting the tone and creating the dynamics for good teamwork.

2. Fostering good communication

A defining characteristic of GVTs is that they have to communicate electronically. The communication tools are therefore much more than mere channels of communication. They represent a shared space in which the team comes together to get the work done. The way the team members interact in this space – both quantitatively and qualitatively – will impact significantly on team processes and project outcomes.

Katja's analysis shows that she initiated most of the discussions in her team, and wrote the most frequent and longest messages. She was also the only team member who attended all team video conferences from beginning to end. The majority of communications were task-related, about organising and moving the team forward. However, Katja also relates how team members shared a joke, engaged in light banter, comparing the cultures of the institutions or the countries they hailed from, and provided emotional support.

A Host Leadership perspective

Research on GVTs tells us that emergent leaders are those with a strong telepresence and capable communication skills. They co-participate, allow others to have their say, invite, connect and integrate ideas. This resonates very strongly with the roles played by host leaders, and Katja's communication behaviour shows all the signs of her becoming an emergent host leader in her team. Getting the tone right and building trust in the team was a delicate balancing act with students from different cultures whose command of English – the team's lingua franca – varied. Three things, according to Katja, were conducive to achieving this. Firstly, using clear, inclusive and positive language that was understandable to all, no matter what the communication tool. Secondly, creating a common understanding about when communication is required (does everybody mean the same thing by "deadline", for example?). Thirdly, and perhaps most importantly, making time for non-project related conversation. This social interaction helped to form bonds between team members and fostered team spirit.

3. Sharing leadership

Katja writes that, although she maintained the role of team manager throughout the project, as the project progressed, different team members stepped forward to lead in aspects for which they felt they had the necessary expertise. For example, one team member led the final presentation due to her strong online presentation skills. Another team member was eloquent in report writing and offered to take the lead in editing the project report. Furthermore, Katja was not the only team member to initiate discussions, nor was she alone in creating the team space. Subsequent to her setting up the first Skype call, another team member took the initiative to set up a team WhatsApp group and, later on in the project, a further team member set up shared documents for the team report and presentation.

> **A Host Leadership perspective**
>
> It is not unusual for GVTs to share leadership. In Katja's well-functioning team, each leader was able to perform host leader roles in their own area of expertise. Following Katja's example, team members stepped forward and moved into the spotlight when they identified a need and stepped back to let others take over at other times. Observing this from the gallery, I have to admire the dynamics of this exemplary team with its multiple attuned leaders. My best hopes are that members derived the same satisfaction from co-hosting this team as I derived from facilitating it.

Looking back and looking forward

In writing this chapter, I have reconsidered the GVTs project in terms of Host Leadership. How might this new awareness be fed into the next GVTs project? In a first step, this might take place by introducing colleagues to the concept and inviting them to consider their own roles as host leaders. It might, in a second step, also take place by embedding the concept into seminar materials to draw students' attention to their potential as host leaders in this and other situations. Finally, if both facilitators and students model host leader behaviour, I hope that further students might be apprenticed into Host Leadership.

References

Daim, T. U., Ha, A., Reutiman, S., Hughes, B., Pathak, U., Bynum, W., & Bhatla, A. (2012). Exploring the communication breakdown in global virtual teams. *International Journal of Project Management, 30*(2), 199-212.

Kayworth, T. R. & Leidner, D.E. (2002). Leadership effectiveness in Global Virtual Teams. *Journal of Management Information Systems, 18*(3), 7-40.

McKergow, M. & Bailey, H. (2014). *Host. Six New Roles of Engagement.* London: Solutions Books.

Misiolek, N. I. & Heckman, R. (2005). Patterns of emergent leadership in virtual teams. *Proceedings of the 38th Hawaii International Conference on System Sciences.* Retrieved online from https://ieeexplore.ieee.org/document/1385332.

Murkherjee, D., Lahiri, S., & Billing, T.K. (2012). Leading virtual teams: How do social, cognitive and behavioral capabilities matter? *Management Decision, 50*(2), 273-290.

Nordbäck, E. (2018). *Shared leadership in Global Virtual Teams: Building conditions for its emergence and team effectivenss.* Aalto: Aaalto University publication series. Doctoral Dissertations 174/2018.

Tuckman, B. & Jensen, M-A (1977). Stages in small group development revisited. *Group and Organisational Studies, 2,* 419-427.

Zigurs, I. (2002). Leadership in virtual teams: Oxymoron or opportunity? *Organisational dynamics, 31*(4), 339-351.

Acknowledgements

I would like to thank Leah Davcheva, who writes about her four-hour workshop on Host Leadership elsewhere in this book, for introducing me to Mark and Helen's *Host* book (McKergow & Bailey, 2014).

Author

Rachel Lindner is Coordinator of Languages for International Business Studies at the University of Paderborn in Germany. She teaches English and communication skills for International Business Studies and is Associate Lecturer of English Language Didactics at the Department for English and American Studies of the Technical University of Dortmund in Germany. Through her own experience of studying, living and working abroad, she is particularly interested in helping students to communicate across borders linguistically and interculturally in both face-to-face and virtual contexts.

8
How Host Leadership handles conflicts

Sieds Rienks and Leo Blokland (Netherlands)

Amongst the many difficult situations in which leaders find themselves, handling conflict is often raised as particularly challenging. Here Sieds Rienks and Leo Blokland share their experiences of using Host Leadership to work with conflict, at work and elsewhere.

We often see conflicts – in our family, in our neighbourhood, in our work, in our lives. And always emotions seem to become involved. Or people get stuck in a debate about right and wrong. And many, many times conflicts end in an apparently unbridgeable gap between the two conflicted people (or groups, teams, clubs). It seems really difficult to end a dispute, a debate or a conflict in a peaceful way.

At work the tragedy of conflict seems sometimes even harder. We argue and debate about vision, power, quality, strategy, money, expenses, competence and more. The effects can be enormous. Effects for people, for result, for teams, for clients even. And all of a sudden people seem to think they have to make a choice between A and B. Sometimes they tend to bow (until the storm is over) or they want to make peace by offering alternative choices. And they forget other possibilities, chances, solutions.

Luckily there are two blessings in disguise. The first blessing is that many conflicts seem to pass. We just hop over to another topic, another problem, another quarrel. The dispute is over, the conflict seems gone, and the fight between people just disappears. It makes it possible to move on. Let us be thankful for that quality!

The second blessing is that a lot of disputes help to bring about something good. If the fight is for instance about old and new, or about formal versus free routine, the dispute can be welcomed to give us better ideas about the way we work. Many new insights and innovations emerge as a product of debate. So conflicts can work out very well for the firm, where intervention and reaction in an early stage can even be harmful to good solutions and innovations.

However, the topic of this article is not about conflict itself, but about the way leaders can react to conflicts, disputes and debates. We want to know how leaders on all levels can improve in handling conflicts in our organisations.

But first, we want to emphasise how conflicts can be harmful for teams or organisations. If for instance the two directors of a company (the new one and the old one, or the managing director and the marketeer) are in an overt conflict, the employees do not know the boundaries and horizons of their position, their work, their choices. The effect is that they become insecure about direction, their pitch, their vision and their presence to clients or services.

And sometimes the fight is even visible and clear in external publications and press. We all know examples of big fights in organisations. In the Netherlands for instance we have seen the fight between KLM and Air France, between the leaders of huge banks, or the management boards of big corporates.

This is not to mention politicians! The effects are mostly huge and devastating. The risk of lower financial results, no growth, no innovation and no participation can be great for the companies and organisations involved.

Conflicts can be everywhere, not only at the top. In every team, segment, department there are differences in character, competence, vision and performance. That gives variance, which is mostly healthy and positive. But sometimes the debates seem to end in conflicts and the members of teams are taken to positions they did not ask for! This leads to detrimental effects on the atmosphere, the results and more.

So, the question for this article is: what can be a proper reaction of the leader (team leader, manager, director, CEO) to conflicts? Let us look a little bit deeper and first see how we mostly deal with conflicts. And let us see if there is an alternative. (We promise you: yes, there is!)

The reaction we all know: the 'tough' response

In our lives we have seen many examples of a 'tough' reaction of parents, neighbours, family members, colleagues and bosses. It is not difficult to estimate that more than 90% of all reactions to conflicts are decisive, one-directional, not inclusive and mainly 'tough'. With 'tough' we mean that the leader stands in front of their people (or a meeting, or a gossip, or a side conversation) and gives decisive, negative attributions to the people or the subject.

Let us have a deeper look at these organisations and reaction patterns of leaders like these:

The 'tough' pattern	Effect
Stop now !	No further debate allowed, frustrating reaction for the people involved
I blame A for not talking well with B	If you blame or accuse one, he is demotivated to give his opinion or to continue the discussion
You act like children !	Frustration, he claims to be better than me !
A is right, and B is wrong	Decisive pattern, demotivating for B
Let us postpone it for another moment	No content, no discussion, no decision. Bitterness.
I want to know the votes now and decide	No process, no debate, no appreciation. Lost interest.
And many more of the same kind	No discussion, no process, no development, no learning.

In our experience none of the reactions described here are healthy for the culture or the atmosphere. They may help for a very short while, but the attributions to the people involved are mostly negative, not helpful and sometimes even damaging to the people, the subject and even the firm. It provides bad management and instead of speeding up progress, development stands still and no change or renewal is seen. This effect cannot be taken lightly!

Conflicts even seem to have some negative consequences in the way people present themselves in the organisation. We see some really bad effects in the presence of the conflicting partners, as described by Gary Harper (2003) in his 'fight or flight' reaction triangle (see below).

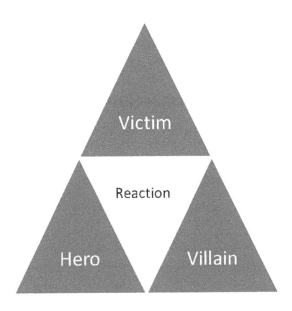

What we see is a common reaction pattern of people around us in conflicts. They sometimes show inadequate behaviour, which is hard to understand. The Victim will say that the conflict is due to the aggressive power, the behaviour of the other party. The Hero will show that he is the toughest of all in this conflict, that the other(s) are losers and that he is the real hero who is on the right side. He is the best at negotiation and he knows the weak spots of the others. And then there is the Villain, who tries to find his interest by gossiping about others, using tricks or changing the rules.

This reaction pattern is often seen but very inadequate for good conflict intervention. We know all these behaviours. In summary: these approaches are not constructive, not helpful and certainly not good for the continuous improvement of team and organisations. We should do better than that! That makes us ready, we hope, for a better approach. In our opinion and experience it is time to swap to these better approaches, as we found in the wonderful book of Mark McKergow and Helen Bailey (2014), *Host*. That will need change, practice and training. But we assure you: it will help!

The concept of Host Leadership

In essence McKergow and Bailey want leaders to change their role and their behaviour to a much more constructive approach. They distinguish six roles and two particular behaviour types – stepping forward and stepping back – that we will mention only briefly here. In other chapters of this field book there will be much more explanation of this wonderful content. We will explore them here in terms of conflict resolution and intervention.

Host Leadership in conflict resolution and intervention

Above we described many conflicts in terms of behaviour, content, pattern and the leadership direction. We described the annihilating effects on organisations and the people involved. And finally we mentioned the effects on the growth, the results, the innovation and the culture of the organisation.

Leadership roles

In this chapter we will follow the content of the McKergow and Bailey book, although we changed the order a little bit for our own purposes. What we want to say is something about a sensible and inviting behaviour pattern that will lead to a better way of understanding debates and dealing with conflicts. With less frustration, more motivation and the best of all, more resilience.

Inviter: "Please come over and talk ..."

When leaders invite conflicting partners (maybe individually, maybe together) and show real interest in the content, the people or the development team will meet more quietness, more rest, more process and more authenticity in the people involved. Particularly when the need for quick answers is less overt and by showing genuine interest in the conflicting partners, the conflict will become more peaceful, more tranquil than before. There is no blame, no accusing of anyone. We have seen many cases that even with this small change the conflict seems to diminish or that good conversation can be restored.

Space creator: "This is not about right and wrong."

When leaders give space to the conflicting team members the dispute tends to become less absolute, less black or white. It can even make people enthusiastic to play with the opposite opinions and make their own future. If people experience space there is room for development and improvement.

Space is a strange thing. You cannot do something (or not do something) specifically but everyone in the room knows the feeling of space. We all seem to think that a solution must be found now, or within a short time. It makes us nervous; we feel tension. If we experience enough space, we know that there is an opening, some rest. Deadlines are famous for producing bad results. Offering some open space can deliver us speed and good results, instead of bad choices because of wrong deadlines.

Gatekeeper: "Do not go further, my boundary is here."

It is very important that leaders show that there are boundaries. Giving space is OK, of course. But setting boundaries is OK as well. We all need to know where boundaries are. That is normal, if the container offers enough space to discuss and to debate. Boundaries and containers can be in space, in subject and in time. Once consensus, agreement and choice is reached in a proper way the dispute can be closed or postponed for the future. A very good boundary is the behavioural one: no accusing, no blaming, no negativity, only constructive and reasonable behaviour is allowed!

Initiator: "Could this be a good idea?"

A leader shows good leadership by giving space for the development of change and new ideas. Or to implement change. Or to initiate the project to move towards new horizons.

And there is also another effect. When the first movement is taking place, there will be room for followers and new adaptors. It is very important that the new change is appreciated, without negative feelings about the past. Leaders should show that the aim is for the future, but that they also believe that the past had its own benefits, needed at that time. Often change is seen as better than the past. Good leaders show respect for the past and give direction for the future. If not, there is potential for disconnect and even for disapproval of the change.

A lot of consultancy agencies offer themselves as change agents. They believe in large scale innovations and seem to offer a better world without resistance. As we see it, this is the best ingredient for failure. Good leadership evokes changes, inspires transformation and gives appreciation to employees and their success. It is cheaper, less revolutionary and offers much more enhancement for change.

Connector: "Both views can have benefit."

In big organisations and institutions there are often rumours between the marketeers (let us be innovative, build up new challenges, go abroad, more growth!) and the back office services (such as finance and HR). The marketeers want to experiment, to develop and to broaden perspectives and chances. The services want to follow rules and procedures for good book-keeping, good organisation or better control. This 'fight' seems eternal.

Good leaders connect both worlds. It may look like a fight but it is just a good way for all parties to show responsibility and carefulness for the well-being of the company. So good leaders connect here and strive for the best of both worlds. They give appreciation and space to the renewals but also to the people who want a good order and a proper transformation. The discussion here is seldom about 'good' and 'bad', it is always more like what can be our goal and what will be the best step to reach for the future. That creates cooperation and participation.

Co-participator: "Can we help each other?"

If the leader joins in to change with his team most disputes will end. We often see a lot of convincing, arguing and disputing in teams and organisations with only negative effects. If team-members feel appreciation, authenticity, respect for their view and even an invitation to move on and go further, they will become enthusiastic and cooperative.

We see a lot of leaders avoiding the arena of disputes and conflicts. They wait for a formal proposal, give a reaction and then do what they always did. That is the best way to stay away from the future, to keep safe and avoid any experimenting. If we react like this, the competitors in our market will conquer our place and leave us as helpless 'old' organisations. So we strongly recommend the leaders to be part of a good discussion, offer space to experiments and give room to progress.

Leadership behaviours

Leaders are aware that the employees are looking to the reactions and behaviour of the management. He or she is always watched, questioned and looked upon. This will not change. Never. People want to know how their 'boss' is reacting: supportive, aggressive, welcoming, confirming, assuring, hosting and any other way. Let us watch the two possible and good behaviours when it comes to conflicts. They are good examples of host behaviour.

Stepping back – being reflective

Good leaders know when to step back. In a conflict it is very necessary to know if there is no intervention needed. That you take time to solve the conflict. That the leader will wait for a good answer in the trust that the employees will reach a good decision and that time is needed, or that space is requested. In combination with the described roles, stepping back can be very effective and helpful. Particularly when the choice for self-organising teams has been made, it is good to wait, even with a certain reluctance to decide already. Setting some conditions is enough. It enriches the atmosphere and makes it valuable for team development.

Stepping forward – being outgoing, showing strength

And sometimes it is very good to step forward. In many situations there is the opportunity for leaders to step forward and to encourage decisions, to make them public, or to inform everybody. Hiding is the worst behaviour. Employees and teams just want to know the direction, the strategy, the route or the 'conclusion' in a deep conflict. And information (not necessarily in detail) about insights, positions, content or decisions are necessary.

But there is a crucial difference between this and the 'tough' role we described in the opening sections. In the tough role the leader shows themselves as the first to decide. They do not give appreciation or respect, and do not describe the process. They just give information about the content or belittling comments about the dispute. The effect is seldom good. Moreover, the effect is that trust and motivation diminish, and the consequence can be that future differences and debates are papered over and maintained.

Do not overlook the missing part: the paradigms!

There are two wonderful books that are very important in this field: *Six Thinking Hats* by Edward De Bono (1985) and *Thinking Fast And Slow* by Daniel Kahneman (2012). Although communication and behaviour are by far the most influential parts in handling conflicts and leadership, we should never forget the important role of the paradigms we hold, when we are looking to the world around us.

For instance, when we watch a football match of the red shirts versus the blue socks, the supporters of red are very certain that the referee is making a bad decision, whilst the supporters of the blues are convinced of the contrary. And when we look in terms of politics we are convinced of the left wing instead of the right wing. This kind of divisive thinking is seen in sports, politics, strategy, religion or any other debate.

We are full of presumptions, and they are part of out history, our education, our school or our peers. And more. And the pattern of the assumptions is called our paradigm: the way we look at the world. When we look at problems around us these paradigms help us to think about risk, belief, chance or view. We do not discuss them. These are our values, they are the way we look at the world. And they are of value to us.

But when we debate, when we interact opinions, we discuss words, events, facts. And we are not always aware of the values and paradigms behind these interactions. Good leadership knows that, good mediators understand the enormous value of our background. And we know how to open our eyes for the value behind the debate, behind the arguing. This is yet another reason to take up the good Host Leadership role and behaviour in this field.

When would you need a mediator?

In most cases, you do not need one. Conflicts and debates just pass. And when there are good discussions under the umbrella of good (and host) leadership most conflicts seem to disappear. There is trust that everything can be discussed safely, that the outcome can be good and that there is no blaming of any kind. That is the true value of Host Leadership.

And sometimes this is not enough. Especially when money, position or exit are involved discussions seem to end ambiguously, perhaps with dangerous side-effects. Normally a good discussion, a good decision and good information can be of great help. But sometimes the fight is bigger than that. In those cases mediation can be of great help.

In our work we are often asked to mediate. In those cases both parties have reached the ultimate stage of conflict and are no longer accessible for good leadership. Whatever the manager does, he is not taken seriously, the normal rules and procedures are no longer followed and every meeting seems to be a fight. And furthermore, the leader as well is part of the debate or even distrusted. The only thing that is left seems to involve lawyers or the court and continuation of the 'war' between parties. That is the stage where mediators often come in. And even in those cases we can be successful. To us, success means restored relations, better understanding, more space and acceptance and clear positions.

Very occasionally good mediation ends in forced exits. We have not yet had to resort to forced decisions in our work. We always succeed in finding solutions. But everything starts with good leadership. Host leadership. So we strongly support the concepts in this book and the earlier work by Mark McKergow and Helen Bailey.

Summary

In this article we made a choice for Host Leadership as the best approach when it comes to conflict. It seems very promising to decide to work 'tough' (quick and dirty) in conflicts but the effect on your employees is mainly demotivating and frustrating. Leading as a host offers teams a welcome and appreciation, support and sharing for the best future of team and organisation. Never ever underestimate the power of good resilience in your staff and employees. So, if you want to go fast, go slow ! And we close this chapter with our own Masters in Conflict slogan: Do you want to be right or do you want to be happy ?

References

Harper, G. (2003). *Conflict Drama: Victim, Villain or Hero?* Retrieved from http://www.joyofconflict.com/articles/ConflictDrama-VictimVillainHero.pdf
Kahneman, D. (2012). *Thinking Fast and Slow*. Oxford: Penguin.
de Bono, E. (1985). *Six Thinking Hats*. Boston MA: Little, Brown and Company.
McKergow, M., & Bailey, H. (2014). *Host: Six new roles of engagement for teams, organisations, communities and movements*. London: Solution Books.

Authors

Sieds Rienks and *Leo Blokland* *have worked together since 2014 as Masters in Conflict. Both have profound experience in the management of big organisations and their original disciplines such as law, psychology and business. Both are very inspired and attached to the world of Solution Focus Mediation after their first courses at Ilfaro Leuven and Marco Ronzani from Basel. They became very successful in conflict mediation for boards, management teams, councils, political organisations and top-level executives. Website with articles, interviews, blogs all in English available at: www.mastersinconflict.nl. If you would like English translations please email sieds@mastersinconflict.nl*

9

Host Leadership as a basis for leadership in a hybrid organisation: Roskilde Festival

Jonas Hedegaard and Hans Christian Nielsen (Denmark)

> *How to lead when an organisation consists largely of volunteers, who are managing and leading other volunteers? In this chapter Jonas Hedegaard and Hans Christian Nielsen reflect on how Host Leadership offers not only a useful metaphor but also a great fit for the hybrid organisation that presents the massive Roskilde Festival every year in Denmark.*

Introduction

Roskilde Festival is an annual festival located in Roskilde, Denmark. The festival has its 50th anniversary in 2020 and has been held continuously every year. The festival is Northern Europe's largest music festival with approximately 130,000 participants, which makes it Denmark's fourth largest city while it is happening. The festival engages about 30,000 volunteers from the participants – some volunteers return year after year. All year around, the festival employs 75 full time staff members and around 1300 year-round volunteers, of whom approximately 750 are volunteer managers. The festival is a charity foundation and all profits are distributed according to the purpose: "To support humanitarian, non-profit and cultural work with special focus on children and youth".

How Roskilde Festival operates

The festival's organisation is made up of six divisions, each of which has several layers of management. The executive board consists of three employees who form the top management (alongside a voluntary board of directors). The six divisional managers are also employed, and they form the top operational management of each division, along with several team managers. Team managers are both employees and volunteers – this means that the top operational management of the festival also consists of volunteers.

The daily life in the organisation of Roskilde Festival is very similar to the life of an NGO or another organisation with many volunteers. As a value-based organisation where many of the members are not paid a salary and many are "called" to the task, there are many things at stake at the same time in organisational life. As you build, run and manage an entire city, it takes a multitude of different and diverse people to solve that task – both volunteers and employees. The different organisational members are thus very different in age, background, experience, education and jobs. This holds especially true among the volunteers where many different people are given the opportunity to participate in the handling of the multitude of tasks.

In this way, there is a lower entry bar to handling a particular task than is often the case in an employed context – more people are given the opportunity to work with different tasks. Likewise, there is a greater dynamic in progression between different levels of management; there are more opportunities to change tasks or teams internally within the organisation, in doing projects and collaborations across different teams and divisions. The different organisational goals might seem to oppose one another (for example the festival is a commercial product, but it is also a value-based event). This is a source of strength – but also a challenge, as diversity requires a lot of trust, understanding and communication.

Complexity, clashes and contradictions

The complexity of the organisation and the management task is therefore greater than in many private or public organisations – due to the great diversity, dynamic organisational life, and the many diverse values and motivations at play at the same time (Smith, Besharov, Wessels & Chertok, 2012). The many differences sometimes clash and can be experienced as contradictions, and this can create paradoxes because it might be impossible to choose one course of action over another, and instead you must choose both at the same time (Lüscher & Lewis, 2008; Smith & Lewis, 2011). This can paralyse organisational members and is often a challenge for management in these kinds of hybrid organisations (Battilana & Lee, 2014; Smith, Besharov, Wessels & Chertok, 2012). When the paradox is broken and a solution is found, it often manifests as a new possibility – a third way – and this creates innovation and developmental growth (Jay, 2013).

This complexity in organisational life is further compounded by the fact that the organisation involves a large number of volunteers, who cannot be present for a full time week as can those in paid jobs – and the volunteers are often not present at the same time or at the same location. This means that the organisation's 'bandwidth' will be lower – there is less time available to take care of coordination, relationships, communication and understanding organisational values. In addition, the volunteers' time is precious and must first and foremost go to solving specific tasks. This makes it harder for each organisational member to make sense of organisational life. Roskilde Festival, however, succeeds quite well in this task – and work satisfaction and commitment of the employees and the annual volunteers always score highly in internal surveys.

Developing leaders to handle complexity

When we work with leadership development, we do our best to support the managers in tackling their responsibilities within the complex organisation that is Roskilde Festival. This means that the leadership development is only in small part "tool-based" and more often focuses on understanding complexity and knowing how to act within complexity. The core premise of the management task is that the managers manage volunteers, and this impacts their task in several ways. The four most central challenges that they face can be described as follows: 1) diversity in the volunteer team; 2) an informal leadership role; 3) organisational paradoxes; and 4) limited time. We can connect each of these with some of the Host Leadership roles described by Mark McKergow and Helen Bailey (2014).

1. Diversity in the volunteer team

As a volunteer managing other volunteers you will very often experience diversity in your work group. This diversity might very well be more profound than that experienced in most teams made up of paid members. Volunteers can be both younger and older than is the norm at a given place of work. The volunteers will have more diverse backgrounds, a wider range of different education and a greater breadth of experience. In addition, the volunteers might work with very different jobs in their professional life – jobs that can be different from the other team members' jobs – but also jobs that can be quite different from the volunteer task.

This diversity can be utilised as a strength, if it is possible for the group to work together without conflict taking up too much time. Too little conflict and the group is not utilising its differences enough and the potential for innovative solutions and a pooling of resources is not maximised. Too much conflict and the team members cannot accept each other's solutions and too much time is spent not agreeing or on mitigating sore feelings. When the group functions just right, there is a bearable level of conflict that also brings the differences of the group members into focus, in such a way that the diversity becomes a strength and a tool for innovation and development – helping the group perform even better than an un-diverse group (Pentland, 2012; Duhigg, 2016; Jang, 2018).

One of the ways we work with the managers to foster this kind of cooperation is by inviting them to be reflective, to seek feedback and to listen more than talk, as well as involving the team members in the majority of decisions that impact the team and the cooperation around their different tasks. This connects well to the concepts of Host Leadership and especially the roles of Inviter, Space-creator and Connector.

2. An informal leadership role

The managers of the different teams at Roskilde Festival are in most cases volunteers themselves – volunteers managing other volunteers. This means that their management role might be formally introduced and sanctioned within the organisational hierarchy, but there is no real formal power sanctioned in formal contracts and the like. This means that the manager will most often have a hard time 'telling people what to do'.

They will instead have to provide boundaries for the task and communicate direction, goals and deadlines, based not on authority but on the premises of the task at hand – and then ask the team members to fill out the boundaries and meet the goals, in a way they themselves decide and find meaningful. It is more about setting up a common shared understanding and then asking questions instead of telling people what to do. This connects well to the roles within Host Leadership of Initiator, Inviter, Gatekeeper and Co-participator.

3. Organisational paradoxes

As mentioned above a multitude of different values, motivations and goals can come into conflict and be experienced as not just different goals that can be aligned and taken care of in order, but as aspects of organisational life that are in opposition and which cannot be handled together. They are not dilemmas but paradoxes. This apparent opposition paralyses both team members and management. This is a growing problem in organisations, as the world around us grows increasingly complex. Working through a paradox is not a competence that one can learn or an organisational procedure that can be implemented. It is a process that needs to be 'lived' where the manager reflects on the situation at hand and tries to reconcile the opposing demands in a way that often means one has to abandon both demands and find a new shared way forward – creating a third alternative – often resulting in innovative and new ways for the team to handle the challenge (Lüscher & Lewis, 2008; Smith & Lewis, 2011).

This process can sometimes rest solely on the shoulders of the manager, but again and again during the leadership development course we have heard from the managers how reflecting on the challenge together with someone else will help in finding a new way forward. Too often the managers feel it is their responsibility to tackle the problem themselves – but actually involving their whole (diverse) team in addressing the challenge is often a much better alternative. In this way the manager stops seeing him or herself as the sole responsible problem cruncher of the team and instead takes on the role of host – inviting the team to crack the challenge together. This connects well to the roles within Host Leadership of Initiator, Inviter, Connector and Co-participator.

4. Limited time

As a volunteer your time is limited – the volunteer task is something you do in the time between your professional job, time with your family and other leisure activities. This means that more people must often be involved in tasks that could be handled with fewer people in a setting consisting only of paid workers, making the volunteer teams larger. This of course creates more complexity as more people must relate to each other and coordinate their communication as decide well as how they solve the task at hand. The manager, who is also a volunteer, can also spend less time getting to know each team member and their different strengths as well as mitigating conflicts and both inter- and intra-group problems of cooperation. Again this can be linked to Host Leadership, where the manager, instead of delegating and coordinating the tasks for the group, invites them to join forces in solving the tasks at hand and decide together how to coordinate and delegate different obligations, in order to achieve the goals set for the team. This connects well to the roles within Host Leadership of Inviter, Space-creator, Gatekeeper and Co-participator.

Conclusions

At Roskilde Festival we have not based our leadership principles directly on Host Leadership – but after having read about the six roles of engagement and the ideas presented in the book, as well as having experienced Mark McKergow live, we have come to realise that in many ways it is what we do at Roskilde Festival, and that Host Leadership has some very relevant and effective ways to understand the role of being a manager in the complex organisation of Roskilde Festival. When you manage volunteers you cannot just hand out orders and commands the idea of seeing the manager (who might also be a volunteer) as a host who invites the other volunteers to participate in a shared task in order to complete shared goals – is a powerful concept. It fits so very well with our work at Roskilde and the fact that the 30,000 volunteers creating the festival are already hosts for the 100,000 invited participants that make up the city, the party and the event that is Roskilde Festival.

References

Battilana, J., & Lee, M. (2014). Advancing research on hybrid organizing – Insights from the study of social enterprises. *The Academy of Management Annals*, 8(1), 397-441.

Duhigg, C. (2016). *What Google Learned from its Quest to Build the Perfect Team.* The New York Times Magazine. Retrieved from https://www.nytimes.com/2016/02/28/magazine/what-google-learned-from-its-quest-to-build-the-perfect-team.html

Jang, S. (2018). The Most Creative Teams Have a Specific Type of Cultural Diversity. *Harvard Business Review.* Retrieved from https://hbr.org/2018/07/the-most-creative-teams-have-a-specific-type-of-cultural-diversity

Jay, J. (2013). Navigating Paradox as a Mechanism of Change and Innovation in Hybrid Organisations. *Academy of Management Journal*, 56(1), 137-159.

Lüscher, L. S., & Lewis, M. W. (2008). Organisational Change and Managerial Sensemaking – Working Through Paradox. *Academy of Management Journal*, 51(2), 221-240.

McKergow, M., & Bailey, H. 2014. *Host: Six new roles of engagement for teams, organisations, communities and movements.* London: Solutions Books.

Pentland, A. (2012). The New Science of Building Great Teams. *Harvard Business Review, April 2012.* Retrieved from https://hbr.org/2012/04/the-new-science-of-building-great-teams

Smith, W. K., & Lewis, M. W. (2011). Toward a theory of paradox: A dynamic equilibrium model of organizing. *Academy of Management Review*, 36, 381-403.

Smith, W. K., Besharov, M., Wessels, A., & Chertok, M. (2012). A Paradoxical Leadership Model for Social Entrepreneurs: Challenges, Leadership Skills, and Pedagogical Tools for Managing Social and Commercial Demands. *Academy of Management Learning & Education, 11*(3), 463-478.

Weick, K. E. (1995). *Sensemaking in organisations.* Thousand Oaks, CA: Sage Publications.

Authors

Jonas Hedegaard is currently pursuing an Industrial PhD with Roskilde Festival in collaboration with Roskilde University. Jonas holds a masters degree in Pedagogy, Educational Studies and Psychology and has a professional masters degree in Social Entrepreneurship. Jonas is also trained in narrative and systemic coaching and consultancy and has for many years worked as an organisational consultant, coach and facilitator with a focus on psychosocial work environment, workplace cooperation and management. Jonas is also involved in civic society in Denmark and is engaged with Advisory Boards and committees of several NGOs.

Hans Christian Nielsen *is Head of the Organisation & Culture division at Roskilde Festival. Hans Christian has a masters degree in political science and has been working in different management positions within HR and communications for most of his career.*

Part Two
Host Leadership in Agile settings

10
How to host a successful stand-up meeting

Rod Sherwin (Australia)

Stand-up meetings are used in Agile software development and many other contexts such as hospitality, event management, the construction industry, health care and sports teams. They differ from traditional status meetings as they are more focused on a team self-managing to progress the work of the team and aim to be completed in under 15 minutes. Host Leadership provides a rich variety of perspectives on how to host a successful stand-up meeting – here Rod Sherwin shares his own way of doing it.

What is the purpose of the stand-up meeting?

Stand-up meetings vary from traditional status meetings due to the purpose of the meeting which I define as:

> The purpose of a stand-up meeting is for the team to self-organise to get the work done.

My experience of stand-up meetings comes initially from participating on agile software development teams and for the last few years applying the format for other business teams such as marketing, human resources and change management teams. The stand-up format is so useful that it also used in hospitality, event management, building sites, shift changes in health care, and sports team huddles.

Why do stand-up meetings work?

Stand-up meetings are used across a wide range of contexts as they add a lot of value compared to traditional status meetings. The stand-up meeting is a regular synchronisation point to align the efforts of the team in the direction they are working. Like an airplane that is off course 98% of the time and continually course corrects, every team needs to keep checking they are on course. The longer the gap between course checks, the further off course you can find yourself.

Since the meeting is for the team to self-organise (or self-manage) to get the job done, the stand-up meeting provides an early opportunity to raise issues rather than waiting for a weekly status meeting. The longer an issue festers, the greater the impact it can have. Raising the issue as soon as it becomes evident often means it can be addressed before the impact becomes amplified.

Knowing that the team will regularly be together at a specific time gives us the opportunity to share information from outside the team into the team, keeping the members connected to a wider context. Updates from within the meeting may also trigger communications to other interdependent teams. For example, a software update may trigger the need for an organisational change management team to kick-off training sessions.

When stand-up meetings are combined with a visual workflow or Kanban board showing work items in different states, the team gains motivation from items moving across the board and seeing the progress being made (Anderson, 2016). This is important for creating motivation and momentum.

Finally, having the team together regularly provides an opportunity for team bonding by the sharing of personal events in our lives such as a child's school achievement, a holiday experience, or friendly rivalry about sporting team wins. Sharing this personal information helps the team create psychological safety and vulnerability.

Characteristics of stand-up meetings

They are called "stand-up meetings" because ideally, everyone is standing up as the meeting is conducted. This has the benefit of keeping people focused on finishing the meeting quickly and preventing them going into a traditional 1-hour meeting trance where everyone sits downs, their posture slumps and their concentration wavers. Standing up helps us stay focused, keeps our energy up and we naturally become uncomfortable if the meeting goes on too long.

A stand-up meeting is usually time boxed to a maximum of 15 minutes to keep the discussion short and concise. The need for longer in-depth discussions may be identified during the meeting but are conducted after the meeting or at another time and place.

Stand-up meetings are ideally conducted at the same time and place each day to reduce complexity. Varying the time and place just adds confusion to our already complex work lives. The meetings are held at a frequency that makes sense for the rate of change that the team is dealing with. In Agile software teams, this is usually daily, whereas for marketing or change management teams maybe a twice weekly frequency makes sense, and when in a crisis mode, maybe a meeting is needed as many as three times a day.

Because of standing space and the short time box, the number of people who attend a stand-up has a somewhat natural limit around the number of people who can effectively communicate in the short timeframe. This is usually 3-9 people but there are some much larger groups that use different communication strategies and still have effective stand-ups.

Structure of a stand-up meeting

Stand-up meetings all follow a basic structure:

1. Start at specific time
2. Team collaborates around progressing the work
3. Other updates for the team as a whole
4. Clearly indicate the end of the official part of the stand-up
5. Optional, huddles as needed for deeper discussions

There are two basic formats for part 2 above and I'll share those here, but the stand-up format works best when you adapt it to the needs of your team. What is the important information that your team members need to share each day? There are many other formats to choose from but here are two popular ones:

Three question format

In the three question format, each member of the team concisely answers a variation of three questions:

- What have you done since the previous stand-up?
- What are you planning on working on between now and the next stand-up?
- Are there any issues or blockers to your progressing your work?

Each team member gives the answers to these questions in a short concise update remembering that the stand-up ideally runs for 15 minutes or less. There are many variations to the three questions and an you can find more examples in this presentation (Sherwin, 2016).

Walking the wall

The second format works when you visualise the workflow of the team in some way. A Kanban wall shows work items moving through different states. For example, from Options in a backlog, through to the work being Completed. A simple kanban wall may only have three columns such as To Do, Doing and Done. More complex workflows might have a dozen or more states. The work is broken down into small tasks that can be moved across the wall as they progress. Here is an example Kanban board:

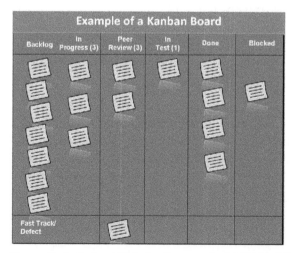

Figure 3: By Dr Ian Mitchell – Own work, CC BY-SA 2.5

With the work of the team visualised on a Kanban wall, the stand-up meeting can focus on "walking the wall" from right to left, operating on the principle of pulling work through the system and focusing on finishing work in progress first, before starting new tasks. The more you start, the less you finish, so the goal is to get better at finishing things rather than starting things.

In the stand-up meeting, you pick an item in the column just before Done, and check with the team members working on that item what they need to finish this item. In the example Kanban board in Figure 1, this would be the item in the "In Test" column. Then move to the next item closest to being finished, e.g. Peer Review, and so on. When the stand-up timebox expires, you have focused on finishing the nearly completed items rather than pushing more work in to the workflow from the left. The team are focused together on the work rather than each individual sharing updates about their work.

There are many more variations of stand-up so pick one to start with and experiment to find one that works for your work and context (Sherwin, 2016).

Exploring the Host Leadership roles

Initiator

Working in Agile software development, a stand-up is often mandated as one of the key team meetings. However, based on the purpose and benefits I've shared above, do you sense a need for a regular stand-up meeting for your team?

Does your team need to have more frequent alignment and synchronisation around their work towards the team's purpose? Do you want to encourage self-management of the team so that you can step back and nurture their confidence and expertise? Do team members need a safe space to share challenges and ask for help?

If you are in the position of team leader, you might sense the need and initiate a stand-up meeting to help the team operate more efficiently and to replace a longer ineffective status meeting.

If you are not in a team leader role, how do you initiate the idea of hosting a stand-up meeting with the leader and other team members? Given the complexity of today's business world, proposing something new can create resistance, so my suggestion is to shape the initiation of a stand-up as an experiment, something to try for a period of time and see what the results are. Use a hypothesis template to shape the idea (Little, 2014).

Hypothesis template

> We think that by <implementing this change>
> we will <solve this problem>
> which will have <these benefits>
> as measured by <these measurements and diagnostics>

For a stand-up meeting, this might look like:

> We think that by having regular team stand-up meetings we will improve team communication, collaboration and alignment, which will have the benefit of moving the team forward, creating visible progress and momentum, coordinating team efforts, creating shared focus on outcomes, and harnessing the collective talent of the team as measured by

- project task completion frequency
- improved quality of work
- the morale of the team and
- reduction of other team meetings.

Pick a regular time and frequency and get started. You will learn more by starting the meeting and seeing how the team interacts and then listen for what's needed to continuously adapt your approach. If this is a new format for your team, give everyone permission to do it badly first, and learn and improve from there.

Inviter

Have you ever received an email newsletter that you didn't sign up for? It's annoying and an imposition on your time and energy. You quickly look for the unsubscribe link to get rid of the annoyance. Yet in the corporate world, how often are changes imposed upon us without a request to opt-in?

Offering an invitation to team members to attend the stand-up and giving them the option to say 'No' will change the energy of the attendees. Take the time to share with the invitees the hoped-for benefits of the stand-up. Tell them that you are conducting an experiment as outlined above, and that you would like both their participation and feedback about the value they find from using this new format.

Host Leadership tells us that a powerful invitation should include three aspects: Acknowledgment, Attraction, and Choice. For our stand-up meeting your invite might be something like this:

Acknowledgement

I would like to introduce a new meeting format called a stand-up meeting. This format is a great way for us to come together and self-manage around getting our work done. I believe we can achieve more as a team by drawing on each other's strengths and creativity rather than using traditional task association and status updates.

Attraction

I know we are all busy and the last thing we need is another meeting. However, the stand-up format is short and sharp and delivers a lot of value in a short period of time. Hopefully, this stand-up meeting will replace several of our other meetings because of its effectiveness and efficiency. The stand-up meeting is not a status update but an opportunity for the team to work together and collaborate on achieving our goals. It's also an opportunity to raise issues and ask for help.

Choice

As this is an experiment for us, you have the option to attend or not. I hope you will join us as it works best when the whole team is present and I hope you will attend to help learn about, contribute to and evolve the format of this meeting to make it the most useful for us moving forward.

I suggest combining the elements of the Host Leadership invite with the 4-Part Game Structure to make the invitation even clearer (McGonigal, 2011). Thinking of the stand-up meeting as a game might seem odd but games give us key elements that help us understand how to execute and succeed in a given activity.

The 4-part Game Structure consists of:

- A clear Goal – How do we win at the game or what is the purpose of the game
- Rules – how to play the game
- Progress Tracking – how to keep score
- Opt-in Participation – it's not fun if you're compelled to participate.

We already have the Opt-in item from the Choice part of the Host Leadership invite and we have also included the Goal. Adding the Rules and the Progress tracking to the invite will help make the invite even sharper. We can add an additional paragraph outlining the rules, depending on which format you're planning on using, for example for the 3-Question format:

> The stand-up meeting will start at 10:15am each day at our team space. We will aim to keep the meeting to 15 minutes or less. Each person will concisely answer 3 questions about what you have worked on, are planning to work on and if you have any blockers. Should a given discussion start to become too detailed, anyone can call time-out and the discussion can be taken offline.

If you're planning to use the Walk the Walk format than you would change the rules to match.

Inviting team members to host the stand-up meeting

With many teams, there is someone in charge and by default they might be considered the host of a stand-up meeting. While the team leader is responsible for setting a direction and explaining the purpose of the work, modern ways of working encourage self-managing teams to work out amongst themselves how to achieve the desired outcomes. So, if the team is self-organising around the work, can the host change as well?

As a stand-up meeting host, I try very quickly to step back from the role of facilitating the stand-up meeting and instead coach the team members to take turns in hosting the meeting. This builds shared ownership for the outcome we are working towards, develops the confidence of team members in speaking up, and helps shift away from the traditional status update format where status is reported to the person in charge but the team isn't necessarily collaborating around progressing the work.

My simple approach to inviting people to take a turn at hosting the stand-up is to hold up a token such as a permanent marker at the start of the meeting and ask, "Who would like to host today's stand-up?" Someone then takes the permanent marker from me and the meeting begins.

Space Creator

Space shapes the way we operate and influences our thinking. In Host Leadership we consider physical, mental and psychological space. Let's start by looking at the physical space in which you host your stand-up.

A training exercise that I regularly run called the Ball-Point Game involves a team self-organising to optimise the flow of tennis balls thrown between all the participants in the team. As we often use a training room with a class-room layout of desks, I see the teams constrained by the physical layout of the room as to what solutions they can come up with. Narrow spaces between tables constrain teams to lining up facing each other in parallel lines. However, when there is more open space, teams tend to come up with more circular configurations. This is how physical space can influence our thinking.

When you are hosting a stand-up meeting where everyone attends in person, do you have enough space for people to circle around and see each other or are you compressed in a meeting room or close to a wall where people need to overlap to gather together? Can you have a comfortable semi-circle with everyone able to see each other and the workflow board?

How comfortable are the team in talking at normal volumes in the space? Are they too close to other teams or are they in an open space where other people nearby are trying to work and your team may be disturbing them?

Is your team able to customise the space to make it theirs? Some offices have rules about the placement of post-it notes on windows and walls and restrict their customisation. Your team may be forced to have their stand-up in a meeting room to prevent the noise from impacting other workers on the same floor but then have to vacate the meeting room without leaving any trace.

Given it is called a stand-up meeting, does your space encourage people to stand-up? I have removed chairs from meeting rooms so that when people arrive, they have no option but to stand. This also needs to be balanced with common-sense where, if someone has a health issue that prevents them from standing, a seat is provided.

Ideal solutions I've seen are for teams to have their own dedicated room where they can put things up on the walls that over time becomes their space. I've also seen large mobile whiteboards used to reflect the work, values, principles, purpose and calendar of a team. The benefit of the large mobile white board is that it is easy for the team to wheel around to wherever they are seated, or into a meeting room during the stand-up.

One small thing that makes a big difference is to provide the materials that the team needs to customise their space. This may be as simple as a good supply of post-it notes, colourful permanent markers, Blu-Tack and string.

If your team is geographically distributed and your stand-ups are hosted virtually either via teleconference or video conference, you need to work even harder to shape the virtual space for your team. High quality video connections and large screens are important to recreate as closely as possible the feeling of meeting in person.

Gatekeeper

In hosting a stand-up, you decide who to invite and who to exclude from the stand-up. The core group of people who need to attend the stand-up are those doing the work. Having organised the stand-up meeting from the perspective of all the Host Leadership roles, the running of the stand-up meeting may be taken on by members of the team as they grow familiar with the format and self-organise to run it. When the host can step back from facilitating the stand-up meeting, the team has reached a good level of maturity with the stand-up format.

The purpose of a stand-up meeting is for the team to self-organise to get the work done. As the host you need to protect this meeting from those not directly involved in the work. When stand-up meetings are new, well-meaning managers may want to participate, yet they can be a distracting influence that disrupts the container of psychological safety created for and by the team. In the Gatekeeper role, you may need to have a coaching conversation with these managers to acknowledge their interest and to suggest they either observe silently from the side or engage with the team at another time.

As the host, I encourage the team to take ownership of their stand-up. I often give them a basic structure and I also expect the format to change and evolve over time to suit the people in the team, the location, and the type of work the team are doing.

The Gatekeeper role helps us engage some of the rules of the game that I explored in the Inviter role. For example, what time will the stand-up be held? Does first thing in the morning work, or do some members come in a little later after dropping children off to school?

First thing in the morning is my most creative time, so I would rather have a stand-up later in the morning so as not to interrupt my most productive time of day. What about if you're working with a team in another time zone? What time is good to overlap with them, or can you have one stand-up at the start of day in your time zone and then another stand-up when the other team comes online?

Having clear signals to start and end the stand-up meeting help the host in the Gatekeeper role set the time box for the meeting. A simple "Let's get started" is enough to kick things off, maybe followed by a mindfulness or check-in process to help set up the psychological container. More on this shortly. At the end of the stand-up, I say the words "Stand-up done" so that participants are very clear when the formal part of the stand-up is complete, and they can return to their work if they are not sticking around for any follow-up conversations.

During the stand-up, the Gatekeeper may encourage the team to use a pre-arranged signal for when a discussion is becoming too detailed. I often use a simple hand signal with one hand horizontally on top of the fingers of my other handheld vertically to form a t-shape to indicate a time-out is needed and the discussion can be organised to continue elsewhere. I have also heard the term ELMO (Enough, let's move on) used by some teams.

If there are guests who need to attend the team's stand-up meeting, be sure to introduce them to the team and clearly convey the purpose of their being there. Take time with the guest beforehand to educate them about the format of the stand-up and when they will be given their opportunity to speak.

Connector

An important part of connecting as human beings is to share our whole selves. One of the simpler ways to do this is to allow time for small talk just before or at the start of a meeting. This occurs naturally for stand-ups happening in person as people gather at the place where the stand-up is being held. There is usually a quick chat about sport games, what people did at the weekend, or where someone is thinking of going for their holidays

With virtual stand-up meetings, I have found that opening the teleconference bridge or video conference five minutes before the official start time gives people a chance to share small talk and connect before the official start of the meeting. For remote workers, this social connection is especially important to combat the social isolation that can impact their wellbeing.

To connect people into the space, or container of the stand-up, I have found it powerful to start a stand-up with a short mindfulness technique.

Once everyone is in attendance, ask everyone to take three deep breaths, in through the nose, out through the mouth, each one slightly longer than the previous one. With each out breath, allow the body to relax into the currently place and time. This has the effect of people bringing their mind to where they body is and helping them be more present.

There are many other forms of check-in that you can use (See Checkinsuccess-com, 2019).

A quick reminder of the team's purpose and goals at the start of the stand-up helps the team reconnect to this purpose, shift their perspective from being lost in the weeds of task completion and consider more creative ways to achieve the team's outcomes. In a physical space, this may be as easy as referring to a poster on the wall which captures the purpose and goals of your team. For virtual teams, it may be screen sharing a slide or two from a slide deck before switching to the virtual Kanban board.

While we want to connect the team together as a cohesive unit, the team itself is one of many teams in the organisation so you need to create connections with these other teams to get work done. Sociocracy 3.0 has the idea of double-linking, where an elected person from one team attends the meetings of another team to represent the source team's interests and provide a channel for information to flow between the two teams (Sociocracy 3.0, 2019). If you need to connect with another team, consider stepping into the Inviter role and shaping a powerful invitation to the other team requesting someone to attend your stand-up, and offering to have a member of your team link with them.

Co-Participant

Remembering that the purpose of a stand-up meeting is for the team to self-organise to get the work done, the host leader will need to carefully coach the team not just to provide status updates directed at themselves as the team leader. Instead, the host will be in their position "with the guests" and direct the attention of the team members to each other as they share what is happening with the team's work. When the host's turn comes around, they will take their position briefly "in the spot-light", share their update but then clearly step back to the position "with the guests" as part of the team.

One tip here is that, if you find your team members giving status updates to you as the team leader, don't make eye contact with them but instead direct your gaze at other team members and the other person will naturally follow you gaze. This is a subtle non-verbal signal to have the team communicate with each other.

If the team is new to the short sharp stand-up format, the host may spend time with the individual team members "in the kitchen" before the stand-up, coaching them on how to make their updates during the stand-up as concise as possible.

Finally, during the stand-up, the host leader will need to have some of their awareness on the host position "in the gallery" to notice how well stand-up is working, whether it is flowing, is it of value to the team, has it grown stale, and can something be changed or re-initiated to continuously improve.

Summary

The stand-up meeting is a valuable structured meeting and can often replace several other less effective meetings when it is done well. It takes time for a team to master the format and all the roles and the positions of the host leader provide different perspectives to make the meeting as useful, efficient and effective as possible. If you're operating with an Agile team, consider applying the host roles and positions to the other Agile workshops such as sprint planning, showcases and retrospectives.

References

Anderson, D. J. (2016). What is Kanban. Retrieved 11 August 2019, from https://leankanban.com/project/wkanban/Checkinsuccesscom. (2019). Checkinsuccesscom. Retrieved 11 August 2019, from https://checkinsuccess.com/

Little, J. (2014). Lean Change Management. (1st ed.). Happy Melly Express.

McGonigal, J. (2011). Reality Is Broken: Why Games Make Us Better and How They Can Change the World. (1st ed.). USA: Penguin Books.

Sherwin, R. (2016, 16 February). How to Host a Successful Agile Stand-up Meeting. Retrieved 11 August 2019, from https://www.slideshare.net/rodsherwin/how-to-host-a-successful-agile-standup-meeting Sociocracy 3.0: Effective Collaboration at any Scale . (CC BY-SA 4.0 2019). Double-Linked Hierarchy. Retrieved 11 August, 2019, from https://patterns.sociocracy30.org/double-linked-hierarchy.html

Author

Rod Sherwin is a solutioneer, coach, facilitator and speaker who uses solutions-focused approaches as a direct route to create Business Agility and respectful lasting change for individuals, teams and organisations. Rod has applied his unique experience to create positive organisational change in industries such as telecommunications, government, civil engineering, digital, banking and consulting. Having seen how Agile approaches have helped improved the way we work at team level, Rod is now facilitating business agility to allow companies to respond and adapt to the rapid pace of change and competitor innovation.

11
Host your team in a Relationship Retro

Olga Kiss and Gabriella Peuker (Hungary)

Just as the relationship between the leader and the team members is a key factor in performance, the relationships among team members are equally important for an agile self-organising team. Agile teams regularly meet to look back and improve their teamwork by learning from their experiences. Relationship Retros are special occasions when the team reflect on their recent collaboration and relationships. In this practical chapter Olga and Gabi examine how the host leader leads by example and helps team members to connect in an open, brave, autonomous way by creating an atmosphere where everyone can be themselves.

Introduction

We always make some sort of contract at the beginning of a retrospective – not only about the subject and the aim of the meeting, but also about the process. Setting the working agreements in a classical retrospective usually requires 10-30 minutes, no more. Derby-Larsen suggests 3-7 working agreements are set. These are meant to be rules; "Having more than seven is too hard to remember and follow" (Derby & Larsen, 2006, p. 49). However, you will find here 13 cards, and I always have empty cards for new ideas to evolve. But as you see, these parts of the agreement belong to each other tightly. One can say that they are all about the same thing – maybe from different perspectives.

This is not the classic working agreement Derby and Larsen talk about, because Relationship Retro – especially with working in depth – is special. It requires deeper trust, psychological safety. As coaches, we are aware of the relevance of stating explicitly all the important parts of the agreement. We make a **psychological contract** at the beginning of a development process. **Dialogue cards** help groups and teams to have really constructive dialogues, to start to hear each other's true voice.

The story behind

For a long time, I supposed that it was enough to ask the participants how we wanted to *work* together, how we wanted to *be* together in the following session. They usually collected some ideas, and we used to vote on each of them. I used to do a similar activity to that described in Derby and Larsen (2006, p. 48-49). All of the parts seemed to be so obvious that I usually spent a very short time with this part of the contract. Half an hour used to be enough. I just (implicitly) supposed that:

1) All of the participants understood the meaning of these words in the same way

2) All of them agreed that we wanted to work together under this sort of agreement, if they simply said yes to them

3) In this way, it was not necessary to discuss the meanings in detail explicitly.

But it has become clear to us that none of these presuppositions are right. We had a group coaching during which a debate escalated. One of the participants was able to express his thoughts very strongly, but it took a long time for him to formulate them in a way which could be satisfying to himself. These were really brilliant ideas, so I tried to leave him as much time as he needed, but some other participants started to be more and more impatient, even starting to laugh at him quietly. At first I felt that their behaviour was impolite. But then I realised that the tension of this process was mainly inherited from other tensions in the company. This situation was simply too much for the group.

This was the point at which I realised the importance of the contract. Since then we spend as much time with the contract as the group needs. Sometimes it takes two to three hours in a two-day workshop/coaching event. But finally, it can become the most important part of the whole programme. We hope that you will see why.

Dialogue cards

You will need ...

- Cards (sometimes I use handwritten cards) with the following labels on them (one expression on each):
    - intention to understand each other
    - pay attention to each other (give undivided attention)
    - respect
    - open-mindedness
    - constructive dialogue
    - partnership, equality
    - empathy
    - trust
    - safe space
    - support each other
    - thinking together
    - collective wisdom
    - unbiased, non-judgemental
- Some blank cards
- Pens

How to use the cards

Each member of the group chooses one or two cards, making sure that everyone has at least one card. We ask them to tell us what the card tells them. How do they interpret it?

Someone starts by saying what that expression means to him/her. Sometimes a small debate emerges around the meaning; the goal is not to have the "right meaning" of the term, but rather a "shared meaning". When we see an opportunity for some sort of synthesis of the different interpretations, we offer the agreement: shall we accept this as a basis for our work for the following hours? Do we agree on it? (Can it be a part of our psychological contract?)

If yes, then OK, we go to someone else's card. (Usually, people say "my card is connected to that one …".) Yes – all the cards are interconnected. They are almost all about the same thing: how can we think together in a way that leads us to collective wisdom (and not the opposite).

Some cards, some requirements will not be accepted. It's okay. The point is to clarify the shared values of the discussion and make the group aware of them. This awareness can change people's habits for the better.

Rationale

Why is this activity so important? Usually participants realise here for the first time that although almost all of them can accept these values, they can mean a lot of different things to them. If they did not clarify these terms, they could agree only in words without really agreeing on the content. They realise that it is not enough to say "yes"; they have to have a shared vision, a shared understanding of the spirit of these terms.

These are not rules of cooperation, because they are not rules at all. They are values, and after the whole discussion we start to have not only an agreement but a shared sense of these values as well. Of course, we have rules: when to start the meeting and when to finish, but this is something completely different.

So why is it so important? Because in many places these small circles of dialogue can give fresh air. People start to breathe together. A different sense of being together can occur.

It is also important that they can understand each other's frame of reference better. It is a good starting point to have better, deeper relationships.

Results – a story

On one occasion at the end of this activity, a girl said: "I have decided to change my behaviour for these two days. Usually, I like to make jokes, but now I realise, that there may be people here who do not know me well enough, and who may be hurt by my sense of humour." As coach, I said thank you to her and told the group how much I appreciate such a gesture because I know how hard it could be for her not to react with her usual attitude. Making jokes can be a primary source of fun. Hurtful jokes will not create a safe space to talk about emotions and feelings. Her decision was important for all of us.

Comments

A story

Once, while we were talking about the cards, a woman asked me why I supposed that they did not have the conversation in this way all the time. "These are such obvious requirements", she said. Then I told her the story of the origin of this activity, and my original mistake when I supposed the same and it let the discussion go badly. Only after hearing that story did she start to accept that such an agreement could be important at the outset.

Special qualities of a Relationship Retro

The normal "usual" retrospectives may work well without such a specific agreement (psychological contract). But when we want to talk about relationships on a deeper level, this requires special trust, special ways of talking to each other. Deepening is risky. It requires an Adult Ego State (in terms of transactional analysis – for more on ego states see Berne, 1969, pp. 23-28). A joke can break this trust, even if it looks innocent. The coach has to see these dangerous actions (speech acts, among others), and address them. But the team has to decide whether they can and want go deeper, or not. At what level of their relationships do they wish to work?

Timing

We usually make this psychological contract at the beginning of coaching processes. However, if you are a scrum master, agile coach or agile leader, it could be also useful to make parts of this sort of contract as the need comes up. Do not worry if you haven't made such a contract with your team yet. The time may come when you feel the urge to do that. Use that time to make such an agreement among team members.

Conclusion

In this activity the host leader (scrum master, Agile coach) leads by example. Through the dialogue cards, a psychological contract is created by the team. This activity helps team members to connect in an open, brave, autonomous way. This is how they can create an atmosphere where everyone can be themselves.

References

Berne, E. (1969). *Games People Play: The Basic Handbook of Transactional Analysis.* New York, NY: Ballantine Books, Random House.

Derby, E., & Larsen, D. (2006). *Agile Retrospectives: Making Good Teams Great.* Raleigh, NC: Pragmatic Bookshelf.

Authors

Olga Kiss, PhD is a coach with 10 years' experience, an academic at Budapest Corvinus University and the VP of Research at EMCC Hungary. Mathematics, philosophy, technical studies and financial informatics, together with her decades-long teaching at the University of Economics and working with CMSs, give her the opportunity to understand many dialects of 'expert language' and fluency in changing frames of interpretation. Her special interest is reflection and self-reflection in retrospectives. LinkedIn: https://www.linkedin.com/in/kissolga/

Gabriella Peuker is an EMCC EIA accredited coach at Practitioner level, team coach, trainer and OD consultant. She is a developer of Agile teams and organisations in Agile transformation. She is interested in the human side of Agile leadership; deepening soft skills. She has more than 15 years of experience in working with groups and teams in the business. Her special interest is emotional deepening, autonomy and psychological contract in retrospectives.
LinkedIn: https://www.linkedin.com/in/peukergabriella/

Olga Kiss and Gabriella Peuker are the founders and organisers of the Self-Organizing Teams Meetup, the Self-Organizing Teams Vienna Meetup, and the Future of HR Meetup. Website: agilehuman.eu

12
Creating a self sustaining community with rotating hosts in a high stakes situation

Michael de la Maza (USA)

Host Leadership makes for an effective way to create and build communities, professional and otherwise. In this chapter Michael de la Maza describes his experience of forming a self-sustaining based online community of agile team coaches in the Bay area of California.

Introduction

This is a story of how a group of professionals used Host Leadership to create a self-sustaining community that helps members become certified team coaches. It demonstrates the power of Host Leadership in a high stakes situation.

The Scrum Alliance Certified Team Coach (CTC) certification is one of the highest and most difficult to obtain certifications in the agile space, with fewer than 200 people having obtained the certification as of August, 2019. CTCs are Certified Agile Coaches (CACs) that work with Scrum teams, stakeholders, and managers to improve value, flow and culture.

Becoming a CTC is a formidable task for even the most experienced professionals. For starters, the professional needs to be an active Certified Scrum Professional (CSP) and also have logged at least 1,000 hours in the past two years as a coach. They also are expected to be active in the agile community, be it through volunteering or contributing to meetups, conferences, continuing education groups, or things along those lines.

There are many benefits to being a CTC. In particular, the Scrum Alliance Certification via Coaching program allows CTCs to recommend up to 50 individuals per year for the introductory level certifications, a very large market opportunity.

Although the CTC certification requires significant time and effort, it's well worth the effort. Certification holders on average earn more money, can take on more complex projects, and achieve recognition of their expertise among numerous other benefits.

Starting the certified Team Coach special interest group

As a Certified Agile Coach I enjoy helping others on their professional development journeys, which is why I became a co-organiser of the BayALN agile user group, the largest agile group in the San Francisco Bay area, with over 3,000 members.

In 2016 as part of our annual retrospective, I found that many of our members wanted more focused groups. After running a poll, I found that one of the topics people had the most interest in was a group for advanced Agile coaches. Based on this interest, in January 2017 I started a special interest group on that topic. While the group originally had in-person meetings, the traffic in the Bay area made it difficult for members to attend, so we shifted to holding online meetings.

Launching with Host Leadership

In the spirit of improving overall professional development, I chose to embrace the Host Leadership model as it provided numerous advantages over using the servant-leadership model or me working as the permanent facilitator.

I chose to embrace Host Leadership because I thought it would be interesting to apply it outside a corporate setting in a group that was volunteer-based. It also allowed me to combine my expertise in becoming a CAC with the ability to shift to different stances.

Initially I acted as the hero – in my case, it was handling initial group logistics, developing a meeting agenda, and being the sole facilitator. However, after the first year, I was able to step back. This chapter tells the story of that particular journey for me. Ultimately, the Host Leadership model provided me with the ability to lay the groundwork for the group, and then allow the members to take the lead, which in turn enabled them to grow professionally (the primary purpose of the group).

Although embracing a new leadership model can seem overwhelming, hosting is something familiar to anyone who has hosted a party, so applying it isn't as difficult as it sounds. The flexibility means that anyone can serve as a host regardless of status, such as being a CEO, mid level manager, or even an entry level employee.

During the early phases of the group, I served as the initiator that worked in the spotlight. As the group took on a steady routine I then shifted my role to the inviter, focusing on growing the group through social media.

Rotating hosts

As the group took off, other members came into the spotlight and facilitated the meetings. In general the roles within the group changed naturally, with volunteers being selected each week to fill the different roles. Today, I'm a co-participator and if you attend one of our meetings you cannot tell that I started the group.

The first significant step that took place was to rotate meeting hosts. At the end of every meeting, members of the group would volunteer to host the next meeting. If no one volunteered, I would continue to host. During this period I was "in the gallery" observing the hosting and supporting when necessary.

This continued for several months until, during one retrospective, one of the top voted items was to rotate hosts. Since that time I have not hosted a single meeting!

Another large change that was led by the participants was the use of new technology. The tools that I had proposed as initiator – an online email list and shared drive – were deprecated in favour of using Slack. This move was entirely driven by the members of the community. I was not familiar with Slack, did not know how it was set up or managed, and now I am a co-participator on the Slack channel.

On two occasions I found it challenging to not be the initiator who was in the spotlight:

- The group is open to everyone and we had one individual join who I found highly disruptive. I was concerned that this person would wreck the group. I considered intervening but ultimately chose not to. In the end, the members of the group discussed the situation and the disruptive individual chose to leave the group. This demonstrated to me that all group members had become leaders who were willing to step in and become gatekeepers to protect the group.

- Sometimes members of the group fail to obtain the certification and vent to others during the group meetings. In these situations I have chosen to be a silent co-participator instead of intervening.

Impact of the group

The group members work in a variety of industries, but the common theme is their commitment to the profession. Upon joining, members commit to attending 60% of all meetings until they achieve CTC certification (or decide not to pursue it), and if a meeting is missed, the member agrees to review the notes and video from that session.

Group members also share the common goal of helping establish Agile coaching as a profession, and they also have a desire to learn about online collaboration tools and techniques, to help improve their ability to work in a world where distributed teams are the norm.

Since the first group session, over 100 people have participated in our meetings, and eight people have become Certified Team Coaches (CTCs). In fact, approximately 20% of the people who have become CTCs while the group has been active have been members.

After successfully implementing the host leadership model in my CTC training group, the biggest lesson I've learnt is that leaders can't be afraid to let go of being "in the spotlight".

They need to let others hold the centre position. It might be hard at first, but time has shown repeatedly that the most effective leaders are the ones that not only delegate effectively, but that also help team members to grow professionally.

Author

Michael de la Maza is the founder of Heart Healthy Scrum and a Scrum Alliance Certified Enterprise Coach (CEC). Previously, he was VP of Corporate Strategy at Softricity (acquired by Microsoft in 2006) and co-founder of Inquira (acquired by Oracle in 2011). He is the co-editor of Agile Coaching: Wisdom from Practitioners *and* Best Agile Articles of 2017 *and co-author of* Professional Scrum with TFS 2010 *and* Why Agile Works: The Values Behind The Results. *He holds a PhD in Computer Science from MIT. https://www.hearthealthyscrum.com*

13
The trainer as a host leader

Pierluigi Pugliese and Markus Reinhold (Germany)

Thinking and acting as a host is open to anyone who works with others, whether that's as a leader, manager, front-line staff member, volunteer, nurse, teacher or whatever. This chapter comes from a discussion at the Host Leadership Gathering about how trainers can take the ideas of Host Leadership to enhance the learning and connections they build.

Introduction

What does it mean to be a good trainer? This question has had many different answers by many different authors in the past. But can Host Leadership as a metaphor gives us some higher level concepts to approach being a better trainer? In our experience it does! In particular:

- Host Leadership unifies different approaches, making the ideas coming from different disciplines more relevant and usable in practise. We could say that while Host Leadership does not give us a specific tool, it allows us to integrate different tools in a systematic way, and guides us to use whatever other trick we have in our toolbox in a coherent and useful way

- It helps us put the training participants in the centre, thus giving us a different way to approach classroom work: participants have knowledge that we can pull in and integrate with the value the trainer provides. The trainer is suddenly not the only one knowing stuff! If you are a professional trainer you can probably appreciate better how important this aspect is, especially in adult education

- The relationship between trainer and participants is now conceived in a way which encourages them to explore together; the co-participating role is an important part of being a trainer

- Through Host Leadership the trainer becomes a positive role model, especially when the training is related to leadership, cooperation, communication – any kind of interaction

- By thinking of themselves as a host, the trainer becomes more approachable, hence making possible a better trainer-participant relationship, with benefits for the learning process. Fostering cooperation over confrontation is beneficial for learning
- When acting as host, the trainer can now also show vulnerability, making them more approachable by the learners
- The trainer is in a better position to accept and integrate feedback from the learners.

Let's now drill down into how the Host Leadership roles (McKergow & Bailey, 2014) can be beneficial while being a trainer…

Initiator

Being an initiator is in any case part of being a trainer: How do I approach a topic? What am I going to say? What exercises shall I set up?…

Host Leadership, with its focus on the interaction between host and guests, promotes a different approach to this role. Suddenly the questions "what do they need?" and "how can I help them?" become the centre of attention when initiating something. In our perspective "thinking host" reminds us we are there for the participants and not to show off how great we are as trainers. It makes us more humble, and at the same time puts us in a better position to cater for the learners' experience.

Inviter

This role is crucial! Properly inviting participants is possibly the most important part of creating a proper learning environment. Invitation is the basic building block to move from "old style" trainer to modern educator, a very important mind shift.

Before the training you could…

- Invite people to participate, stating how important their contributions are
- Appreciate your participants, inviting them to be an active part of the learning experience
- Set and frame the expectations of the participants regarding their participation and contributions

- Inform them of (or at least propose) the basic rules to know in advance: start/stop time, breaks, team agreements, ...
- Provoke a smile and use a little humour

During the training you could...

- Invite people to participate
- Invite openness about someone's needs
- Invite people to take care of themselves: participants should monitor how they are doing and be prepared to ask for breaks, further explanations, fresh air, coffee, ...

These are invitations that are worthwhile offering constantly during a training!

After the training you could ...

- Invite people to continue learning and integrating knowledge (and perhaps suggest some routes to doing that)
- Invite people to share experiences (and maybe offer a way to do that)
- Invite the group to stay in contact (for those who wish to do so) – collecting and circulating contact details for those who wish it, setting up an online group, sharing pictures, and so on.

Space Creator

For a trainer, being a good Space Creator is also extremely important! It is also a very complex role, as you have to deal with all the aspects of "space":

- Room settings
- Setting stages for experiences (including mental state)
- Break settings (time, space, access to food etc., fresh air, ...)
- Preparing questions/materials/exercises/...
- Preparing and looking after interaction space – so that participants feel 'safe enough' and confident to participate with the trainer and each other
- Offering headspace time for reflection and personal meaning-making.

In this role you often have to confront yourself with the limitations you will find: constraints coming from the client, the location, the mood of the participants ... You will need to be at times very creative in order to create a good space despite all the problems you'll find. However, focusing on guests is the crucial factor in determining how we act. One way to handle this is to actually ask your participants to help! This can even be beneficial for the training experience. Helping people feel involved and engaged is particularly helpful. As the late and much-missed accelerated learning pioneer Dave Meier used to say, "Never do for learners what they can do for themselves, or for each other".

A personal story of one of the authors:

> "One day I was preparing for a training. But when the participants arrived, it was clearly not the perfect day. The company had just announced a restructuring that was going to result in a massive downsizing. As a trainer I had to do something and work on the mental and interactional space. As a first activity, just after the initial introduction to the course, I invited them to discuss how the material they were supposed to learn in the course could become useful in their professional career, even if outside of that company. After that, I rarely saw such a committed group of learners!"

Gatekeeper

The Gatekeeper role is part of your constant activities as a trainer:

- How to deal with the different personalities of the participants in training: Host Leadership allows for contextuality ...
    - 'Alpha' people (very outgoing and strong)
    - Shy people
    - People who think they know more than they do
    - People who always wait for others to speak first
    - People who don't give space to anyone else
    - And many more ...
- What rules do we need to give? What can we leave open?
- What rules/limitations/... coming from the outside (company, management, ...) do we need to consider? How much flexibility do we have with these?

- What about the participation of people who do not belong to the group, in particular somebody who could endanger the psychological safety of the group: the manager, or some 'external observer' that might be perceived as a 'spy' by the group.
- Whatever rules are given or agreed, you need to be sure they are clear for everybody and accepted as broadly as possible
- One particular case of the previous point is the description and set-up of the activities performed during the training, as they are usually crucial for a proper experience of the activity.

Remember: you are still the host! So while you might delegate the gatekeeper role, as a trainer you are the "final" gatekeeper in the room, responsible for the training experience.

Connector

As a Connector you should help people work together as a group and make sure they have a shared context to build the training experience on.

You could also help the learners connect also after the training: working group, peer groups for exercises, communities of practice, and so on.

Co-participator

Modern training is also about co-participating: make your training a group effort, have your participants share their knowledge and their experience, and help them learn from each other.

One way you can usefully co-participate is to go first when an activity has to be modelled, to show the participants what you expect. Mark McKergow always goes first when it's time for introductions in his own trainings, so that everyone else knows the kind of thing he is after from them. (Note that to do this properly you need to be able to set aside your need to be a particular show-off! There will be other times for this if it's really what you want to do.)

In our experience the basic question you should ask yourself in this role is "how could I make it a collective effort, a 'group concert' rather than 'my training'"?

Conclusion

The role of trainer offers many opportunities for using Host Leadership skills to build engagement with your guests (learners). This is in contrast to the old 'heroic' teacher model that used to be common in schools decades ago – the teacher is the last to arrive, the learners rise and obediently greet the teacher, who takes control of the room. From a host leader viewpoint where the trainer is both the first and the last, the host trainer is the first to arrive (so they can prepare the room and greet the learners) and also the last to leave (having brought the session to a close and said goodbye to the learners).

Similar thinking can be applied to many other organisational roles: facilitator, internal and external consultant, project leader, meeting host, coach and so on. Let your imagination and good sense tell you how to experiment with Host Leadership and see the response for yourself.

References

McKergow, M., & Bailey, H. (2014). *Host: Six new roles of engagement for teams, organisations, communities and movements.* London: Solutions Books.

Authors

Pierluigi Pugliese is founder and managing director of Connexxo GmbH and active as Agile Coach, Systemic Consultant and Trainer. He has a long experience in various roles in software development organisations and complex international projects. As an expert for Agile and Scrum works flexibly in various functions: consultant, coach, trainer, facilitator, ... depending on whether the client wants to implement Agile methods in just one team or spread the agile values and principles to the whole organisation. https://connexxo.com

Markus Reinhold founded CoCOO in 1999. He supports organisations to improve their way of working. This includes work in engineering activities as well as work on social and organisational topics. Markus is a conference speaker and has contributed to more than eight books in the area of process improvement. CoCOO is a network of independent agile / lean specialists that help their customers in various areas with training and coaching. Markus serves the team as a host leader. Working in complex environments has taught Markus that appropriate leadership approaches are essential – which has led him to favour the Host Leadership metaphor. Markus can be contacted via email at info@cocoo.de

14
Can it be that simple? Cases of a minimalistic use of the metaphor

Géry Derbier (France)

Host Leadership is notable for being both a metaphor and a model. While the model has many rich aspects, the metaphor on its own can be hugely powerful in connecting with both experienced and new leaders. In this chapter Géry relates his experience of engaging people with the simple metaphor of leading as a host.

Introduction

Considering the vast amount of literature available, it seems leadership and management in organisation is a complicated matter. But is it? Since Mark McKergow told me about Host Leadership for the first time in Bad Piedmont six years ago, I have run several workshops in conferences and incorporated the material in the Agile Management trainings I give with Laurent Sarrazin (see his chapter in this book) at Rupture(21.

Each time the response of the participants in these events has been very positive. But the most satisfying results I have seen came from rather simple conversations.

The presentation review

A team asked me to help them for a high-stakes presentation they had to deliver in front of a panel of executives of a business unit of their company. They had in mind showing me the presentation so that I could review it. Instead, I started exploring what a successful presentation would be for them. At that moment in the conversation, the team conceived of itself clearly as the owner of the success of the event. Then I continued:

- *You've been asked for this presentation...*
- *Yes, at the end of the last one we made.*
- *Who asked?*
- *The business unit.*
- *Who among the people that will attend the next presentation?*
- *Hum...*
- *Who invited you? You've been invited, right?*
- *Oh yes. Peter T. did. He is the head of the business unit.*
- *Peter T. invited you?*
- *Yes.*
- *So, he is the host of the event.*
- *Yes.*
- *What are his success criteria for the event?*
- *...you mean we should ask him?*

Deference for hierarchy was a hallmark of the management culture in the company they worked for. Now in the conversation, it was clear the team had reframed its view of the situation. The introduction of the idea of being guests of a host seemed to have enabled them to talk about going to Peter and asking him about what would please him and the other guests. They saw themselves as helping Peter to host a successful event.

They did ask. Peter changed the agenda and put the presentation first in the schedule to have time for discussions. The presentation was a success.

The newbie project manager

Sebastian has been promoted to a position of project manager. He would have to work with couple of dozen people in the team. He had no previous experience of project management. The unit he was working in had no culture of project management.

His boss suggested that he could copy the daily meeting some teams in the IT department were practising and that seemed to get good results. The meeting would last twenty-something minutes, they would use a whiteboard where the necessary information would be displayed. Sebastian was a bit lost. He could only afford thirty minutes for a coaching conversation with me. He started:

"I told them I had no experience in project management whatsoever. And I don't understand what is expected from me at the meeting. I've been told the people attending the daily meeting should self-organise and say themselves what they have done and what they intend to do for the next day. So, what's my role? What am I supposed to actually do?".

He continued describing what he thought a good project manager was like. The picture soon looked like an omniscient super-hero dressed in an orchestra director suit. Then I interjected:

"Look, imagine for a moment that in your situation you are a host and the people are your guests. What does a good host do?"

Sebastian and I continued the conversation exploring the interactions between the host and his guests. After a couple of minutes Sebastian said:

"Oh yes I see. You know what? In real life I'm a pretty good host. I can manage it. Thank you."

A couple of weeks later, we had a short meeting where he told me he was managing his way through reasonably well.

The flourishing new manager

Clara is a young woman who has been promoted to a management position. She had no previous experience of management and initially she was not really interested in becoming a manager. Even so, she accepted the challenge of developing a unit located a hundred kilometres away from the Paris-based headquarters. When I started the work with her, the team had about ten people. Now the team has more than doubled in size and the company plans to grow the unit even more as the idea has proven successful.

During one of the coaching sessions, I introduced the metaphor of leading as a host by simply describing it and illustrating the idea with some of her situations. I simply suggested that she could bear the idea in mind and she could draw upon what she already knew about her good hosting manners.

Some time later, Clara participated in a 45-minute Host Leadership introductory workshop which Laurent Sarrazin and I gave at a conference she happened to attend. She got the book we wrote (Derbier & Sarrazin, 2017). (The book liberally translates the core of Mark McKergow and Helen Bailey's description of the metaphor and illustrates with specific field experiences Laurent and I had with the use of the ideas). Clara says:

> "These tools helped me to use words to make sense of what I have been feeling, experiencing. It gives you a reassuring basis that helps to tell yourself "ok, all this is quite normal". Even if you feel you've failed a little bit. I became less judgmental with myself. In case of trouble I can come back to the model and figure out where I am and what to do next. I am no longer telling myself 'oh, gosh, I should never have done that. Now I give myself the right to fail."

As the team is growing, Thomas, a team member, is now promoted as the team manager while Clara slowly develops into a site manager. Clara is now coaching Thomas into his new role. She says:

> "With Thomas, for example, I've been able to discuss directly with him about the way I interact with him. After re-reading the book a bit, I felt maybe I was stepping in too much. We had a very good discussion about that. The day after the conversation, both of us could already notice signs of progress! This, I think, has been possible thanks to the Host Leadership tools."

Handling a conflict with an invitation

Julia, a seasoned manager, had a hard time with one member of her team; a young woman described as a strong diva-like personality by Julia and the HR person as well. During the coaching conversation I had with Julia, I quickly introduced the host metaphor and spent a while on the inviter role. As Mark did with me during the 2018 Host Leadership gathering in Paris, I brought the attention to one key aspect: an invitation is an acknowledgment.

- *Right, she said, with a diva you have to be firm, but you have to listen too.*
- *So, what could you invite her to?*
- *Well, in fact I don't think the point she is making is very important. But it seems so to her. So, I imagine I can invite her to be herself the host of a workshop with the rest of the team! They would find a solution together, with me stepping back. Whatever came out of this workshop would be suitable as I*

think there is nothing that big at stake in the first place. But it must be acknowledged.

A couple of weeks later, Julia reported the invitation had worked very well. During the conversation she had with her team member, she managed to both bring her ideas to the table, with solution focussed questions she learnt from our conversations. She told her team member: "Who knows the problem you insist on being addressed better than you? I suggest you take the lead and run a workshop with the team to solve the problem. I can help before and during the workshop, but you will be the host!" She accepted and, during the workshop, Julia said, there was even an alliance between the two of them.

"I still think the subject was not so important, she told me, but as it seemed important to her, I had to welcome it, help her find her way. All I had to do was to give some time, offer my help if necessary. Taking care of your collaborator is a mark of appreciation, and that is important for getting engagement. Acting as a host with guest is very respectful and that is what I like here. This is my style indeed."

Conclusion

I had many occasions of coaching leaders with a pretty lightweight conversation about what the host-guest relationship is about and what it could translate into in the situation at hand. In many cases it quickly gave birth to some possibilities of moving on.

I will leave the conclusion of this short piece to Clara:

"You know, it's like the book is a companion for your life. You can use it for many situations. It is not a book you read and then it becomes passé. As you have new experiences, the metaphor will always teach you something in your context."

References

Derbier, G., & Sarrazin, L. (2017). *Host Leadership: Invitez-vous à un leadership ordinaire donc extra.* lulu.com

Author

Géry Derbier mainly helps companies to get a better organisational agility to sustain their development. His lightweight coaching style blends Agile principles with a Solution Focus approach and some other beautiful ideas such as the leader as host. He started his career in the late 80s as a software engineer, then occupied various positions of manager and technical director. He is a pioneer of the Agile movement in France. Passionate about the Solution Focus approach, he teaches it frequently and has written one the very few books on the subject in French. He is a contributor to the SFiO international network of solution-focused practitioners (http://sfio.org). He can be reached at gery.derbier@rupture21.com

Part Three
Host Leadership in organisational change

15
Hosting stakeholders for engagement in generative change

Gervase R Bushe (Canada)

Gervase Bushe's work in the developing field of Dialogic Organisation Development (Bushe & Marshak, 2015) has put him at the forefront of those working with inquiry-based change processes, helping individuals, groups, organisations and communities take on complex challenges and wicked problems. This overarching field includes both Solution Focus and Appreciative Inquiry and is based on attending to narrative, emergence and generativity, rather than the more customary problems of diagnosis and analysis. A key element for engaging stakeholders in dialogue is a possibility-focused purpose statement that captures something they all care about. The most powerful purpose statement is a 'generative image' which offers a new way to see attractive possibilities, ideas and connections. Here Gervase writes about the importance of hosting, rather than facilitating, stakeholder groups in these processes.[1]

The generative change model

In the literature on how leaders can manage in complexity, there are basically two solutions. One is to find ways to reduce the complexity to the level of complicated so that rational data-driven problem-solving models can be used. The other is to manage complexity by working in an iterative way, using 'probes'; relatively small innovations which explore the space of what works and give vital feedback to guide next steps. The Generative Change Model is based on the second solution.

The idea is that in complexity, it is not possible to understand what affects what except in retrospect. So to figure out what to do, try a little fail-safe experiment

---

[1] Adapted from Bushe G.R. *The Dynamics of Generative Change*, BMI Publishing (2019).

and see what happens. Some people have called these experiments 'probes' (Brown & Eisenhardt, 1998; Jackson & McKergow, 2002; Snowden & Boone, 2007), a term I will use here. Collins and Hanson (2011) call this process "fire bullets, then cannonballs". Rather than assuming anyone is smart enough to anticipate all the possible permutations of all the factors influencing a situation ahead of time (the 'vision'), assume you can't really predict what will work. Instead, launch as many probes as possible and learn as you go. When something works, scale it up. There are many other names for probes, like experiments, pilot projects, prototypes, and so on. What you do, essentially, is to keep firing bullets until you hit something, then you bring in the cannon.

The Generative Change Model (Marshak & Bushe, 2018) identifies the steps required to engage the people who will have to change in conversations where they come up with new ideas (probes) they are willing to act on. They are encouraged to self-initiate action while leaders pay attention to what's working and what isn't. The good ideas and innovations are scaled up. More importantly, however, the generative change process creates a more adaptive, agile organisation, better able to tackle increasing complexity and produce far more change far more quickly than anyone familiar with planned change would consider reasonable.

As shown in Figure 1, Generative Change begins by identifying the "adaptive challenge" that leaders are willing to put time, effort and resources into managing. I say managing, because adaptive challenges are never "solved" – which is a major reason why spending a lot of time and resources identifying "the vision" is generally not useful. This then needs to be re-articulated into a "purpose" that will frame the adaptive challenge in a way that captures something stakeholders care about and attract them to engage in generative conversations. The difference between a vision and purpose is that the former describes a clear end state, and often the path to it. A purpose, on the other hand, describes what the organisation is trying to do every day, and may never fully accomplish. Typically, there are many different ways to accomplish a purpose, which increases the potential for generative conversations to take place.

Most Dialogic OD methods (see www.dialogicod.net/toolsandmethods.pdf for an up-to-date list) are ways to design generative conversations. Learning these different methods is very useful as it offers you a wide array of "tools for your tool belt" – but using them in a simple "paint by numbers" way will lead to inconsistent results. Dialogic Organisation Development is a theory base for

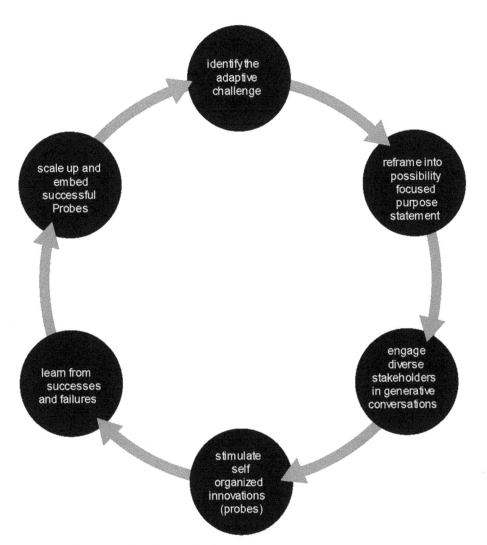

Figure 1: The Generative Change Model

how to use any method in a way that will lead to more consistently successful change. You want to be able to mix and match different methods with the best chance of achieving the desired outcomes with this group, at this time, in this place with the opportunities and constraints it faces.

Preparing for generative conversations

When using a generative change process, I tell my clients "the ideal is to close down the whole organisation and put everyone in the same room for a couple days. If we can't do that, let's work back from that to what we can do". I look for ways to work with the natural ebb and flow of this organisation's life. One of my mantras is "whoever will need to change needs to be invited to the conversation". It doesn't mean they have to show up, but a fundamental assumption about generative change is that more change happens more quickly the more stakeholders are involved in the same engagement events. If people are forced to show up, however, you don't know if they really are interested in or engaged by the purpose. Worst case scenario is that they are opposed to the purpose and work to sabotage the event.

Making attendance at engagement events voluntary makes it more likely that everyone there is predisposed to positively contribute. In many organisations there will be a group of people who are not interested in getting engaged. Typically, they are older employees with just a few years of service left before they retire. Not everyone has to engage for generative change to happen. Work with the willing. On the other hand, it is often the case that some key people or groups need to be part of the event for it to be successful. Think of people with control over key resources. People who control organisational processes. People whose opposition to an idea could kill it. The last thing you want to do is hold an engagement event that gets people excited and builds momentum for change and then gets killed by some authority who doesn't understand what is going on or doesn't support it.

Think about the purpose you are trying to accomplish, the stakeholders who are key to accomplishing it, and the kinds of changes they are likely to propose. Now think about who else will have to support those changes – those people need not only to be invited to the event; they need to have the generative change process explained to them as well as why they are so critical to its success. Hopefully, the purpose will be of interest to them as well, and the event can be scheduled so they can attend. Sometimes the group can make changes internally without needing the consent of others. In other cases, however, when a whole other part of the organisation has to be part of the process, you will need to take the time to ensure that the right person from that part of the organisation is co-sponsoring the event, or someone higher up that both groups ultimately report to is a sponsor; that they understand the generative change model, and sign off on the purpose and design of the process.

A key to increasing the creativity and innovation that emerges from engagement events is increasing the diversity of participants. Innovation is often found at the margins of organisations, among those who have not had much voice or ability to influence the organisation. It is through different perspectives rubbing up against each other that new ideas are born. Open Space Technology, in which participants design the entire content of the event during the event, can be incredibly transformational or produce very little and this seems to depend on the amount of 'heat' in the room – the more heat, the more transformation. Harrison Owen (2008) has identified the following ingredients as necessary for successful Open Space: a purpose people really care about, conflict, passion, urgency, diversity of views and voluntary presence. When there is a lot of energy and desire for change amongst the group of stakeholders, you don't need a lot of design. When there is less urgency or passion, some structure really helps. But in all cases, you need different perspectives in the mix to produce something new, and people who care enough about it to mix it up.

Hosting, not facilitating

A facilitator is someone who helps a group of people work together effectively by guiding conversations, asking questions, helping spread participation, capturing ideas, suggesting processes for group work and then leading them. Normally, they don't have a personal interest in the issues being discussed, so they can guide interactions to produce outcomes the entire group is satisfied with.

However, there are some who question whether this kind of facilitating produces less generative conversations (Goppelt & Ray, 2015; Zubizarreta, 2014). When a consultant stands at the front of the group, capturing what people are saying on a board, all eyes are on him or her. This is not a conversation among stakeholders, this is a conversation where stakeholders are feeding the consultant what they think they are being asked for. Often, the outputs are clichéd, easy to justify, and abstract and while they might look like a great list rarely power any change in behaviour. I am now of the opinion that if the people in the room are talking to me (the consultant) instead of to each other, something's wrong.

Hosting, on the other hand, is about creating 'containers' that support people to have new and better conversations (Bushe, 2010). Typically, these are not facilitated; one reason is that it would require a small army of facilitators to have one for every small group. Instead, engagement events need to be designed so that small groups can work on their own. How much structure will be required depends on the group, its size, and how familiar or foreign the tasks they will be asked to do. It's not unusual to design a workbook that describes to participants what each step in the day is, provides cues and questions for small group discussions, and so on. Overall, generative conversations need to be designed to step people through a sequence of activities where the following questions are answered:

1) Do people know why they are here? If not, design a process to make that happen.

2) Are people willing to say what they really think, feel and want? If not, design a process that will make it more likely that people will.

3) Do people know what they need to know in order to come up with practical new ideas and innovations? If not, design a process that will help them discover what they need to know.

Good hosting requires paying attention to the energy and being ready to redesign on the fly when unexpected things show up (Bushe, 2010). You will want the design to be sequenced so that it naturally leads to people self-selecting themselves into groups focused on something they want to work on, producing applicable new ideas and experiments they will be motivated to act on.

Checklist for hosting generative conversations

- ✓ You have a clear purpose that people care about, and have identified what is in bounds and what is out of bounds.
- ✓ You have the right space for people to be able to move around, as needed.
- ✓ The key sponsor(s) will be there at the beginning to explain the purpose and process and answer questions, and there at the end to hear and bless probes. If they can be there for the entire event, even better.
- ✓ Your design will ensure that people know why they are there, can say what they think, and will get whatever information they need to come up with practical ideas.
- ✓ You have provided just the right amount of structure so people have a sense of the beginning, middle and end of the event, and can step into productive conversations they want to be having.
- ✓ You create opportunities for the large group to check in on what is happening without long, labourious 'report outs'.

✓ Your design helps people who don't know each other very well uncover who has similar interests, motivations and ideas and lets them team up to create a probe.
✓ There is some way of supporting/amplifying people's commitment to acting on their ideas.

References

Brown, S. L. & Eisenhardt. K. M. (1998). *Competing on the Edge: Strategy as Structured Chaos.* Boston MA: Harvard Business School Press.
Bushe, G. R. (2010). Being the Container in Dialogic OD. *Practicing Social Change,* 1(2), 10-15.
Bushe, G. R., & Marshak, R. J. (2015). (Eds.). *Dialogic Organization Development: The Theory and Practice of Transformational Change.* Oakland, CA: Berrett-Kohler.
Collins J., & Hansen, M.T. (2011). *Great by choice.* NY: Harper Business.
Goppelt, J., & Ray, K. W. (2015). Dialogic Process Consultation: Working Live. In G. R. Bushe, & R. J. Marshak (Eds.), *Dialogic Organization Development* (pp. 371–399). Oakland, CA: Berrett-Kohler.
Jackson, P. Z., & McKergow. M. (2002). *The Solutions Focus: The SIMPLE Way to Positive Change.* London: Nicholas Brealey Publishing.
Marshak, R. J., & Bushe, G. R. (2018). Planned and Generative Change in Organization Development. *OD Practitioner, 50*(4), 9-15.
Owen, H. (2008). *Open Space Technology: A User's Guide.* (3rd ed.). Oakland, CA: Berrett-Kohler.
Zubizarreta, R. (2014). *From Conflict to Creative Collaboration: A User's Guide to Dynamic Facilitation.* Minneapolis MN: Two Harbors Press.

Author

Gervase R Bushe is Professor of Leadership and Organization Development at the Beedie School of Business, Simon Fraser University, Vancouver, Canada, one of the top 100 management research schools in the world. Gervase's career spans over four decades of transforming organisational structures, culture and processes away from command and control toward more collaborative work systems. Gervase is an award-winning author of over 100 papers and four books on organisational change, leadership, teams and teamwork. His latest book, The Dynamics of Generative Change, follows a case of Dialogic Organisation Development to explore each phase of the Generative Change model. You can download his papers at www.gervasebushe.ca

16

Hosting company-wide process improvements

Jessika Jake (USA)

> *Jessika writes about using Host Leadership in a project management role in an internet marketing company. She finds many different ways to use the hosting suite of ideas and tools, such as deciding to initiate projects and making some very creative use of invitations. She addresses the question of what to do if folks decline your invitations, and also uses the four positions very well in her work – the kitchen can be such a useful place!*

Due to my interest in helping out and my background as a consultant who used to get hired as a fixer (fixing processes and issues in agencies), I was asked to work with the Chief Financial Officer (CFO) on company-wide process improvements. At the time I was the Director of the Project Management Office. I interacted with all departments on a regular basis, but had no authority over the other departments. I was also newer to the company than the directors of the other departments. The CFO worked from offsite, and came to our office a handful of times during the year. We needed to take care with every move we made, both because of our roles and relationships and because these people had seen prior initiatives amount to nothing.

We also knew that we would need to invite the help of, well, *everyone* in the company. In stepping back, we decided to keep our initial invitations for participation to a very simple ask. I had previously worked as a consultant for agencies and had a huge stack of assets and questionnaires to draw from, but with the guests we had in mind this time, simplicity and directness were key. We created and distributed a small questionnaire. It was but a few questions, asking about top 3-5 pain points across a few areas (company, department, and other). (You can read more about 'pain points' in Mark McKergow's chapter in their book on *Hearing What Is Being Called For.*) This left the guest with the discretion to merely list 3 things or to tell us their life stories. The goal was to find the common and most pressing pain points, and then we would iterate through improvements.

The response rate was overwhelmingly positive. However, the responses themselves told a less positive story. Specific company-wide pain points were uncovered, as well as departmental and cross-departmental issues. Most participants wrote at length, often in ways that had me concerned about protecting the jobs of the respondents. Though I had to report findings to the CEO and CTO on a per-department basis, I decided to combine some groups together, so that cited issues would not be able to be mapped back to a single individual when small departments were involved.

The CFO and I headed back to the kitchen to reflect. The plan became one such that we would invite other team members to host their own process improvement teams – we had identified a half dozen to start with: a Requirement Gathering team, a Statement of Work Team, and so forth.

At that point, the CFO was pulled off the initiative, and I was on my way to lining up process improvement teams and team leaders. In creating space, sometimes a big key was to NOT set up space in the form of formal meetings. These employees were already concerned with the number of meetings that were happening, and what transpired within those meetings. In fact, one of the improvement teams would be working on "Meeting Etiquette and Productive Meeting Formats."

Stepping back to the gallery and stepping forward among the people/guests helped facilitate a lot of the right conversations and invitations. Since this was all being done on a volunteer basis, the timings ('due dates') I chose needed to be balanced based on the need to keep the momentum going versus all of the work that people already had on their plates, which were already overfilled.

In inviting others to host their own process improvement teams, it gave them the chance to be host leaders to their own group. I was able to take on different roles as these sub-'parties' played out. Sometimes I needed to step into the gatekeeper role and ultimately replace some of the team leads due to lack of progress. I acted as the connector quite a bit – connecting the right people with each other.

Additionally, I was invited as a guest to most of the sub-parties, and took on a proper guest role within each I decided to attend. This meant, if my host was on the stage, I listened. If my host asked for ideas, I participated and collaborated. If my host connected me to a few individuals so we could work together on a piece of the solution, I valued those connections and contributed alongside this 'sub-team'. As leaders and managers, we may be living in the host role to varying percentages of time. For some, it may be 100% of the time. For others, maybe 90%-10%. Being able to know when you are not the host allows you to set your fellow host up for success as a leader by being the very best guest. You also set the example of what being a great guest looks like!

In Host Leadership, one of the questions that often arises is "What do you do when guests decline your invitation?" In this scenario, the answer was: "Invite them to a really enticing private party". For example, the Director of Development had declined a team leader's invite to participate on the "Statement of Work" (SOW) improvement team. He also had declined my invite to participate on the "Requirements Gathering" team. This team focused on gathering requirements for eCommerce projects that were development heavy.

There were a lot of issues relating to development that needed to be resolved or improved. For example, development work was chronically under-scoped by the Sales Team. In looking at the data, we could see that we would need to at least double the line item for development work on a standard eCommerce website SOW. But other issues that we needed to contend with were the vague language of the SOW, some items in the SOW were "just wrong," and so forth. Having the participation of the Director of Development was critical to our success. He had been with the company practically since its inception and was incredibly talented at his job, to say the least. He would definitely be getting another invite, but it had to be one he wouldn't want to say no to. Inviting him to help create something was viewed as a waste of his time because: "*Who were these new people thinking they will make a change here? This never works, etc.*"

I took a step back and decided to extend invites to a front end developer and a back end developer. In our private party we were able to make headway on the development aspects of the SOW and Reqs team processes. We were also able to start addressing cross-department issues. It was clear that processes in other silos needed to change in order to fully resolve a majority of issues we were seeing. I didn't let that go unnoticed and was able to spur a new "Cross-Department Processes and Handoff" initiative which ultimately resolved those. Over the course of stepping forward and back with new iterations of the Reqs and

SOW processes, we got to a place where we were ready to invite the Director of Development. The invite was an impromptu one, by me, with printouts of our work. In other words, this was a super-simple invite: put your eyes on this here paragraph! Well, in seeing something concrete, the Director agreed to look it over and make edits.

The other way I was able to deal with guests declining invites was to rephrase (and actually adjust) what my actions would be. Instead of waiting for approval on the new processes from the CEO and CTO, I would say "Hey, we are launching this process on Wednesday. Let me know if you have any feedback." The feedback never came, but the processes launched. This is the second way I dealt with the "What do you do if a guest declines your invitation?" The answer is to create a "party" whereby it's a win whether or not the party actually happens.

Going forwards, everyone was also invited to share with me the changes and improvements they recommended. I could invite the appropriate guests to 'buy in' to the change, finessing it as needed, and then use the same launch process. We got this so dialled in that improvement ideas were able to be launched same-day.

Author

Jessika Jake, MS, PMP, CSM, ITIL-F, WELCOA Faculty, Brain Health Coach. Jessika creates and leads programs at the nexus of wellbeing and leadership, helping individuals and organisations achieve purpose-aligned impact at spectacular levels. She's a master of the art and science of performance, purpose, and positivity. She's been contracted for companies large and small – from small to mid-sized to Fortune 500 and Fortune 100, weaving in neuroscience and the science of positive psychology, science of achievement, and hard and soft skills to create custom solutions for increasing engagement, productivity, efficiency, morale, professional certification acquisition, inspiration, fulfillment, alignment, collaboration, client satisfaction/account growth, and the bottom line. You can find her online at JessikaJake.com

17

Helping engagement with messy experience: Organisational transformation at Assimoco Group

Gian Carlo Manzoni (Italy)

> Hosting and facilitating are two related, but not identical, ways to work with groups and organisations. In this chapter Gian Carlo Manzoni shows how Host Leadership ideas helped with a major organisational transformation project at the Italian insurance company Assimoco Group. Host Leadership informed both the ways of working with the clients, and was also key in helping the facilitation team work together, gauge their work and develop their professional practice.

Introduction

In 2018 Gian Carlo Manzoni, E-consultant's director, and Marco Ossani, associate partner, delivered a big facilitation project for Assimoco Group, the insurance company of reference of the Italian Cooperative Movement, with which it shares a heritage of history and values. These values are:

- Attention and care of people: Assimoco establishes a relationship that comes from continuous listening and develops through professional competence and personal involvement, with the aim of implementing a common growth path

- Responsibility: Assimoco exercises its role with care and is aware of the result of these actions

- Cooperation: Assimoco pursues an individual approach that develops abilities to work together towards common goals

- Transparency: Assimoco dedicates time and attention to sharing information and promoting direct and sincere communication

- Simplicity: Assimoco makes complex things simple
- Learning: Assimoco can be distinguished by curiosity and desire to learn, that is to say people are not satisfied with the results achieved. They innovate by learning
- Passion: Assimoco works with commitment and enthusiasm, and actively contributes to its growth.

In general Assimoco believes that only a superior organisation can achieve superior results, in full respect of all stakeholders: customers, distributors, collaborators, shareholders and the community.

Assimoco is a B Corporation (a benefit corporate, a new kind of business that balances purpose and profit). They are legally required to consider the impact of their decisions on their workers, customers, suppliers, community, and the environment – https://bcorporation.net/) They have a facilitative mindset, able to implement valuable conversations as a basis for innovation (thanks to this project), creating a context that supports the adoption of agile methodologies which improve internal decision-making processes, encouraging the ambition to develop networks with business partners and external organisations.

When we started, the Assimoco Group was facing an intense transformation programme, in order to acquire a distinctive positioning in the panorama of Italian insurance. Assimoco realised that, to face this huge transformation challenge the entire organisation needed to evolve the ways in which people generated conversations, on a daily basis. The main objectives of the project were to make facilitation a new way of looking at group dynamics and co-innovation processes, upskill and increase internal Assimoco facilitation capability and capacity, and embed facilitation as a core competence of the internal leaders. So building facilitation skills and competence, especially starting from team leaders, really developing and enhancing existing skills and finally providing a broad understanding of facilitation tools, techniques and processes is the 'stargate' for a new generation of internal leaders.

We won the International Association of Facilitators (IAF) 2019 Golden Impact award for this project (see https://www.iaf-world.org/site/award-winner/building-internal-facilitation-mindset-shape-sustainable-future). One of the main things we delivered in this project was about recommended, useful and relevant facilitation resources to support the internal community of practice for facilitators. This internal community needed to be both consolidated and reinforced, and pushed to do more internally and externally, based on well-defined skills and processes and facilitation approaches – and all this while respecting the corporate objective to push the adoption of a more facilitative/conversational approach in general.

At the end of the project we gave frameworks to evaluate internal processes and, specially, to evaluate themselves as real internal leaders able to host and engage internal and external stakeholders. Actually the internal facilitators are now running one or two facilitated interventions every week. This amounts to around 10+ interventions a month internally and across their direct and indirect customers. So stepping forward and back, which is core of the Host Leadership process, was not only a metaphor but a practical and concrete approach to measure and assess their own capabilities as leading facilitators, increasing internal performance.

The delegates had engaged internal leaders in their project work, getting direct facilitation experiences during their internal meetings and kick off. They shared exercises done together, facilitating the class directly under our coordination and supervision. So they expressed their own leadership planning, inviting, introducing, providing, encouraging, giving space and joining in. They understood the value of knowledge and experience shared both in this project and in the internal community of practice: they became real hosts!

The percentage of employees who have benefited from at least one meeting to understand the potential of facilitation is 100%. We think that is a great result. Due to the fact that the community of practice has to increase the percentage of employees and external partners who can be involved in a facilitated activity, we decided to deliver and offer frames (such as U theory and Appreciative Inquiry) through which many dimensions of leadership can be viewed and Host Leadership was ultimately a support to these.

Host Leadership became a common approach to assess personal approaches to different facilitated intervention planning and preparation of interventions. In fact Host Leadership is a ladder of facilitative influence and has been used as a check in and check out personal and professional feedback tool. Through exercises to organise and invite professional and private meetings (for example very complex birthday parties according to the guests and available resources), the participants understood what they had to do as hosts before, during and after the event. The participants had to both give themselves votes and give votes to their abilities and ways of welcoming people and respecting the process. Having the six roles in mind made them reflect on the extent of the possibilities and criticalities to be handled by them directly or by the group. And this became a mirror: first they saw the facilitator in his different roles as a unique figure, then as through a kaleidoscope they saw the various colours and phases of the various colours. The connection of these colours and these roles with specific process phases and/or facilitative techniques was also nice.

The 25 voluntary employees selected to become Key Internal Facilitators held generalised discussions of small group and also plenary processes about leadership as relationship, before starting their own leadership processes evaluation through the six new roles of engagement. For example, let's imagine a plenary session like a fishbowl conversation. That evoked many more memories and details about their roles. One story sparked another.

And then importantly, they were able to write on the wall the messy experience of these roles together in a way that communicated much more. The different roles were put on individual sheets on different walls. After an official description of the individual roles, the participants gave their definitions, which were even more relevant to their current reality. By doing this they rearranged the ideas about what they were doing and saying in plenary (often they said ... "we are only able to do this" ... or "we are not able to do everything") and have therefore transcribed the most effective ways to interpret that role, that is, to live it concretely with the public in certain circumstances. Although the focus on a specific project would certainly have given more order, the ideas became clearer and little by little the ways that could be useful were defined, not only as an attitude, but as "activation" of a given process ("Ah ... so that time I could do this!").

They felt able to share their on-the-ground experience in a way that would truly help their colleagues to shift and shape their roles depending on the goal and on the situation. For instance, there was huge amount of understanding about the roles of engagement and about the progress made or not about these. The interaction among the participants told more of the specific style and behaviour and impact done leading the concrete role to support the community of practice and the target audience.

We compared the roles to some specific IAF competences such as developing working relationships and designing (Connector), preparing for facilitating processes (Initiator and Co-participator), creating a participatory environment (Inviter and Space Creator), and guiding the group to useful outcomes

(Gatekeeper). As Connectors the participants created dedicated teams to analyse the customer's situation together and then design the most suitable process and method, and of course facilitated internal meetings to spread facilitation processes. As Initiators and Co-participators, they collected stories and exercises and we invited participants to then find "their best final story" and techniques in the group by dot voting.

All facilitation events were prepared with preliminary meetings by objective definition with the client, based on what the most appropriate methodologies were. Participants had to commit to *participating* in planning before and during our seminars. As Inviters and Space Creators the delegates were more aware of the environment settings and took advantage of those settings to improve the group collaboration. Increasing active listening, clarifying conflict resolution, consensus building among team members were all tasks that they achieved by creating a participatory environment. Finally, as Gatekeepers they enhanced the focus on what the client wants and needs. Delegates gave practical examples of using high quality materials and step by step processes to get results with the client choosing appropriate methods. We helped the group to facilitate meetings on the new products process they mentioned during the masterclass.

Then the delegates learnt the four ways to dance the Host Leadership process managing the given information. They matched on scales of how often and how effective they were for each position (in the spotlight, with the guests, in the gallery, in the kitchen) in order to engage participants and themselves better through the performed modes of new thinking and learning we shared together. They shared present experiences where they carried out and embodied those roles (why, what, how, when, where, with whom) and also shared proposals to build and embody new roles in the future (examples, suggestions, positive spaces and locations have been shared among the participants). At the end of the masterclass everyone had to assess himself as a facilitator and as a leader. One way to do this was therefore to allow people to recognise themselves in at least three or more prevalent roles and discuss them together (including how they didn't choose other roles). Also the fact of knowing if they were performing well in the spotlight (or how they prepared themselves to be) or they were better prepared being alone (in the kitchen) or with someone – they became moments of awareness and possibility of future change.

Helping engagement with messy experience 137

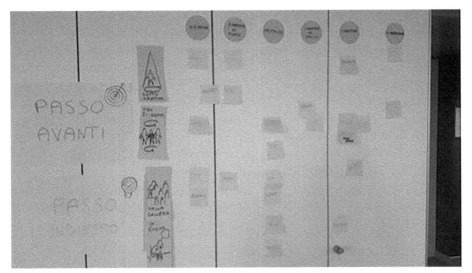

A wall showing how participants connected with the six roles (horizontally) and four positions (vertically), in deciding whether they needed to step forward (passo avanti) or step back (passo indietro) next.

Roles and positions can be chosen, defined in groups beforehand or covered by someone else if necessary. This was a useful mental and operational order at the end of a journey to reaffirm that everything can be tried by planning it first. It was a revelatory experience, a great photo and map about how to increase their effectiveness. They had a chance to talk, see and feel what was conveyed between them leading and those stakeholders entering. Picking roles and positions was the main step to encourage the whole group to build shared understanding in another way than in a circle, giving them a map and a new vision for the situations they were facing.

Conclusion

Assimoco has to share the results and the facilitative team spirit in order to accomplish their new challenges.

The natural inner transformational changes of the people was fantastic indeed: more engaged with more wisdom about the usage of the methods depending on the target. They told us at the beginning:" We cannot do and deliver all the stuff you're sharing" ... and at the end they say: "Awesome ... and wonderful what we have done together". And from our perspective we were also surprised by our new capacity to inspire a good fusion of different approaches, respecting the processes and the philosophy behind them. When people speak new languages and create new words, it's the moment you really say: "Aha!" That's really and truly wonderful.

We encouraged host principles at the beginning and it was clear for us the Host Leadership involves a direct social influence and happens within an organisation in different styles. Style is everything and we know, thanks to Mark and Helen, we have six new styles and super-powers. There is also indeed empirical evidence that Host Leadership results in a deeper bond between employees and the organisation if there is a good facilitative flow. Only when you pick the appropriate Host Leadership style and role will you be able to facilitate better and better.

Author

Gian Carlo Manzoni is a Certified Professional Facilitator (IAF), Certified NLP Trainer(R. Dilts), Certified Coach(ICF), Certified Counsellor (Assocounseling) and management consultant. He is an author with over 20 years experience and more than 10 books about management, after his career in global companies including Microsoft and NEC/Packard Bell. He has been involved in designing, organising and delivering facilitation and development projects in Europe. He focuses on innovative and integrative approaches, based on design thinking, mindfulness and leadership. He puts strong emphasis in Metalog EOL (Experienced Oriented Learning), transformational strategies, and visual thinking. He is the managing partner and director of E-CONSULTANT and METALOG ITALY in Italy. www.econsultant.it. www.metalog.it www.giancarlomanzoni.it

Part Four
Introducing Host Leadership in organisations

18
Attracting people to the host metaphor

Veronika Kotrba and Ralph Miarka (Austria)

Host Leadership is both a metaphor and a model. A key aspect of introducing Host Leadership to any situation is to use the power of the metaphor – connecting people with their own experience, skill and awareness of hosting and setting this into a new context of leading. In this short chapter, Veronika and Ralph share their experiences of how to achieve this, and why it's important.

Introduction

In their book *Host*, Mark McKergow and Helen Bailey propose the host metaphor for leadership (McKergow & Bailey, 2014). They elaborate on the concept by picking up on two other existing metaphors: the leader as hero, and the servant-leadership metaphor of Robert Greenleaf (Greenleaf, 1970; 1977). The intriguing questions posed by Helen and Mark are: "who are the others?", "how are they viewed?" and "what behaviour is presupposed by this relationship?".

Exploring leader-follower metaphors and relationships

In our trainings on Host Leadership, we start with an exercise about collecting leadership metaphors. We ask the people to call out metaphors that they use, have heard or experienced when they think about what leadership is. We collect them on a flipchart written graphically for later use. Here is a short list of metaphors that have been brought up by our participants:

- Captain
- Mountain guide (this is in Austria!)
- Shepherd

- Gardener
- Tour guide
- Chieftain
- Coachman
- Drummer
- Story-teller
- Kindergarten teacher
- Helicopter
- Visionary
- General
- and more...

Next, we ask the participants to provide names or roles in each case for the ones that are the "others". For example:

- Captain => seaman/crew/passengers
- Mountain guide => hiker
- Shepherd => sheep and sheep dogs
- Visionary => enlightened ones

And so on. We add them to the leadership metaphors in a different colour and with iconic drawings. Then we ask everyone, what is the impact on the followers to be considered in such a way? The discussion shows the participants that the choice of the leadership metaphor is shaping a picture of the followers and also a particular kind of leadership behaviour.

Let's take a little detour here. Rini van Solingen (2016) wrote the book *De bijenherder* – the bee-shepherd (*Der Bienenhirte*, translated by Rolf Dräther into German). An experienced shepherd was asked to look after bees, the next big business opportunity. First, he used his tried and tested leadership tools from herding sheep. Quickly he and his dog noticed however, that these tools did not work on bees. So he had to learn new ways, adapt to leading bees in a unique way. Bees are a different kind of follower. They fly around, find the flowers on their own, bring back the pollen and produce honey. They need someone that takes out the honey on time. They certainly don't need a sheep dog.

It is similar with the other leadership metaphors and the associations with them. We often hear from people that in their company it is like in a kindergarten. What do these people imply by that? We guess it is not that the "followers" are strong minded, very creative, socially active human beings that need very specially trained "leaders" to help them achieve their learning objectives. Hosting kids, for example, needs a lot of initiatives, invitations, well prepared spaces and a lot of gate-keeping and also connecting and co-participation. Reflecting on this helped a lot of training participants to gain new insights into hosting and applying Host Leadership to their environment.

After discussing the complex leader-follower relationships given by the participants, we move on to introduce the metaphor of a host as a leader and guests as "followers". What does this mean to the trainees? What do they know about good hosting? When have they experienced great hosting or done it themselves? Collectively, we re-create the Host Leadership model.

Conclusion

We like this approach as we co-create a picture, building on the strengths and resources of the participants, their experiences and knowledge. In this way, we hope that the host-guest relationship they know well becomes intuitively part of their repertoire for hosting different situations.

References

Greenleaf, R. K. (1970). *The Servant as Leader*. Retrieved from https://static1.squarespace.com/static/51473514e4b0090a1cad74f9/t/5194e399e4b0b0879dc2e8ef/1368712089353/Greenleaf+essay+part+one.pdf

Greenleaf, R. K. (1977). *Servant Leadership – A Journey into the Nature of Legitimate Power and Greatness*. Mahwah NJ; Paulist Press.

McKergow, M., & Bailey, H. (2014). *Host: Six new roles of engagement for teams, organisations, communities and movements*. London; Solutions Books.

Solingen, R. van, (2016). *De bijenherder: leidinggeven aan zelfsturende teams, hoe doe je dat?* Uitgeverij; Atlas Contact. German: *Der Bienenhirte – über das Führen von selbstorganisierten Teams: Ein Roman für Manager und Projektverantwortliche*, translated by Rolf Dräther. Heidelberg: dpunkt.Verlag.

Acknowledgements

The authors would like to thank Mark McKergow for his helpful comments on both their chapters in this Field Book.

Authors

Veronika Kotrba is a solution-focused coach, consultant and trainer. Together with Ralph Miarka, she has been supporting people with management tasks in an agile corporate environment since 2012. In 2015, the two of them founded sinnvollFÜHREN GmbH in Vienna. Veronika is co-author of the book Agile Teams lösungsfokussiert coachen *(dpunkt.verlag), has been training solution-focused coaches since 2018 in her in-house course, together with Ralph and a top-class team of trainers, and tirelessly finds new approaches to facilitate cooperation at eye level in the business and working world.*

Dr Ralph Miarka lives in Vienna and has worked for many years as a solution-focused agile coach, consultant and trainer. In his work, as a well-read practitioner he constantly incorporates new findings from scientific research. Since 2015 he has been managing director of sinnvollFÜHREN GmbH and co-author of the book Agile Teams lösungsfokussiert coachen *(dpunkt.verlag). He is interested in the effective cooperation of people – both at large and small scales. To this end, he supports all those in companies who make decisions and bear responsibility – from leaders to team members.*

19
Introducing Host Leadership to your organisation: An integrating metaphor

The Host Leadership Gathering Collective

One of the questions that often arises is along the lines of "Hey, I love the idea of Host Leadership! How do I get my organisation to adopt it?" We admire the enthusiasm and energy in this position ... and yet, getting your organisation to adopt Host Leadership (whatever that means) is probably not the first step. There are lots of useful ways to start, which themselves will also help your organisation to become more engaging and responsive.

Introduction

So ... how do you sell a leadership concept to management? How do you 'sell' Host Leadership, especially when the organisation might already be using some other leadership concepts? After all, as Stephen Josephs observed in his Foreword to *Host* (McKergow & Bailey, 2014, p. xi),

> *Has this ever happened to you? It's the end of a day and you're contemplating the problems that demand your attention – fires in operations, unpleasant surprises in a key customer account, complications in relations with your board, a troubling employee survey, and long-term strategic plans that are perpetually on hold. And then it hits you like a bolt of lightning. You push back from your chair and say aloud, "What we need around here is a better metaphor!"*

Hardly anyone suddenly wakes up wanting a new metaphor, of course. But how many people would like their teams, organisations or relationships to be more engaging and mutually productive?

There are a few things to consider. Many companies are buying leadership concepts, ideas and methods. Yet it seems most of them are opting for some variation of a heroic leadership metaphor: how should YOU be and behave as a leader. Crucially, they are missing the aspect of the interaction among people. They are also focusing on the tools required to be a leader, rather than having a look at the way that interactions between people work, thus missing a crucial parameter for understanding leadership.

Furthermore, as time is money (and leadership consultants cost money as well), there is a clear tendency to consider leadership as something that can be learned in a classroom in one or two days, rather than an evolution path for the people involved.

Because of the issues above and also because Host Leadership is an easy metaphor to begin to grasp, many people to whom we have presented this concept tend to stay at a very superficial level of understanding. This is better than nothing, but it's a pity; one of the great values of Host Leadership is the possibility of an in-depth exploration of nuances and possibilities, a richness that is rarely present in other leadership metaphors. How do you then invite a management team in an organisation to go beyond the basic metaphor of the host?

Here are some ideas from our collective experience about ways to engage people in your team or organisation.

1. It's not about selling, but showing

Sometimes your clients might come to you to 'buy' a way towards leadership. Good for you. But if they don't, why not simply show how you could be a good host, be a role model for your guests! Maybe after a while your guests will realise the value of your behaviour, attitude, mindset, … and, in our experience, they will ask for more of that, and so become engaged in how you work.

One of the great advantages of Host Leadership is that you can start, right here and right now. Think of yourself as a host. Who are your guests? What would you like to encourage them to do? What do they need, in order to do that? What are your next steps?

Make a start and begin to build your own experience. Then you will have a story to tell people in your organisation which is not about a leadership metaphor but about you actually achieving something that matters.

2. It's about attitude, not recipes

Very often leadership books and consultant teach managers that a leader does X or Y or ... While advice like this might be operationally useful, these strategies are often used at the level of recipes. This is better than nothing, but even to use a recipe well you still need the right skills in terms of cooking!

We believe Host Leadership implies a set of principles you can use to make your actions more contextual, organically fitting different situations. From this perspective, Host Leadership is not about being an alternative to other leadership "methods", but it is rather a compass giving the general direction, a true north towards using and integrating together other techniques in a more ethical way, where ethical in this context means "in the interest of your guests". From this perspective we could call Host Leadership an integrating metaphor – it's about your guests first, and you last.

3. It's about roles, not rules

Host Leadership, being a metaphor, allows for flexible translation to the reality of your organisation. This is an obvious advantage as it allows you to create a 'version' of being a host that is culturally consistent with your organisation.

However, there is also a disadvantage: the model does not give specific rules. It might be difficult to implement in the beginning, and anyway does not give you pre-defined solutions. As a coach helping your clients to implement a leadership metaphor it is your responsibility to guide them through a deeper reflection and exploration of all the nuances that might be beneficial.

This is where the idea of roles, not rules, can come to your aid. Rules are things you follow – probably all the time. That's over-rigid for us, as it leads in the direction of 'magic bullets' which can be fired once and solve your problems for all time. Roles, on the other hand, are ways you can step forward when something is needed.

The *Host* book presents six roles: Initiator, Inviter, Space-creator, Gatekeeper, Connector and Co-participator. One great way to start using Host Leadership is to look at the situation and see which of these roles seems to speak to you, seems to be something that's needed next. Then, think about how you as a host leader can step into that role and do something for your guests that will help things along.

4. You can start straight away, then you can explore the nuances

Sometimes we notice that we do not get enough traction in the organisation; some companies are culturally not ready to talk about leadership, even if they claim they want to. As Host Leadership is an easy metaphor to understand, in our opinion it is OK to just start and see how the idea is used by the people you are working with. (The chapter by Géry Derbier in this Field Book contains some very revealing stories about how simply introducing the metaphor can have instant and yet profound effects.)

In a leadership development scenario it might be a strategy to start by presenting the idea to a group of people and see what they make of it. Some will get it and will want to explore it more, and then you can expand and develop understandings and practices with that group as a next step.

5. Loud enough?

The Host Leadership metaphor speaks very loudly to some people, but not to all. We believe it's OK to have different attitudes and speeds in approaching Host Leadership. Don't push, wait for hosts to begin to appear. Also in this case, being a good role model will help others understand the value of this work.

And you can also gently let people know that you work as a host leader, and this is how you develop your work and thinking. Why not download the posters created by Leah Davcheva in her chapter of this book and put them on your wall, or leave them lying around to be discovered and discussed by members of your team? In the end, anyone who trumpets the idea of being a host leader is not really being a host leader; putting our guests first is more a matter of quiet observation and action than self-aggrandisement.

6. Strategies for promoting Host Leadership

Host Leadership is inherently an emergent practice, so promoting the 'next step' in using the idea seems to be a very good strategy, and there are a lot of tools that can be useful:

- Think of yourself as a host. Who are your guests? How can you support them?
- The question "what else [can you do in the role of …]?" seems a great way to explore options.
- Solution Focus scales – "On a scale from 1-10, how much are you using host leadership? What makes it that high already and not lower – what is working already? What might be a next step to add to or build on that?"
- Exploring the metaphor embedded in each role: "what does it mean for you to be (for example) a Gatekeeper?", "How do you know whether you as a Gatekeeper are helping the group?", "Which role might you switch to next?"
- Don't forget the four positions of a host leader: in the spotlight, with the guests, in the gallery and in the kitchen. Those who want to shout loudly about Host Leadership may be want to be in the spotlight, when working in some of the other positions might be more useful to start with.

References

McKergow, M., & Bailey, H. (2014). *Host: Six new roles of engagment for teams, organisations, communities and movements.* London: Solutions Books.

Author

This chapter emerged from the collective wisdom of the Host Leadership Gathering in Oberschleissheim, Germany.

20

Pick your poster: Getting started on a learning journey with Host Leadership

Leah Davcheva (Bulgaria)

> Leah Davcheva has introduced the metaphor, ideas and practice of Host Leadership into many different contexts over the years. Here she reveals how she uses interactive methods and involvement to engage people, so they can start to appreciate and use the ideas within a short timescale.

Introduction

Leader as host is still a new idea and a novel set of practices for many organisational, corporate, and community contexts. A quick introduction to the approach and to the metaphor underpinning it might possibly be a lecture, i.e. let people *hear* "IT". And yet, there is another way for novices to engage with the new hosting perspective on leadership, a way which inspires them to act, sparks off new learnings and creates a fruitful environment for growing new skills.

Once or twice a year I initiate a half-day Host Leadership workshop, open to all who are interested in modes of leading whereby engagement with people and flexibility of performance are key. Among its merits is the generous space the workshop offers for the participants to connect with pioneering ideas and with each other, to develop, on the go, their own meaningful content and make progress in their leadership thinking.

Here I will tell the story of a short, four-hour edition of a Host Leadership workshop. Occasionally, I pause in the telling and voice my reflections on what made me think that the workshop did a good job. My best hopes are that this written outline will be able to provide a basis for Host Leadership practitioners and consultants to introduce Host Leadership to their clients by giving them the pleasure of collectively exploring its territory and constructing their own small steps into it.

Invitation

I invited prospective participants, by a public announcement, to come and:

- explore the metaphor of leading as hosting and hosting as leading
- relate the new metaphor to leadership situations in their own contexts and develop a view on what the benefits might be from using Host Leadership practices
- consider how with Host Leadership thinking they might further "engage [their] people by drawing them in" (McKergow & Bailey, 2014, p. 9).

Those who responded to the invitation – 21 people – had diverse professional and vocational backgrounds. There was a teacher among them, the CEO of an international trading company, a beautician, an experienced project manager, the HR Director of a bank and her deputy, an NGO activist. Closer to the day of the workshop and by way of sparking off their curiosity I sent them three postings. The first one gave them an overview of the programme as well as some practical detail concerning the workshop venue and timings. The second message featured an inspirational quote: the opening paragraph of the first chapter of the book *Host* (McKergow & Bailey, 2014, p. 3). The third one referred them to a film, *Sully: Miracle on the Hudson* (2016). I drew attention to this film because the true story of aircraft captain Chesley "Sully" Sullenberger, saving the lives of everyone aboard, connects powerfully with the old Arabic proverb "The host is both the first and the last" with which Mark and Helen both open and finish their book.

Reflection note 1

A not so obvious thread in my design of the workshop but one I hoped would eventually emerge into the participants' awareness, was me doing my best to perform host leader roles and move in and out of the four hosting positions. The Invitation stage provided me with a good opportunity to elaborate on my Inviter role. I expanded the invitation beyond a single formulaic message sent through the social media. I hope I thus made it engaging and calling for commitment of time and intellectual energy.

Physical space

We worked in a spacious seminar room with the chairs arranged in a circle in the centre of the room. There were also loosely arranged work stations in various other places in the room itself and in adjacent areas.

On the long wall of the room I had hung 12 posters showing through text and image the two steps, forward and back, the six roles of engagement and the four positions the host leader may take up. (The posters are reproduced at the end of this chapter.) Randomly, on the other walls of the seminar room I had put several other posters with thoughts / proverbs / sayings relevant to the theme of leadership which I thought might possibly arouse the interest of the participants and / or help them bring to mind some previous experience. The music of Yiruma (South Korean-British pianist and composer) sounded in the background and warmed our space.

> *Reflection note 2*
>
> While preparing the physical environment of the workshop, I was careful to leave plenty of room for emergent re-arrangements and for people to move naturally and freely in what was going to become their space. A principle which guided me in creating the initial setting for the workshop was that the space should support the interactions I was hoping to stimulate.

Welcome at the door

As they were arriving, I welcomed my guests at the door, chatted to those I knew and exchanged words of introduction with the ones I was meeting for the first time. I also kept an eye on what was going on in the room and was pleased to notice that some of the people were busy talking with each other while others, attracted by the posters on the wall, were looking at them.

As the workshop was about to formally start, somebody arrived at the door. She admitted that she had come across the announcement for the workshop just an hour ago and had immediately rushed to the venue. She was unsure she would be allowed in and was delighted to be heartily welcomed.

> *Reflection note 3*
>
> Greeting people cordially and welcoming them comes quite naturally to me but at this particular moment, before the start of the workshop proper, I was aware of performing the role almost deliberately. Later on, during the workshop I found a suitable moment to return to those initial moments to illustrate the gatekeeping role of the host leader. Furthermore, I was lucky to have this unexpected participant arrive unannounced to exemplify the possibilities of either opening or closing the door.

Flow

Stage 1: What difference might this workshop make?

To get the workshop going, I took my place in the circle and greeted everybody again. Following a short introduction with an emphasis on possible personal benefits from the workshop and its collaborative dynamics, I asked them to form pairs with the person sitting next to them and take turns to ask and respond to the following questions:

- *What difference do you think this workshop will make to the way you approach leadership issues in your situation next week?*
- *How will you notice – tomorrow / on Monday – that the workshop was useful?*

After their private conversations, some of the participants volunteered to share what they thought would be of interest to the others. For example,

- I'll share a couple of ideas about this workshop when our colleagues ask me how come I look so pleased and excited.
- In the morning, as people come into the office, I'll greet them warmly, complimenting them on the way they look and smile.
- I'll call a team meeting and invite people to ask me questions about this workshop.
- There will be a small turn for the better in the way I lead my company.
- I will buy the Host Leadership book.

- I will have jotted down every new idea that emerges in my head during this workshop.
- On Monday, I'll send a brief note to my team, letting them know how the workshop was.

> *Reflection note 4*
>
> I noted here the widening of the interactional space. The 'difference' question triggered off a chain of responses and clearly voiced hopes.

Following the excitement of this first exchange I next stepped forward to set the scene for the workshop and sketch out the 'big picture' of the content. I also made it clear that we were free to trace other routes should we want to do so.

Stage 2: Timeliness of the metaphor

Before stepping into the core learning stage of the workshop, I wanted to softly steer the participants to further develop their sense of the modern 21st century global context and some of its demands on leadership. Using a light lecture format, I let the participants "encounter" (Meier, 2000. p. 81):

- some of the challenges which today's leaders face when addressing "wicked problems"
- the history of hosting and its modern expressions
- leadership metaphors and the types of relationship they imply
- the timeliness of the leader-as-host metaphor

The task which I invited the participants to complete after the brief talk was the following:

> *If you had to explain to a colleague why you think calling attention to a new metaphor for leadership is important, what would you say? Write this down in a sentence or two and keep for future reference* (Bowman, 2009).

With their writing pads still at hand and by way of smoothly transiting into the next stage of the workshop, the participants were asked to accomplish another task:

"Think of a current leadership issue you are facing right now and sketch what it is, where it occurs, who is involved." (McKergow & Bailey, 2014)

Reflection note 5

Two times more into the workshop, the participants were going to return to this first description of their leadership challenge, modify and expand it with new ideas. The purpose of interweaving this strand into the flow of the workshop was to enhance the practical value of the learners' experience and have them build new meanings for themselves.

In addition, working individually gave the participants an experience of some "kitchen time", i.e. one of the four host leader's positions where, in a more private and intimate space, they reflect and prepare for their next task.

Stage 3: Two steps, four positions and six roles of a host leader

Reflection note 6

Stage 3 constituted the core of the workshop and it is the one which, to a great extent, contributed to the value of the participants' learning experience.

* Acknowledgement: I first came across a prototype of this activity at the 2015 SolWorld conference in Budapest. My gratitude goes to Hannes Couvreur http://superblyhuman.be/

Step 1

As the participants finished drafting the description of their leadership issue, I signaled the beginning of a new phase in the workshop process. The moment was ripe to examine the host leader's two steps, six roles of engagement and four positions. The participants were going to do this first individually, then in self-forming groups, and finally in plenary, while building a new language and constructing for themselves a scaffolding for learning what host leading was about.

I first passed a bowl full of big colourful buttons (real, plastic buttons for garments) for each of the participants to pick one (see picture). Secondly, I drew their attention to the twelve A3 posters arranged along the wall, saying that they represented, in images and text, the host leader's two steps, four positions and six roles, i.e. the components of the host leader's framework. I invited them to view the posters and spend as long as they wanted taking in their contents and images. Perhaps they were going to find a poster the contents of which they associated with something they had once done, or it might be that they did not quite understand and wanted to find out what it was all about, or they had a story to tell which the poster reminded them of. Upon deciding which of the posters grabbed their curiosity and / or intrigued them in some way, they would put their button on the floor underneath the poster.

With the buttons (and people) thus distributed among the posters, we had six self-formed teams. The groups picked their chosen poster off the wall and found a suitable space to work together, either in the seminar room or outside it, in the adjacent areas.

Some of the posters remained on the wall, i.e. nobody had put their button there. There were also posters which had only got one button. That meant that only one participant had taken interest in that particular poster. Without too much ado, the person joined a bigger group but also remembered to take their originally chosen poster with them. The instructions were:

> *Study your poster and share with the others in your group what made you pick it. What drew your attention? How can you connect the poster theme to some of your personal experience? Is there a word or a phrase which is important to you and reminds you of an experience you have had?*

One or more members of the groups were to take notes by way of recording significant points in the conversation for reporting later, in the next step of the workshop. Soon after the groups settled down, I could hear the lively buzz of work, murmurs, louder voices, laughter, emphatic statements and assertions.

Step 2

Now, all the participants got back together. I noticed how the original seating had changed: all the poster groups were now very much sticking together. Poster by poster, the groups reported back. Typically, one person would give the gist of the group's conversations from the previous step while the rest of the group would add a detail or two, modify the account, ask the odd question, tell their own story. The spirit was high. Conversations flowed as the participants built on each other's ideas, told their stories, offered diverse interpretations of the steps forward and back, the six roles and four positions.

> *Reflection note 7*
>
> As I was closely following what was being said and, also, what was being left out, it occurred to me that the room had begun to resemble a construction site where common ground of ideas and experiences was being built and new insights were being arrived at and multiplied by the group's energy. It would sometimes be that the participants turned to me with a question and I would grab the opportunity to make clarifications, provide input, or refer the groups to those posters which were left on the wall. In Host Leadership terms, I performed my Co-Participator role, contributing to this unique process of knowledge generation.

Stage 4: Using the six roles and four positions

After the participants had spent a good chunk of time encountering Host Leadership through their own experiences and resources, some time for reflection was very welcome. I invited the participants to each go back to their notes about the particular leadership challenge they were currently facing. In their own quiet space, i.e. "In the Kitchen", the participants developed further their original descriptions. I reminded them to think in terms of the two steps, four positions and six roles. Acting by the principle that they were experts in their learning process and their lives more generally, and trusting that they could build on each other's expertise, we stepped into the last stage of the workshop.

Stage 5: Reflecting teams

Bearing in mind the time we had till the end of the workshop, I asked whether there would be a volunteer among the participants to present her leadership issue. Luckily, there was one.

We loosely followed the Solution Focused Reflecting Teams model (Norman, 1998) whereby the presenter explained her case and identified a practical issue that she needed to resolve by collecting wisdom from the group. It was once again becoming possible for the participants to get involved in a real-world learning experience and offer their piece of advice to their fellow participant. She accepted that gratefully.

> *Reflection note 8*
>
> The way Reflecting Teams flowed turned it into a spontaneous debriefing activity whereby the participants re-visited their Host Leadership thinking, put their Host Leadership language to use and rehearsed their understanding of key aspects of the method. Step by step they collaborated in building their own content and re-assured themselves of its pragmatic value for resolving challenges in their day-to-day work life.

Stage 6: Now what?

We were now heading towards the completion of the workshop. The participants took turns to say what one new thing they would be doing differently in the week following our event. Below are examples of what they said, uploaded from the flipchart notes.

I will

- tell my team how Host Leadership thinking can change our life in the company and will invite them to a workshop I am going to develop
- read Mark and Helen's book in English
- explore possibilities to take part in one of the international Host Leadership gatherings
- set up a series of meetings with our middle management to present the Host Leadership positions and roles

- watch myself when I am meeting clients and be aware which roles I am performing and whether I am not stuck in my step forward
- let my colleagues know how and what names to put to what they are already doing as host leaders
- clean and wet the doorstep of our beauty studio at least five times during the day so that our clients feel welcomed.

Reflection note 9

It is no big surprise that the participants each had a different idea for the 'next small step' they were going to make after the workshop. I regard this diversity of ideas as one of our jointly generated achievements. Clearly, Host Leadership and the way the concept and the approach were tackled had touched people differently, all depending on their state of mind, their desires and the larger context they operated in.

To my practitioner self, the main value of this particular workshop and of its numerous other editions is that word about Host Leadership spreads. Encouraging participants to take their learning in their own hands and therefore connect with the new approach meaningfully and usefully guarantees the germination of good outcomes.

References

Bowman, S. L. (2009). *Training from the Back of the Room*. San Francisco, CA: Wiley & Sons.

McKergow, M., & Bailey, H. (2014). *Host: Six New Roles of Engagement*. London: Solutions Books.

Meier, D. (2000). *The Accelerated Learning Handbook*. New York: McGraw-Hill.

Norman, H. (1998). Solution Focused Reflecting Teams. In W. O'Connell, & S. Palmer (Eds.), *Handbook of Solution-focused Therapy*. London: Sage.

Author

Leah Davcheva, PhD, is the founder and director of AHA moments – Centre for Interculturality, Solutions Focus, and Host Leadership. She works both locally and internationally, developing coaching and training programmes for organisations, teams and individuals in a wide range of settings. Leah has contributed to and was instrumental in building up the foundations of intercultural education and intercultural communication training in Bulgaria and beyond. Having studied Solutions Focus and Host Leadership with Mark McKergow, a more recent focus in her work is supporting people in their desire to make progress. She is also a researcher, and (co-) author of books, articles and learning materials. www.ahamoments.eu

Leah's posters

(Printable PDF copies can be downloaded from the Host Leadership Field Book website (hostleadership.com/field-book) using the code LEAH.)

A KEY QUESTION FOR A HOST LEADER

Should I step forward or step back ... next?
o How do I step forward? How do I act when I step forward, in which role and in what position?

o How do I step back and allow things to happen? Switch off? How to stay alert? How to watch out for what is happening in the space I have created?

FOUR POSITIONS IN THE DANCE OF THE HOST LEADER

o IN THE SPOTLIGHT – up front, in full view

o WITH THE GUESTS – public, yet intimate

o IN THE GALLERY – overview

o IN THE KITCHEN – more private & intimate work

A host leader adopts these positions as she he engages with her learners, people and events

In the Gallery

- Standing back
- Taking an overview of what's happening
- Don't just do something, stand there
- Can be a physical place, state of mind or both
- See the wood and the trees
- Spotters
- Ruiko Aoki
- Be ready to jump in

In the Kitchen

- A more private and intimate space
- Preparing and reflecting
- Time with confidants and advisors
- Coaching, mentoring, developing, learning
- Reflective practice, e.g. a teacher's diary
- Re-generating time, "sharpening the saw"
- Making materials
- Making time for creativity!

IN THE SPOTLIGHT

- Being in the focus of attention
- Out front, on stage
- Making things happen

- Intention:
  - What difference do I want to make here?
- Preparation
  - Confident opening
  - Warm up
- When will it be time to step back?

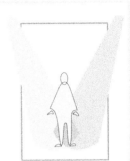

WITH THE GUESTS

- Still out front but being 'one of the group'
- Mingling with the guests
- Not the centre of attention
- Get out and get under

- Personal time
- Informal time
- Listen more than talk
- Ask questions
- An excellent opportunity

HOSTING IN PRACTICE: SIX ROLES

INITIATOR	INVITER	SPACE CREATOR

GATE KEEPER	CONNECTOR	CO-PARTICIPATOR

INITIATOR

Stepping forward and back as an initiator

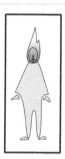

Responding
- Listen for what is being called for
- Avoid "ant country"
- Keep awareness of what's happening

Getting things started
- Form a hope, dream or intention
- Get things moving – small steps
- Respond with dynamic steering

INVITER
Stepping forward and back as an inviter

Giving choice and space

Inviting with soft power

- Think about whom to invite
- Offer choice and space for an authentic 'yes'

- Start with the soft power of the *Ask*
- Make it personal & acknowledging
- Extend a welcoming hand

SPACE CREATOR
Stepping forward and back as a Space creator

Allowing people to use the space

Creating the space

- What would be a great space? Physical? Interactional? Headspace?
- What message is your space conveying?
- Hold the space while people use it

- Create a space to support what you want to happen
- Focus on the details as well as the big picture
- Keep the space refreshed, invigorated and evolving

GATEKEEPER

Stepping forward and back as a Gatekeeper

Excluding and Defining
- Take note of the thresholds
- Be observant of the borders. Can they be changed?
- Step back and welcome people from other boundaries and spaces

Including and Allowing
- Welcome people in and establish defining routines
- Change container size when needed
- Be prepared to exclude topics and people – temporarily or (if you really must) permanently

CONNECTOR

Stepping forward and back as a Connector

Allowing contact
- Look out for not yet connected
- Look for opportunities to build connections between others
- Be aware of connections all around

Making connections and intros
- Connect with new people and their walk
- Connect others
- Respond to new awareness with openness – perhaps a new call is forming

Pick your poster 167

CO-PARTICIPATOR

Stepping forward and back as a Co-participator

Joining in *Initiating and providing*

- Look for opportunities to serve others first
- Step forward to provide care and support, serve others first (in the spotlight)
- Take a turn with everyday tasks
- Be alert to the pinch points (in the gallery)
- Join in the "eat the same food" (with the guests)
- Be prepared to intervene when necessary

21

Hosting new beginnings: Bringing together a 'cellular company'

Paul Hookham (United Kingdom)

> *There are many occasions when a Host Leadership stance can be helpful. One key time is at the dawn of a new group or organisation. Here, Paul Hookham describes his endeavours to create a world-class software company in England.*

At the turn of the 20th century, I was manning a stand at a software conference when I was approached by an ex-colleague who was attending as a delegate for a rival professional services company. After a brief catch-up, she explained that her company was in the early stages of establishing an outsourced IT company based in the south of England. Its major investor was a household name in telecommunications who needed a high-performing software organisation to assist in the delivery of their market strategies.

Would I be interested in being interviewed? She believed I would be a good fit, given her previous exposure to my leadership style, and it would be a great opportunity to get involved right at the start and shape their future. Her 200-strong professional services company also needed something that could demonstrate what world-class software engineering looks like to prospective customers; so it was a win/win!

My heart was not fully engaged in my current role, so I thought – 'Why not?' In two weeks, I was interviewed and accepted in what turned out to be my first opportunity to introduce what we now know as Host Leadership.

The foundation of the team comprised around 30 ex-employees of the investor company, with a budget to recruit a similar number to bring fresh ideas and new ways of working.

Personally, I had become disillusioned with the 'command and control' style of leadership that was pervasive in my previous employments. I knew there had to be a better way; one that would not only lead to success but also put a spring back in everyone's step. After all, the date changes that had to be made to accommodate the turn of the century had been successful. It was time for investment, for optimism and new beginnings. (Popularly known as the millennium bug, any 2-digit date fields containing only the year had to be updated so all systems could recognise the century change and process accordingly.)

I was determined to do three things:

1. Lead how I would like to be led.
2. Only do the things that only I can do.
3. Attend to the needs of the people doing the work.

The team was highly intelligent, talented in their sphere of expertise and needed to be given their heads to not only experiment but also challenge the old ways of working. They had clearly been suffocating within a micro-managed, hierarchical organisation.

The obvious thing to do was to ask them what they were missing, what they didn't like about their old way of working and drive the outline organisational design from there. I believed the buy-in would be pretty good as the people doing the work would have the lion's share of the input (without the patronising pictures of wild animals on the office walls – everyone knew the customer was king).

As I joined the company, a number of externally facilitated workshops were being held around people, process and technology, the output from which would be used to shape the design of the new organisation. Everybody was given the opportunity to contribute and the excitement of being engaged led to a real possibility of doing things differently and more effectively.

It was clear from the outset what they didn't want:

- A management hierarchy, in any shape or form. No line management overheads.

- Being told how long it should take them to complete their activities. They had a massive repository of data that would drive the estimates, so why should they take any notice of uninformed opinion, especially from management?

- Poor communication and no feedback. They never got to hear anything other than where they needed to improve, once a year, at appraisal time.
- Limited personal development other than the training courses that head office thought would be a good idea; how to give effective presentations being a particular favourite.
- Inflexible working practices. Remote working, where they could be more productive, was an absolute no-no. There was a complete lack of trust, evidenced by the need to sign-in and sign-out every day.
- You must do it like this. Thou shalt always follow this process.
- Only lip service being paid to customer and employee satisfaction.
- No closed-door team meetings. Very little is confidential in an IT organisation. They wanted regular open and honest communication not a conclave of management where no white smoke would ever appear.

It was fundamental to the successful organisation of the future that every single one of these was considered to form the new vision and values. Things began to take shape and this is what we came up with and in a remarkably short period.

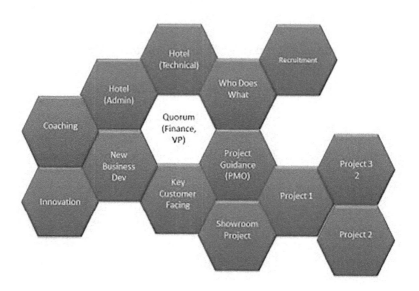

A cell-based structure of self-managing, autonomous teams. Each cell consisted of members and members were encouraged to belong to more than one cell. Cells were both permanent and transient depending on the requirements. However, as the Q-Cell was a profit centre, now in charge of its own destiny, project delivery was its life-blood.

Patronising posters were replaced with the new vision and values.

1. To become a high maturity software engineering and consultancy business.
2. To be a role model software company for small and medium-sized enterprises.
3. To be totally focused on customers by delivering world class quality and delivery precision.
4. To create a culture of employee shareholders.
5. To excel at building high-performing teams.
6. To implement decision-making at the informed level.
7. To exploit new technologies and services for the benefit of both customers and members.
8. To be successful in multiple market sectors.
9. To make a significant contribution to the financial health of the parent company.
10. To encourage, empower and reward innovation.
11. To continually challenge the status quo.
12. Communicate – Communicate – Communicate.
13. Evolution not Revolution.
14. To be agile and responsive and treat everybody with humility and respect.
15. Great teams – Great Results – Great Fun.

We were well and truly on our way. I knew it would be a challenge for everybody, including myself as the host leader of a newly-formed organisation, but we were all excited at the prospect. As with almost every major change or transformation, there are individuals at various stages on the Change Curve. Some were in denial that anything would change, others were sceptical and concerned with the speed of the change but the majority could see the benefits of membership and the empowerment it delivered. They went for it!

Let's look at the cells in more detail starting with the permanent ones.

Quorum

Initially we called it the Court, but this had a flavour of punishing people when there were issues and our desire to be a learning organisation was far more important. Quorum had two members, a Financial Controller and myself. It would allocate budgets to individuals for personal development and remuneration that reflected their contribution to both the culture and customer delivery. It was rarely used in anger to discipline anybody, but if it was necessary – it did.

In terms of annual pay rises, three respected members allocated the budget to the members based on their contribution. How could I possibly make a salary decision at the individual level? It had to be done by the people working at the coalface. This certainly raised more than a few eyebrows at head office, but the outcome was fair and well received by everybody because it wasn't management making an ivory tower decision.

As a leader, this was definitely one of my better decisions. To me, it was logical to act as a host, bringing together the reviewers, the reviewed and the budget.

Hotels

These two cells (IT and Administration) provided quality services to the membership in exactly the same way as one would expect from a five-star hotel – hence the name. Activities included employee relations, licensing, desktop and server management, network management and buildings management. There were three or four people doing this who were specialists in their area of expertise. They were enabling cells that kept the engine running.

Who does what?

This cell had a rotated membership. It allocated individuals to both projects and support cells and was far more effective than using a resource management function. Every vacancy was advertised internally and members applied. Each week, the cell would meet, consider the applications and fill the vacancy. It was important that they never made the obvious choices every time as it would not have stretched the member concerned. Comfort zones had been left in the past.

Both successful and unsuccessful candidates were informed without delay and reasons given for the decision. As this was made by the members themselves, there were very few negative reactions. Its performance exceeded all expectations.

New Business Development

This cell was responsible for the pipeline of work flowing into the company and establishing relationships with prospects across multiple market sectors. I took the decision to allocate the task to an experienced engineer, in exactly the same way as the other cells. Why should this cell be any different?

The answer, of course, is because it was. I should have rejected this approach as soon as it became obvious that we were over-exposed to one customer in one specialist market sector. I realised this when it was too late to have much effect. A salesperson, augmented by an experienced software professional, would have been the best decision with the benefit of hindsight.

Coaching

Success would simply not have been possible without this cell. As many of the members were from a hierarchical, command and control background, it was imperative that they were helped through the change process. It was painful for some; others navigated the challenges with ease.

We made a significant investment in training. This was critical to ensure a professional and credible service that offered real personal development opportunities to the members. It was an eye-opener for some as they assumed the coach would tell them what to do in any given circumstance. Of course, that is not coaching. The coach's job is to ask the challenging questions and get the member to find the way forward. It's far more powerful and effective that way as people are more likely to execute an action plan if they came up with it themselves.

A golden rule – the service was totally confidential. The output was never used as input to the annual pay review. It operated as an optional, peer level service in order to build the rapport and trust necessary to make it work. My coach was a Java developer and she was brilliant!

I strongly recommend that anyone considering a move to Host Leadership adopts a coaching culture and uses trained coaches to deliver the service.

Project Guidance

This was a peer-assist cell as the name suggests and not a forum for inquisition into why things weren't going to plan. It was staffed by experienced project and programme managers and met weekly to offer help and direction to the projects. This made the experience totally transparent and everybody was open and honest about what was going well and not so well. Good practice was shared as well as some 'Please don't do these things.' It showed we were becoming a learning company.

As host leader, I was invited as an attendee, not to lead the sessions but to use my experience and judgement.

Key Customer Facing

This cell was for the 'account managers' on our most profitable or potentially profitable customers. It was a one-stop shop for customer issues as it was critical that they had a direct line into a member who really understood their business and had a good grasp of project progress. The most effective relationships were those where a high level of rapport and trust had been built-up so there was no need to iron over any cracks; much better to gouge them out, fill them in and smooth them over.

Showroom

This was our continuous improvement cell. The concept was introduced as a mechanism to show prospects what world-class software engineering looks and feels like. It acted as custodian of all the processes and tools in use across the cells and the evaluation and implementation of new ones. I equate it to a Formula One garage on race day – busy, spotlessly clean and professional – well two out of three isn't bad!

Recruitment

This is the first of the transient cells and provided an end-to-end service for the addition of great candidates to our membership. The members placed the job advertisements, performed the interviews and agreed the remuneration package with the successful candidate. It was critical that we introduced people who shared our vision and values as this was equally as important as technical ability. There is no point in having great people and then throwing a technically competent wasp at them. It would cause disruption and undo a lot of the good work.

Personally, apart from providing budget and encouragement, I only got involved on the candidate's first day, after the hiring decision was made. The cell was totally empowered and trusted and this was reflected in the outstanding quality of the people who joined us.

Innovation

Another transient cell where proofs of concept were tried and tested on new ideas and if only one out of ten were passed to the Showroom for implementation, then we would be delivering our vision of being a leader in new technology and challenging the status quo. It was here that we started our experiments with what is now universally accepted as Agile although we didn't know it at the time.

… and last but by no means least –

Projects

These were our life-blood and everything we did was focused on delivering a successful outcome for our customers, in terms of quality, delivery precision and valuable features. The revenue generated funded the support cells and enabled us to continue with what we believed was a unique and hugely successful operating model.

However, explaining the detail that underpins the Q-Cell structure is one thing but the proof of any pudding is in its eating. What about the business results, I hear you cry? There is no point in having a high-performance sports car if it runs like a carthorse.

Here are some of the highlights: -

- ✓ Voted No 1 design centre worldwide for quality and delivery precision by its key client
- ✓ Monthly return on revenue of 30%
- ✓ Externally assessed as high maturity by our major investor's assurance team

- ✓ Increase of 30% in customer satisfaction from the initial baseline
- ✓ Increase of 50% in employee satisfaction from the initial baseline
- ✓ ISO9001 certification by the British Standards Institute
- ✓ Defect density of 300% above customer driven target
- ✓ No dates missed – EVER

This was pretty impressive stuff and achieved in an amazingly short timescale. It would sit quite happily at the top of the folder labelled 'Doing Things Differently'.

The last few items are not cells but worth a mention:

Office Design – software engineers are very practical people and like to keep a keen eye on getting value for money. They saw no reason whatsoever why professional tradesmen should be hired to design, decorate and install the way we wanted the workplace to look and feel. So, they did it themselves with impressive results.

Afternoon Tea – admittedly, a totally British concept. This was our weekly all-hands communication session where I gave updates on what was going on in the company and others were invited to present on project progress, sales and marketing activity or the social events that we were planning, and of course tea and cakes were included.

Measurement – as one very wise man said, 'If you can't measure it, you can't manage it'. It was worth every penny to have a full-time software measurement expert in place. A huge repository had been created to enable us to predict defects found in testing, validate estimates and provide defect density and productivity data as requested. Without it, all statements would be based on opinion and not data, something we wanted to avoid at all costs as that's the way it used to be.

Member Surveys – were distributed and analysed once a quarter. It was an excellent temperature gauge on how we were doing, through the eyes of the members. We always acted on suggestions and opportunities for improvement. There were always a Top Three on display along with the progress being made against each one. The talk had to be walked – and walk it we did. There is little point in urging people to return the surveys and then do nothing.

Well that's it. An example of how cultural change can happen and produce outstanding results. The biggest lesson I learnt from the entire experience is this:

"PEOPLE DO OUTSTANDING WORK IN A COLLABORATIVE ENVIRONMENT, FREE OF FEAR AND BLAME, WHERE THEY ARE TRUSTED, SUPPORTED, ENCOURAGED TO INNOVATE AND ALL SHARE IN THEIR COMPANY'S SUCCESS."

In conclusion, it is worth pointing out that over the years, many people have been sceptical about the scalability of this organisational model.

Recently, and for the first time since Q-Cell was formed, I did some work for a Central European technology company who have implemented a cell-based organisation. They have based their cells on competency centres (e.g. Intelligent Digital Workplace, Retail and SAP). Their culture is based on empowered, self-managing teams. They now have well over 500 full-time employees and are growing rapidly. They would not work in any other way now.

Sadly, the original Q-Cell only lasted for a few years. As previously mentioned, we were over exposed to one customer in one sector – telecommunications. When this market 'fell out of bed' followed by the inevitable downturn in the economy, the customer had little choice but to move its engineering capability to South America, where the resources were cheaper. They are on record as saying that 'Q-Cell is great – but we can't afford to stay in the UK'.

I have continued to work as a host leader ever since Q-Cell. It gets the best results, people are much happier, customers are delighted (generally) and continuous improvement just happens. I like to think the main part of my job is not just looking after my people but creating an environment where ordinary people are encouraged, supported, trusted and empowered to deliver extraordinary things.

I'll conclude by listing a few things that have worked for me. I won't apologise for any repetition as some of these are vital to implement Host Leadership and a new way of working. It just doesn't happen by magic; it takes hard work, constant communication and the belief that there is a better way – a much, much better way.

- Always show you care. Ask questions. Be curious.
- Attend to your people's needs. They will then attend to your customers.
- Always walk the talk. Be that role model.
- Be approachable. Encourage challenge.
- Only interfere when asked to or it is so obvious that you have no choice.
- Reward outstanding teamwork. Sometimes 'thank you' is enough – not always!
- Provide high quality coaches for personal development.
- Let people have their own individual training budgets – trust them.
- By all means host visits but engage your teams – involve them as they are your best advocates.
- Communicate and cater for all needs at these sessions as not everybody is comfortable in group sessions.
- Act on feedback – you don't have to implement everything but at least explain why if you don't.

However, it's not all plain sailing. Expect some turbulence. There will be times when the going gets pretty tough and certain individuals don't want or refuse to engage with the new ways of working. They have become embroiled in their comfort blanket, despite the fact that it really isn't that comfortable. You've tried everything you can think of but nothing is changing. You are being challenged – openly.

You have little choice. A difficult conversation needs to be had and quickly. It's sad but some people need to be helped out of the organisation and to find something else that meets their needs. You do not want the teams to be brought down to the lowest common denominator. It's time to say goodbye.

Fortunately for me, this has only happened on a handful of occasions and often, the person involved has thanked me afterwards for being so open and honest. There is always a square peg that just needs to find a square hole.

So, let's finish on a positive. The world of business is changing at light speed. Customers are much more demanding and knowledgeable. Speed is king but not without quality. Your people and the relationships between them are your greatest asset. If you focus on their needs and support them in their work, startling transformations will occur. Process and technology can follow on closely behind BUT first of all – get the culture right.

You need to equip your people with the skills they need so that they can work anywhere – but their choice is always to work with you – as a host leader. If you haven't tried Host Leadership then why not give it a go. There is always help at hand to start you off and accelerate progress along the way but bear in mind that no one-size fits all and the actions of the host leader will need to be tailored to fit the needs of the organisation.

Author

Paul Hookham is a highly experienced delivery executive in both technology and business change. He has worked at all levels within some of the world's most demanding companies and thrives in an environment of change and transformation. He is currently the project management associate at Business Simulations, an experiential learning company where simulations are used to introduce new concepts in high performing teams, project management and business acumen. He is also a master practitioner of NLP (neuro-linguistic programming), a master coach, a published author and conference speaker. He can be contacted at paul@businesssimulations.com

Part Five
Developing as a host leader

22

Hearing what is being called for: What's next in your team, organisation and life?

Mark McKergow, Leah Davcheva, Rolf Katzenberger, Luca Sturaro, Dario Campagna, Olga Kiss, Jessika Jake

The first role of a host leader (in the book Host by Mark McKergow and Helen Bailey) is the Initiator role; deciding that something is important, needs to happen and getting things moving with small steps. However, as the authors make clear, there is a necessary precursor to this; first of all, we need to hear what is being called for. What is important enough to initiate? How do we pick out something from the great emergent confusing mess that is life? How can we begin to notice what might be important enough to start work?

There are many aspects to Host Leadership. However, one of these aspects precedes all the others; what are the priorities, needs and topics which are worthy of attention? This is hardly ever a matter of totally free choice, even if we are in a designated (or simply self-chosen) leadership position. Additionally, we can find ourselves in all kinds of contexts which are potential sources for topics to initiate. These include:

- **Co-participator:** Where we are just joining in with something, whether as members of a team, participants in an online community, players in a backgammon club, residents of a town and so on. In this situation we often don't have a formal role or responsibility for generating change, but you may find yourself noticing something that matters, something you start to think might be important.

- **Team/Organisational leader:** There are all kinds of situations where we might have a formal leadership position. This might be a small or large group, it might be at work or in another setting (voluntary group, charity organisation, sports club etc). Generally speaking, you will now have some kind of explicit responsibility for improving things and generating positive change, as well as keeping things running and preventing them from getting worse.

- **Agile coach/ scrum-master / facilitator /coach:** In this context we are not really 'members' of a team but we meet with them from time to time to host conversations and activities which are supposed to lead to improvements. Here too it is important to find and build support around topics which are felt to be important and deliver enhancements.

- **Life:** Irrespective of our work or other settings, we all have our own lives to lead. So these topics for initiating can include all kinds of things from deciding to move house, enter (or leave) relationships, change jobs, start a business, begin a new pastime for our own enjoyment and recreation, and so on. These can be some of the most important things to think about! So getting better at noticing what is important and when is a really key skill for everyone.

Sometimes we can experience a call from the future when we are explicitly looking for it. At other times, however, these calls can arrive anyway, when we are not expecting or looking for them. Indeed, Mark McKergow was not looking for a new leadership idea when he heard the quote 'The host is both the first and the last' at a workshop in 2003 – but it immediately struck him as an idea about leading as well as hosting, and life for him has never been the same again!

So let's start by looking at hearing what is being called for when we aren't looking for it, and then move on to ways to develop and refine this in more formal settings.

1. Develop habits and rhythms for checking in with yourself

It is often easier to put these feelings into context if we develop habits and rhythms for checking in with ourselves. There are many different ways to do this. Some people like to practise mindfulness on a daily basis, taking the chance for a period of stillness and embracing of experience. Others have daily and weekly routines, perhaps taking stock at the beginning of the day what seems to be important right now, or at the end of the week thinking about what new has emerged and what is important to take forward. The key is to do it regularly – programming a reminder into your phone or calendar is one way to get into the swing of it.

2. Notice feelings and sensations

Often the very first sign that something important is beginning can be an unexpected feeling or sensation in the body. Of course we all experience this kind of sensation; the key here is an unexpected or unusual experience. Sometimes people are nervous of paying attention to internal sensations. By all means be wary, but as a first sign that something new and important is beginning, this is still a vital indicator. Don't rush to try to understand it, just notice that something is happening and congratulate yourself on noticing it!

3. Build verbal and written descriptions

Once you start to notice that something is important, develop it at your own pace. That might be very fast or very slow. If it begins to feel like a big burden (as opposed to an exciting or important new strand) then perhaps it is less vital than you first thought. One way to do this is to start to talk about it with someone else – maybe someone who knows you and that you trust, someone with whom you can speak in confidence and be sure of a supportive relationship. In Host Leadership terms this is an 'In The Kitchen' activity – something to do in private at first, to explore it and see how it emerges and develops as the conversation progresses. An alternative and even more private way to do this is with journalling – writing down your thoughts, making them concrete in some initial way and allowing the words to flow and develop as you go along. This is also something which can be good to do on a regular basis; writing a diary is one form of journalling, and there are many other ways to do it. Make a mind-map if you prefer.

All these methods and ideas work well for calls from the future which are coming to us as individuals. Where you have some kind of formal position in leading a group of people or helping to generate change as a coach, there are many other more structured ways to build conversations about what is important. Here are a few ideas which we have used and might be good places to start.

4. "What would make your life/work easier and better?"

This is a wide open question. It is deliberately wide open, in order to help people think widely and start to engage with the idea that things might be able to be improved, even if that seems initially improbable or unfeasible. Often people give an instinctive answer, like "more time!" or "more money!" This might indeed be a bit flippant, but we can take is seriously by asking "Ok, and what difference would that make?" Rather surprisingly, the answer to the follow-up is often the beginning of a more practical conversation. For example, more time could be seen as a route to making fewer mistakes or giving better service, which are in turn potential starting points for a worthwhile initiative.

5. Pain points

One snappy way into this kind of conversation with groups or teams is to ask them "where are the pain points"? People immediately understand what this means – the moments where things don't flow well, the things which seem like a waste of time, the pointless processes, the feeling of 'grit in the wheels'. Although this might seem like a negative conversation, it can quickly point to the things that matter to people, and where some kind of progress (to lessen the pain or at least keep it to a minimum) will produce clear potential benefits to the people. It is often said that 'people resist change', but they are often more keen on something that reduces their pain! Note that as a host leader you can listen for these pain points at any time and in any role. The With The Guests position can be an excellent time to hear about people's views.

6. Problem to solution

One very useful framework if people have a whole bunch of pain points is the Problem To Solution framework. Put a line down the middle of a flip chart. On the left hand side, list the pain points, problems, bad things. Now, go through the list with the group and discuss what to write on the right hand side. These are what we want *instead* of the pain point etc. It's curious, but it turns out to be much easier to replace something with something else rather than simply remove it. So the right hand column, the list of things that people want, gives a much more meaningful direction to move towards. If you don't know where you want to go then any direction is the right direction, as someone once said. Some people even tear off the left hand side of the flip chart at this point and only work with the remaining right hand side – that's where most of the value is.

7. Build stories

A story can be richer and more meaningful than a series of bullet points. So another way to hear calls from the future is to encourage people to develop stories. These can be stories of pain in the past, and stories of how things can be in a better future. Some approaches such as Appreciative Inquiry have a strong tradition of having people interview each other to build these stories, which can also be recorded for later reference. Often the exact words and phrases really matter in making sure that people feel heard, and that their ideas and wishes are being taken seriously. Listening to people with an open and accepting heart, hearing their words, showing that you have been listening, are all key skills for a host leader. Also tools like Sensemaker from Cynefin can help here to organise multiple stories.

8. Spotting non-compliance

As a team leader or Agile coach, it is often our role to spot non-compliance. Where are people doing things against the established rules and standards? Of course at one level it is our role to stop this non-compliance. But what if it happens again and again, despite warnings and instructions. One way to look at this is to start to look at the wider context here – how come people are continuing to do things this way? This can show the way to new calls from the future, places where change is really needed to resolve the conflicts which are clearly there between what 'should' happen and what does happen. So, persistent non-compliance might just be the key indicator for the next initiative.

9. Desire-lines

We have all seen the phenomenon of desire-lines in action (even if we've never heard of it). A park has carefully designed and laid-out pavements and paths, beautifully constructed – and here and there are muddy tracks where people actually walk, not in accordance with the official paths. These unofficial walkways are 'desire-lines' – signs that people want to do (and indeed are doing) something that's outside the design specified. Of course one possibility would be to erect fences and barriers to stop them. A much more interesting possibility, however, is to start to think about changing or adding to the 'official way' to include these crowd-sourced possibilities.

This is not simply about footpaths of course. As some followers of the new 'Safety II' philosophy (Hollnagel, 2018) have it, why people didn't do what they were supposed to tells you little or nothing about why they did what they did. If people are doing something, then there's clearly a good reason for it – it's quicker, easier, shorter, more convenient. This could raise a project either way – to enable the easier routes and make them official, or (if they are really unsuitable) then do something about it.

Conclusion

This chapter suggests ways to discover what's next for your team or organisation, or indeed your own life. This list is a starter – there are many ways that these things come to us, intentionally or out of the blue. However, this is a key topic; if we're setting off to climb a ladder it's as well to make sure that it is leaning against the right wall! One way to check this out is to go through the User's Guide To The Future process to see how it all stacks up (see Chapter 25 for a good way to do this using coaching processes), and perhaps check it out with some trusted colleagues or friends.

References

Hollnagel, E. (2018). *Safety-I and Safety-II: The Past and Future of Safety Management*. Boca Raton FL: CRC Press.

McKergow, M., & Bailey, H. (2014). *Host: Six new roles of engagement for teams, organisations, communities and movements*. London: Solutions Books.

Authors

This chapter was written by several authors at the 2019 Host Leadership Gathering by several authors hosted by Mark McKergow. Mark pioneered the idea of hosting and leadership starting in 2003 and wrote the book Host: Six New Roles of Engagement with Helen Bailey. He is a speaker, author, consultant and trainer who brings new ideas into the world of management. He loves ideas that make things easier, simpler, shorter and more effective than people thought possible. Mark is based in Edinburgh, Scotland. His previous work in accelerated learning and Solution Focus has taken him around the world.

23
Shapeshifting, beaming and the chameleon shuffle

Rolf F Katzenberger (Germany)

The Host Leadership approach is both a metaphor and a model, with six roles and four positions for a host leader to adopt from time to time as required by the situation. In this chapter Rolf looks at how to make the most of these ideas by exploring the art of moving between these roles and positions – how hosts can get the most out of (as yet) unfamiliar roles, and boldly go to (as yet) unfamiliar positions.

Introduction

When applying Host Leadership in our own contexts, we might realise we're not yet fluent with playing *all* of the six roles it suggests, or with moving smoothly between *all* of its four positions.

It helps to start from familiar ground, taking cautious steps to and fro, shuffling as some chameleons are seen to do (look up "chameleon shuffle" on Youtube, for a smile). It is also helpful to consider what is supportive of the fluency and smoothness we're striving for. Trust in proven skills and knowledge enables a group to benefit from role changes. Genuine presence, the offering of relationships, turns positions into resources. This chapter presents a simple tool and activity for exploring these topics, and it summarises what has emerged so far from working with that tool.

Hosts in their performance zones

The host metaphor is so attractive partially because it presents us with roles and positions that look and feel familiar to us. There are roles we love to play, and positions we enjoy taking. It's where we can apply our expertise, skills and knowledge to the fullest, working on things that matter to us. While it is common to denounce this as "staying in the comfort zone", a term like "performance zone" is a much better fit.

Looking beyond our favourite roles and positions, at our "growth zone", we may sense a vast number of new options. Growth is hiding in the roles we are not used to playing (yet) and in the positions we are not yet used to taking. Sadly, all too often we confuse adopting new roles and taking new positions with a burden of additional accountabilities, and with abandoning our home or strongholds.

However, we can learn and master both the art of fluently adopting any host role, and the art of moving smoothly between all host positions, once we take a fresh look at both and understand why such moves are helpful.

Shapeshifting, the art of fluently adopting roles

Shapeshifters, in mythology as well as in sci-fi, are beings that can morph into the shape of any other being, and become an indistinguishable twin. The fascination with shapeshifters has always been a worldwide phenomenon, yet the stories told are mostly stories about broken trust.

Trust issues are what shapeshifters share with people having to play multiple roles. We are told that everybody else needs to *see* clearly what hat we are wearing at any given point in time. Seeing isn't believing, though; we can put on the helmet of a gatekeeper, claiming that role for ourselves, and still fail to inspire the trust and confidence of others in our performance and motives. To them, what our head is intending and capable of clearly matters much more than our headgear.

What is needed, then, for shapeshifting between roles to work as intended? And once that is in place. what becomes possible when we've started to view unfamiliar host roles as promising bundles of new skills, and new knowledge?

The Circle of Trust

Successful shapeshifting is powered by a Circle of Trust:

- Mutual trust enables a group to favour overlapping skill sets, and adopting roles out of a feeling of responsibility, over assigning and enforcing static accountabilities, disguised as "roles"
- Favouring overlapping skill sets fosters "T-shaped" people, who combine a considerable depth of skills and expertise in a single field (symbolised by

the vertical bar of the T), with an ability to collaborate across disciplines (the horizontal bar of the T)

- T-shaped people reduce the need for elaborate handover procedures, and collaborate in more seamless ways
- Seamless collaboration allows for perceiving shapeshifting as an authentic and helpful contribution to teamwork, not as a game of privilege
- Every experience of authentic teamwork, in turn, reinforces mutual trust.

Tips for successful shapeshifting

Fluency in adopting roles is not something you can practise as an individual. You learn it together with others. As a group, you build more capacity in all of your members to give an effective response whenever needed, not just an account when it's due.

To be trusted, you need to become more responsible, and settle less with everybody being just accountable. Here are a few success tips.

Verbs, not nouns

Start seeing, and talking about, host roles as being verbs: Initiating; Inviting; Creating Space; Gatekeeping; Connecting; Co-Participating. That way, roles morph into bundles of required skills and knowledge. Plus, the efficacy of the roleplay becomes the focus, instead of certainty about who is held accountable, no matter the outcome. People are trusted not because they have been assigned a role and an associated accountability, but rather because they can both perform responsibly and skillfully in that role, and shape-shift between roles, to help out as needed.

Learn to learn and teach to teach

Host roles are learnable, and teachable. Trust evolves in stages, in parallel to growing skills and knowledge. Since medieval times, this thought has manifest itself in the triad of the apprentice, the journey-person, and the master.

Alternative notions include Shu / Ha / Ri ("protect" / "detach" / "leave" – a Japanese martial art concept which describes the stages of learning to mastery; see https://en.wikipedia.org/wiki/Shuhari), which is very popular with Agile teams; or the Dreyfus model of competence acquisition (with its successive stages: Novice, Advanced Beginner, Competence, Proficient, and Expert) as described in Dreyfus and Dreyfus (1986).

Masters are supposed to be teachers, and apprentices learn to become masters. Building on such popular notions makes it possible to both learn to learn host roles, slowly letting go of thinking in terms of immutable personality traits and talents; and to teach to teach, by becoming a host role model for others, demonstrating how to let go of thinking in terms of ownership and mere delegation.

Praise performance, not the person

Praising the person over their performance is like typecasting an actor. It ignores and ultimately thwarts their shapeshifting potential. And if the same is done to you, unchallenged by you, you will finally settle with the 'role of your lifetime". As a host, in the gallery, invest time into noticing specifically what a person succeeds in, and give accurate praise for that – as opposed to merely "watching the show", and applauding the ensemble only. Praise growth, and the adoption of unfamiliar roles. There is hardly a better reason to step into the spotlight, is there?

Beaming, the art of moving smoothly between positions

One of the most famous 'technologies' introduced by the Star Trek sci-fi franchise was beaming – teleportation (mostly) of humans using a mysterious "transporter". Today, the idea of being able to turn up anywhere quickly, and literally out of the blue, is still as fascinating as it was in the 1960s.

And as frightening, of course. Which relates beaming to a familiar story that many team leaders and other executives keep telling themselves: "Sorry, I can't just drop by and intrude into the space of my teams – hell, they'd think BOSS ALERT! OH MY GOD, WHAT WENT WRONG?" Even co-workers themselves similar stories about their peers.

For several decades, there have been attempts to popularise "Gemba walks": leave your desk, go and see the actual processes, understand the work, ask questions, and learn. Still, this is not yet what McKergow and Bailey (2014) hinted at with "Get out and get under!" (p. 66) – get out and actually *take part* in the work.

Given that history, what is needed for smooth quick moves between positions to appear less frightening? And once that is achieved: What becomes possible when people are free to move to an unfamiliar host position – free to put this additional degree of freedom to good use, for everybody involved?

The Circle of Presence

Successful beaming is powered by a Circle of Presence:

- Being present, in any position, means becoming aware of what is possible right here and consequently, offering and maintaining relationships, right here (this concept of presence was introduced into pedagogy by Haim Omer – see Omer, H (2010), and Baumann-Habersack, F. (2017) for its application to leadership topics)

- Tried-and-tested relationships allow for deliberate changes of positions, to increase collaborative efficacy

- Deliberate changes of position turn positions from personal realms into shared resources, to be used for the benefit of the whole

- Beaming, i.e. smoothly using positions as resources, ceases to be considered an intrusion; instead, this form of fluency is perceived as manifestation of care

- Continuous evidence of care, in turn, makes it easier to accept offers of new relationships, at any position.

Tips for successful beaming

Like shapeshifting from role to role, moving smoothly between positions can only be learned together with others. As a group, you build more capacity in all of your members to engage more in positional pla*y*, and less in standing one's ground.

To be present, you need to move more, and stay less. A few success tips:

Devise an integrated routine

Beyond staying aware of the purpose of every position and thinking in isolated options only, *integrate* your movements between positions into a personal routine that results in circuit training for your host skills. For example, follow the Deming Cycle (**PDCA**) – **P**lan, in the kitchen / **D**o, with the guests / **C**heck, in the gallery / **A**djust, in the spotlight.

Take your time to take a position

As a host, you cannot get into the gallery without taking the stairs. Even Captain Kirk has to walk into the transporter room first, to be beamed elsewhere. It is not an inconvenience, but rather an instance of what is called "ma" (間), in Japanese: the concept of an appreciative, empty space or phase between things or events, that allows for letting go of what was, and becoming open for something different. Include ma in your schedule, for winding down. Include ma in your spaces, between your positions, so positions and their respective purposes don't compete for your attention.

Use a white box approach for purpose and positional tactics

As a host, don't make your guests wonder why you are standing in the gallery. If you want your guests to watch for pinch points too, you need to be clear about what the purpose is. If you can't be in the gallery and want "spotters" (McKergow & Bailey, 2014, p. 70) to proxy you, they need to know what to monitor. As individuals forming a team, learn to have open conversations about tactics, for example using Objectives and Key Results (OKRs) as a vehicle. The more transparency you can establish, the clearer it becomes what has to happen in the kitchen, in the spotlight, in the gallery and among the guests. The less secrecy, the more people feel enabled and encouraged to take various positions, as needed. As a result, witnessing smooth moves between positions become less frightening too.

Where to start? The Chameleon Shuffle

Tentatively leaving familiar, and exploring unfamiliar roles and positions may look like a "chameleon shuffle". It is a natural way of moving under unfamiliar and potentially risky circumstances. At the same time, from an observer's perspective, humans doing a chameleon shuffle can be a un-nerving sight, provoking outbursts of impatience and bold calls for "professionalism" or "accountability" – unless the Circle of Trust and the Circle of Presence are both understood, and firmly established.

There is no way of talking yourself and others into trying a chameleon shuffle away from a position or role. Instead, to take courage, you need to have a conversation on that with yourself, both as an individual and as a team.

You might be tempted to sit down before a full matrix showing the six host roles versus the four host positions, and give your best at trying to appreciate the richness of the host metaphor by conquering the matrix square by square – as if taking courage was just a matter of combinatorial logic. It isn't.

Instead, use tools for individual or group reflection like the chameleon shuffle sheets presented below. They are based on two ideas:

- It is helpful to visualise the chameleon shuffle, i.e. to clearly state that leaving a specific role or position is always reversible, for good reasons, until you feel comfortable with your answer to "Should I stay or should I go?"
- It helps to reduce the plethora of role-and-position options by a visual focus on either your preferred positions and roles or on the most promising ones that you have hardly explored yet.

You can use flipcharts for hand-drawing such shuffle sheets. Also, printable sheet templates as well as sheets containing a bit of sample reasoning are available free at *[https://hostleadership.de/chameleon-shuffle-sheets/]*

Sample role and position shuffles

Let's assume the host role of Initiating was one of your favourites. That role, shown at the top, is where your inner chameleon loves to be *now*. Reflecting upon this role, either as an individual or as a team, it is probably easy to fill the column on the right with sticky notes full of good reasons why we would want to adopt the Initiating role, leaving other options behind. Also, it's probably not too hard to fill the note at the center with good reasons for continuing to play that role.

From the safety of your starting point, it feels ok to consider additional options offered by other roles. From your experience so far, start to explore good reasons for leaving the Initiating role, and for adopting another one. List as many reasons you can think of, and be as specific as possible.

Also, think of opportunities for *testing* such moves. With the Circle of Trust doing its magic, you *can* start exploring roles by doing the chameleon shuffle, because shifting your shape is part of the game.

Once you feel comfortable with starting your reflections from a familiar role, try starting from an unfamiliar one. You'll notice how easy it is to collect good reasons, within the left column, for leaving such a role. Collecting good reasons to adopt an unfamiliar role, in the right column, then becomes the challenge.

Leave this role now? «		« Play this role now?
	 **INITIATING**	
	What is my quest? What am I looking for? ...	
Take the first step of the journey. Stand by my idea. ...	**INVITING**	Be open for a change in direction. Announce an incubator. Elicit real world needs.
Grant head space to others. Exercise due diligence. ...	**CREATING SPACE**	Seed activities. Encourage low-risk experiments.
Protect our enthusiasm. Usher out naysayers. ...	**GATEKEEPING**	Welcome newbies. Highlight options and opportunities. Suggest better / alternative spaces.
Let our voices be heard, we are many! Listen to the stories of others. ...	**CONNECTING**	Promote my idea.
Target a narrower, specific purpose. ...	**CO-PARTICIPATING**	Improve continuously. Ask for best hopes. Dare to dream bigger.

In a similar fashion, the chameleon shuffle principle can be applied to beaming, the art of smoothly moving between the four positions of a host leader. Rest assured that Scotty, the space ship engineer, is keeping an eye on you while you are down on the surface of an unfamiliar planet, his fingers on the transporter button, ready to beam you back to your former position, on your command.

Page 198 has a sample sheet for the position of being *in the spotlight.*

IN THE SPOTLIGHT

Leave this position now? »   « Take this position now?

Hold space during gaps.
Divert the river of action.
Be an anchor during crisis.
...

Give way to conversations.
Communicate on equal terms.
Forgo status and privileges. Eat the same food.

WITH THE GUESTS

Speak up.
Contribute an idea.
Give orientation.
Suggesting a course of action.
Ask a question. ...

Hide in plain sight.
Encourage individuals, individually.
Help out.
...

IN THE GALLERY

Walk down the Grand Staircase.
Start / move on with agenda.
Pinch points require action.

Make others aware of meta-issues.
Remind others of principles and agreements.

Let others shine.
Timekeeping for activities.
Step aside after starting signal.
Become referee.
...

IN THE KITCHEN

Establish a frame.
Present with sparklers.
Sprint review.
Become visible as contributor.
Presenting theories. ...

Give space.
Cave-and-commons switch.
Enjoy freedom of action.
...

Conclusion

This chapter suggests a tentative approach for expanding your 'performance zone': consider potential benefits of Host Leadership roles and positions that are unfamiliar to you as yet. As a starting point, choose a role or position you're familiar with. The dynamics of trust and presence were described as the the enablers for the expansion; and cautious moves, "chameleon shuffles" to and fro, were introduced to frame your experiments as reversible, low-risk, and quick-win moves.

References

Baumann-Habersack, F. (2017). *Mit neuer Autorität in Führung. Die Führungshaltung für das 21. Jahrhundert*, 2. Auflage. Wiesbaden: Springer Gabler.
Dreyfus, S. E., & Dreyfus, H. L. (1986). *Mind over Matter*. New York, NY: Free Press.
McKergow, M., & Bailey, H. (2014). *Host: Six new roles of engagement for teams, organisations, communities and movements*. London: Solutions Books.
Omer, H. (2010). *The New Authority: Family, School, and Community*. Cambridge: Cambridge University Press

Author

The ideas and activities described in this chapter were collected by **Rolf F Katzenberger** *over a period of several years of coaching teams and individuals. For over a decade, Rolf's work as a facilitator, coach and mentor has led him to integrate approaches like Solution Focus, Accelerated Learning and finally Host Leadership into his tool set and framework for hosting change. He maintains the German-language website https://hostleadership.de/, and you can find his web presence at https://pragmatic-teams.com/ .*

24

The role of guests/followers: Risk and permission

Roddy Millar (United Kingdom)

'Host' is a word for a relationship – the relationship between host and guest. In this chapter Roddy Millar looks into the guest side of the experience and finds two key ingredients for the relationship – risk and permission. Balancing these is a key role for leaders of any and all persuasions.

Introduction

Adaptive, Agile, Authentic, Autocratic – leadership styles are many and varied – those are just some of the As after all. A trap into which many in the leadership sector fall is presuming that the typical supervisor, manager or executive is bothered about the nuances and semantic differences between the varying styles. In the modern world we tend to think of ourselves in terms of how we have trained – so we are doctors, lawyers,r marketeers or in finance. Very few get out of bed in the morning thinking about their day and how to finesse their leadership skills.

Leadership is an amalgam of meta-skills, those skills which allow you to leverage more functional skills. At its core good leadership is about heightened awareness of the context you are in and moving into, how the people around you are responding to that, and certain actions that you can take to best enable enhanced outcomes. The difference between adaptive, agile and authentic, for instance, is difficult for most people to articulate without reference to the manuals, the key variances being ones of emphasis rather than direction (autocratic leadership is clearly a different direction to the others).

Host Leadership – an intuitive style

Where Host Leadership (McKergow & Bailey, 2014) wins out over its many leadership style competitors is that its name intuitively embodies its meaning. We all intuitively know what a host does – and importantly, what a bad host does. We know also that hosts come in many guises and behaviours themselves, so it is not too prescriptive. A good host needs to be adaptive and agile, as well as authentic – and perhaps in times of crisis even autocratic.

What a host also needs, and leadership practice often fails to focus on this sufficiently, is guests. You cannot be a host without any guests, and you are not a leader if no-one will follow you. The dynamic between host and guest, and leader and follower is, by definition, a two-way one. What the host needs to do is completely driven by the behaviour of the guests; it is not too much of a stretch of the imagination to describe a party where the guests have selected the host and his or her venue, brought the food and drink, put on their own music and chosen when to leave. In these circumstances what exactly is the host's role? Is he or she really a host? They may well be delighted to have the activity and recognition going on around them, but are they in charge?

There are plenty of organisations and teams where this leader-follower dynamic exists. If the host/leader is supportive and co-operative with this situation, a willing participant in the 'open-house' approach, we are moving towards a self-organising and holacratic structure, which can be hugely energising. In many ways this is an ideal structure, if everybody is 'on-board' and there is a common goal being pursued with positive intent.

If the host/leader is not a willing but just a weak player in this scenario, then trouble looms – and we can expect that the host/leader, in animalistic fashion, will not be deemed a leader for long. Clearly, the opposite of this scenario is when the host/leader commands the guest/follower attendance and insists on their particular kinds of behaviour, regardless of the willingness of the guests'/followers' desire to participate or act in such a way. There are all too many examples of this kind of leadership in organisations too.

I describe these extremes to highlight the importance of the follower in the leadership dynamic. Ultimately, it is the energy and passion that the guests bring that makes or breaks the party, and so with teams. The host/leader role is to capture that energy and vitality and direct it towards the desired outcome.

Everyone has a leadership role to play

The key is that everyone has a leadership role to play. While the host takes the titular, visible leadership role, which will carry ultimate responsibility, there is little that he or she can achieve without the guests/followers donning the mantle of leaders too. The first module in almost all leadership development programs is 'lead yourself' or a variation on that. This is the idea that you need to know and understand your own biases and dysfunctions (we all have them!) and discipline yourself to correct and corral them, so they do not divert you from the task at hand and reaching the common goal. In its most primitive state, this may just be not downing all the wine and eating all the canapes as soon as you arrive, but having an awareness that a) these are to be shared with others and b) your resultant behaviour will most likely not enhance the party.

The host as leader, if they have done their job properly, will have excluded from the guest-list those who are most likely to behave like this, and only invited those they believe to have the self-discipline and self-leadership to behave correctly. This is a ludicrous example – but it highlights the unwritten contract between leader and follower, and takes us to the core of all effective teams, organisations and communities; there has to be trust between leader and followers, and also between followers and followers. The stronger that level of trust the more positive the outcomes from the group will be. *Speed of Trust* author Steven M R Covey points out (in his Foreword to Peterson, 2019, pp. xiii-xiv) that trust is an economic driver. "Put simply, high trust is a dividend, low trust is a tax."

The contract between host and guest, leader and follower, works best when it is entirely mutual and freely-given; in most organisations there will be a parallel legal contract that commands certain behaviour in return for pay, but this extrinsic contract does not bring the energy and passion that is really needed to move things forward, it is transactional with little if any relational element to it. The focus must therefore be on the intrinsic contract.

As we identified at the outset of this chapter, it is easy when we start to peel back the layers and nuances of leadership to create a complex leadership framework, and where we place the emphasis will shape its look. Few of these models are wrong, but in their diversity they will inevitably suit some situations better than others. Some interchangeability between the models is often required. The Host Leadership model retains an intrinsic flexibility and agility as the metaphor it encapsulates covers a diverse range of situations too.

Risk and permission

I like to reduce the elements a leader needs to think about to just two ingredients: Risk and Permission. The leader's role is to create an environment where the followers feel they have permission to operate freely, in the best way they can, to deliver a common goal. This requires of the followers certain leadership capacities of their own, as outlined by Ira Chaleff in his Courageous Followership model (Chaleff, 1995). They must take responsibility for both their own actions and how that progresses the team/organisation's journey to the common goal; they must serve passionately, bringing their energy and alertness to emerging needs to achieving that goal; crucially they must feel obliged to challenge the leadership when they think it is veering from the correct path; and they should have a clear moral purpose which allows them to stand-up to the leadership, to refuse to go in certain directions, if they believe it violates their moral stance.

By creating this environment where follower/participants in the team are given this freedom to operate and apply their discretionary effort, the leader relieves themselves of micro-managing things, but takes on a significantly enhanced quantity of risk. This is, to my mind, the real job of a leader, it is the ability to weigh up risk (not just of the financial kind) and make value-judging assessments, to see how much permission they are prepared to enable. Yes, they have to be clear about common goals, that is foundational, but it is their aptitude in giving permission to others to operate without close supervision, enhancing followers, sense of their own value and energy to input that discretionary effort, that marks out their real ability to lead.

When trust is given, it gives back far more than it diminishes. I heard Warren Buffett and Charlie Munger, the two great leaders of Berkshire Hathaway, the stellar investment company of the last century, discussing this at their 2014 AGM (also reported in Sorkin, 2014). Munger noted that "by the standards of the rest of the world we 'overtrust' – but I think a lot of places work better where there is a culture of trust." Buffett then reflected on their 'lack of supervision' of companies. "We think giving managers this degree of freedom allows them to accomplish a lot more – our lack of supervision does mean we miss some things.... but on balance it is a benefit." This approach has taken the share-price of Berkshire Hathaway from $275 in 1980 to over $315,000 today. Looked at this way, overtrusting has paid back a very healthy dividend.

There is another whole book to write on how to develop the ability to make good risk judgements – but a great deal comes down to experience and the wisdom that develops with that. Wisdom is a quality that indigenous peoples value immensely, but the West has largely stopped valuing today. We prefer to accrue the tangible benefits of power and wealth and direct them towards our own entertainment (holidays, houses and hedonism) rather than wisdom (which brings its own Hs of harmony, health and happiness).

Buffett is also known as 'The Sage of Omaha' for his wisdom. It takes self-discipline and the preparedness to take the *risk* of creating the *permission* to operate environments that has allowed this stellar return to occur. Risk and permission are two vital levers leaders should operate to control the balance of their organisation's progress – when done adeptly it allows the followers to fulfil their side of the contract far beyond most people's expectations.

References

Chaleff, I. (1995). *The Courageous Follower: Standing Up to and for Our Leaders*. Oakland CA: Berrett-Kohler.

McKergow, M., & Bailey, H. (2014). *Host: Six new roles of engagement for teams, organisations, communities and movements*. London: Solutions Books.

Peterson, J. (2019). *The 10 Laws of Trust: Building the bonds that make a business great*. (Expanded edition). New York NY: HarperCollins Leadership.

Sorkin, A. R. (2014). *Berkshire's Radical Strategy: Trust*. Retrieved from https://dealbook.nytimes.com/2014/05/05/berkshires-radical-strategy-trust/

Author

Roddy Millar is Editorial Director of IEDP Developing Leaders (www.iedp.com), an online platform that reports on executive education in large organisations, and its magazine www.developingleadersquarterly.com He is also founder of www.IdeasforLeaders.com, a website that houses a library of short, readable and applicable summaries of the latest business school research, predominantly on leadership and management practice issues. He can be reached at rmillar@ideasforleaders.com

25
Coaching with the User's Guide to the Future

Peter Röhrig and Mark McKergow (Germany/UK)

The User's Guide to the Future is a powerful model developed by Mark McKergow and Helen Bailey for working with the future in an emerging and uncertain world. Here Mark and Peter Röhrig extend the framework to make it an effective coaching tool to help those working on challenging and complex projects. You can use this as a coach, or as a self-help tool to aid your own thinking.

Model

In their book *Host: Six New Roles of Engagement* (2014, pp. 45 – 59) Mark McKergow and Helen Bailey present the following model which illuminates the responsiveness of hosting and helps host leaders (and indeed Solutions Focused workers) think about where to put their focus, how to connect long-term hopes and objectives with short-term action. It outlines a way of working with uncertainty that is both efficient – getting lots of action for less effort – and responsive to the unfolding future.

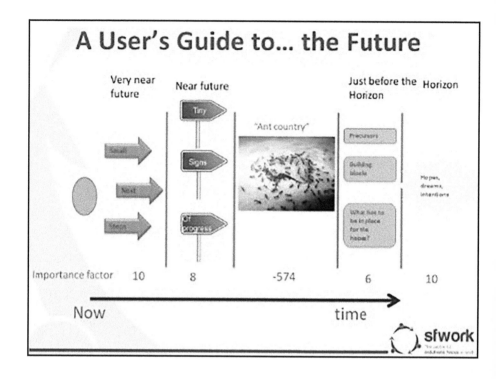

It contains some well-known Solution Focused elements combined with ground-breaking new ones:

On a timeline starting from the right we find the **hopes, dreams and intentions** of a particular project – on the horizon. They might be big or small, global or very local. Whatever, something that sets a direction of travel is vital.

Looking nearly to the horizon, we can think back a little. Supposing we were to achieve a better future – what **precursors** or building blocks will have to be in place to support that? This is about adding a bit more flesh to the bones of our hopes and can help in large-scale projects, involving many people, or those with long term scales.

Back to the left of the timeline, **small next steps** connect the present with the future. They may well be to look not at a plan to get all the way beyond the horizon, but at some next steps right now. Even the biggest project has started with some small steps.

Another helpful adjunct is to think a little way into the future. What might be the first **tiny signs of progress**? Things that will let us know we're on the right track. Signs are an interesting way to think about this – they are things we'd notice, not things we would do.

Somewhere in the middle distance, in between the signs of progress and the precursors to our hopes – is an area beloved of accountants and micromanagers, looking closely at things that might happen in one to three years, perhaps. Mark calls this a "Business Planner orientation". Instead of worrying too much about this middle part, we should think about it as the "**Ant Country**", being aware of the limits of predictability in life and take the mathematical models of ant colonies as examples of successful work in complex systems. Interacting agents (in this case ants) respond and react to developing circumstances and each other to produce rich, useful yet unpredictable behaviour. (Mark was himself a business planner in the British nuclear energy industry some 30 years ago, so should know what he is talking about!) Ant Country is not really plannable, but it will emerge in due course (and when it gets nearer, of course, it becomes signs of progress and a new Ant Country zone appears).

The User's Guide to the Future shows that not every element of the future is seeable or useable in the same way. It proposes embracing dynamic steering and avoiding getting trapped in worrying about "Ant Country" – take action, make adjustments, keep learning.

Coaching tool

In his work with organisations Peter Röhrig found out that the User's Guide can be utilised as a tool for coaching managers facing challenges with complex projects. With some small adjustments the model becomes a powerful tool to help people who feel stuck or overwhelmed by the complexity of the challenges ahead.

- In a sense of "Platform Building" it is useful to find a **name for the project**. A good name inspires customers and the project team equally, stays in the memories and stands as a representative for the project.

- The **horizon** is a way of defining the lifespan of a project that is quite different from the idea of a deadline. It is more fuzzy and undetermined giving an impression when the project will probably be done. This may not

be a full Future Perfect or miracle picture – you can work with just some headlines at this stage.
- Even if we do not pay too much attention to the "Ant Country", it can be useful to remember all the **resources** available to surmount difficulties on the way. This helps to build up confidence that possible occurrences can be mastered.

In a coaching session, you can address the elements with the following questions:

1. Platform building
    - What is the name of the project? or What would be a good name for it?
    - What is your horizon? When will the project probably be done?
2. Hopes, dreams, intentions
    - What do you want to achieve?
    - Suppose … it all went perfectly… what would be happening?
    - What difference would that make to you? To others?
3. Precursors, building blocks
    - What needs to be in place for that to happen?
    - What else?
4. Resources for "Ant Country"
    - Which of your resources will help you to surmount difficulties on your way through the "Ant Country"?
5. Tiny signs of progress (For each of the precursors)
    - What will be the first tiny signs you are making progress? What else? (and what else…)
    - What will be the first thing other people notice, that will be a sign of progress? What else?
6. Small next steps (For each of the precursors)
    - Given all that… What are the first small steps you can take, in the next 72 hours? What else?
    - (If step is still big) And what would be a small step towards that?

The answers to the questions can be written down successively on a prepared flipchart. The coachee immediately gets an idea of a useful structure that helps to reduce complexity. The answers are visible and can be communicated with the team or other stakeholders. This is about getting into action quickly and positively.

The template can easily be used for project reviews, checking the tiny signs and small next steps in an agile way every few days while the hopes dreams, intentions and resources might be checked every few months.

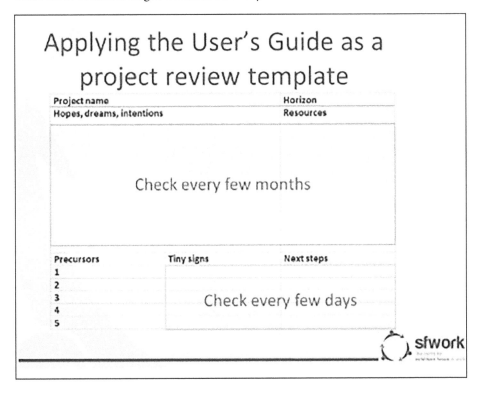

Peter uses the tool mostly standing with the coachee in front of the flipchart, gradually filling the template with useful ideas. Such a "standing session" usually lasts only 30 to 40 minutes, even with very large and complex projects. Coachees report that this brings about change which starts immediately and is sustainable through time. Mark has found that it can also be used to reduce stress with coachees who feel overloaded and have a lot of things on their plate; to turn that into some small do-able and relevant steps can be a great relief.

Reaction from coachees

Peter and Mark have applied this model in various ways, including at a conference workshop. The coachee's responses to her experience with this framework are useful; they show some of the advantages of working in this way. She says:

- *Some people like models because they give them structure. I don't like models for the same reason. This model, however, offers combining easy-to-follow logic with free surfing to explore a project's fullest potential.*
- *Many people in business might say the model is not "complete" without stakeholders and risks analysis, but I didn't feel I was missing them.*
- *I like the word "Horizon"; what a contrast to "a deadline" or "completion date". With a horizon you've got both a certain expected measurable fixed goal(s) and the "unlimited lifespan" of your idea.*
- *Precursors is another great suggestion I think. For me, it's more about "how you would sense that you are approaching" rather than "how you would know that you are moving in the right direction" and for people who "feel" more than "think" it a useful practice to tune in to an emotional and energetic state of a desired reality.*

Reference

McKergow, M., & Bailey, H. (2014). *Host: Six new roles of engagement for teams, organisations, communities and movements.* London: Solutions Books.

Authors

Dr Peter Röhrig is a senior partner of ConsultContor in Cologne,/ Germany. He is an organisational consultant, solution focused business coach and leadership trainer and works a lot in conflict management in organisations. He was one of the first practitioners in Germany who applied and taught the Solution Focused approach in organisations. His book "Solution Tools" is a rich collection of Solution Focused activities for workshops and team events by consultants from all over the world.

Dr Mark McKergow is co-director of sfwork – The Centre for Solutions Focus at Work in Edinburgh, Scotland. He is an international consultant, speaker and author. Many people around the world have been inspired by his work in Solutions Focus presented with his inimitable blend of scientific rigour and performance pizzazz. Mark is a global pioneer applying Solutions Focus ideas to organisational and personal change. He has written and edited many groundbreaking books and articles.

26

The elegant art of noticing: Utilising what happens to improve the quality of interactions

Wim Sucaet (Belgium)

A key skill for the host leader is noticing; noticing what's happening, noticing what needs attention, noticing signs of progress, noticing that things may be about to go off-track. In this chapter Wim Sucaet offers some ways to train your 'noticing muscle' to become even more skilful and resourceful in the art of noticing.

Introduction

Organisations are used to setting out goals and working towards them. It's a way of working that's common in profit and non-profit. However, we live in a very volatile and uncertain world in which defined goals aren't always achievable or effective anymore. Describing the horizon of a project helps to create a more open space in which goals can develop. The User's Guide to the Future by Mark McKergow and Helen Bailey (McKergow & Bailey, 2014) offers you a guideline to walking through this future in an efficient way.

When you've described the horizon of your project, formulated the building blocks and the next steps to take, it's interesting to know what further signs of progress will be. Observing great stuff that happens in the meantime helps you to describe these signs of progress. It's in this observing where the resources unfold.

A lot of unpredictable things occur whilst working and people do a lot of good things in handling these. Only when this great stuff isn't being noticed does it keep being underexposed and so in a way it doesn't exist.

"An unrecognized difference (since it goes by unnoticed) will not receive the amplification needed and will remain a difference that does not make a difference. A simple difference, often just some doubt, can be enough to begin changing a lifelong pattern or way of thinking." (de Shazer, 1986).

In my view the most important asset of being a host leader is noticing bits and pieces of the great stuff that people do and being genuinely curious about it. Especially when things don't work out as planned there's a lot to discover.

"The biggest reinforcing influence on our innate ability to re-tune comes from caring interaction with others. It is so simple for you to increase the benefits of re-tuning among people you truly care for by simply becoming an eager witness of their re-tuning ... As you ask them curious questions, new perceptions will get created in the dialogue with that person. And while you co-create fresh realizations, consciousness about new possibilities arises for both of you." (Szabó, 2019).

Everybody has the potential to be a host leader as long as they keep an eye on the horizon, think in little steps towards it and notice which great stuff happens in the meantime. This also resembles what artists do, according to Will Gompertz.

"If you spend too much time on the little details, you get lost. But if you only think about the large entity you don't create anything and you also don't make any connections. These two have to work together. Otherwise you can forget about it." (Will Gompertz, 2015).

While I was facilitating a change process ...

A couple of years ago I was asked to facilitate a change process to achieve a renewed working structure and model in the organisation I work in. While I was facilitating this I constantly switched between stepping forward and backward in my meetings and conversations with my colleagues and stakeholders.

Knowing when to stand up and take the lead, and knowing when to step back is one thing. If you want to maximise the effect of it then the right context and time to do this is crucial. Otherwise your interventions might just be a blank.

While stepping backward I observed how the process was flowing and gave back the observations that served the purpose of the project by asking questions about it. This is a subtle way of bringing tiny signs of progress to life.

For example:

> "Hi, you managed to have a good meeting with that team although the circumstances weren't easy. How did you do that? What else did you do? By having this experience, what would be a next sign of progress in our project?"

> "Hi, it has been a while since we've seen each other so I don't know the current situation. So what have you noticed that went well lately? What did you do that contributed to this? How can this be a benefit for our project?"

Noticing these bits and pieces create a work environment in which employees:

- feel strengthened in their possibilities
- start to apply the skill of noticing more in themselves and to others.

This results in:

- increased self esteem
- an improvement of the quality of interactions and team work
- better progress in the work that they do.

People are often not conscious of the things they do or minimalise what they do well. By noticing and highlighting these little 'wow' moments in everyday situations and interactions I not only facilitated the change process but also facilitated a better quality of interactions. It was great to see that colleagues picked up the art of noticing and started to apply it in their teams and other working contexts. Maybe they practised it at home too, who knows?

In a way this kind of noticing is an elegant way of acknowledging people. Asking questions about great stuff that happened and being genuinely curious about it is like saying:

> "Hi, I see you and I want to give you a little present but you have to open it yourself because it's yours."

When you give a present to somebody mostly they want to do something in return. And so it happened that colleagues also noticed great stuff I did I wasn't aware of, which accelerated my own learning.

I strongly believe that we often think too much. People frequently search for explanations why things go as they go or have a hypothesis about a problem so that they can work out a solution. In these cases Solution Focus practitioners prefer to stay on the surface and rather go deep into the descriptions of the useful things that happen. In my view this is a more empowering and efficient way of (re)discovering bits and pieces of things that work well.

"Wittgenstein's way of describing things reminds us to observe what is going on and reminds us to look at everyday life – including language as it is actually used – as the home of our concepts and descriptions. It is these descriptions of everyday life that replace the explanations and theories of traditional philosophy and psychology." (de Shazer, 2005).

How to train your noticing muscle

Noticing and being genuinely curious about things that work is like training muscle. The more you train it, the stronger it gets until it becomes a habit. It will also increase the fluidity of your practice in everyday situations and interactions. You can train this muscle in several ways by asking these questions:

1) When you reflect on your own or have a conversation partner:
    - what did I notice lately in my work that I'm satisfied or intrigued about?
    - which great stuff did I notice that other people did and how did I react so that it is likely they will do more of it?

These questions are derived from the three questions to lead a good life from Luc Isebaert (2017).

Be aware that having a conversation partner who asks you these questions often generates more inspiration than when you reflect on your own. According to Dominik Godat and Elfy Czerny (Godat & Czerny, 2019) having a conversation partner is some kind of 'friendpower'. They think this is an essential element of Solution Focus.

2) When you notice somebody has done great stuff:
   - How did you do that? What else did you do?
   - When this happened, how did you cope with that situation?
   - Out of all things you did, what was according to you the most important thing that helped you at that moment?
   - What did you do that made you bend that situation into a better situation?
   - Which signs of progress have you noticed lately?

3) When you want the person to notice things in the nearby future:
   - Imagine things go well, what will you be doing then?
   - How will others in that room notice you're doing a fine job?

All these questions are just some examples of useful solution focused questions. After all, these questions are all variations on the same theme as you may notice. There certainly are a lot more questions that you can ask. I invite you to create your own questions in a style that suits you.

Which position to take?

In their book *Host*, Mark McKergow and Helen Bailey talk about four key positions which a host leader can divide their attention between:

- being in the spotlight
- being with the guests
- being in the gallery
- being in the kitchen.

These places symbolise a position a host leader can take. Now how do these relate to the art of noticing?

When you're standing **in the spotlight**, you've stepped forward and are taking the lead. Your attention is needed to make things happen at the moment itself so focusing on noticing is not the best idea to do then.

Being **with the guests** as one of the group gives you a lot of opportunities to notice and ask questions. This can be done while you're attending meetings but also while you're having a coffee break with others.

Standing **in the gallery** is about stepping back and taking a helicopter view. You connect all the little dots, from the horizon until the next signs of progress and ask yourself 'How do the things I've noticed lately fit in this overall view?'

A position we often take too little is being **in the kitchen**. This is where we reflect and work on our own development. It's an excellent position to be aware of the great stuff you did lately.

Of course these are just metaphors. It's up to you to find out which places and moments suit you the best. Don't underestimate the importance of a good place and time in which you are the most at ease and inspired.

For example:

When I'm cycling home from work I'm often in the position of the gallery or the kitchen. Maybe it's the bilateral stimulation that activates my reflective mind? I don't know and frankly I don't care. I just know that it works for me. If you're somebody who likes to take notes of your reflections then cycling probably isn't the best option.

When you don't have the possibility of going out of your office you can also create spaces in the room. For instance, to the right side of that table on the blue chair is where I will sit when I want to be in my gallery or kitchen. When I leave that place I go back to my other work. This helps you to be in the moment. Being with the guests is the best place to put your noticing into action. Just remember that the question you ask is very important. As long as it reveals great stuff it's a good question.

Conclusion

Whether I'm facilitating a change process, working on a project, having a coaching conversation or even a therapy session, the common thread I practise is noticing bits and pieces of great stuff that happen in everyday interactions and being genuinely curious about it. It even happens that I don't always have to ask questions about it. The noticing itself already amplifies the useful things that happened. Especially as a leader, giving back what you notice is important – whether this is by asking questions or just giving back what you noticed. It's a way of taking the lead without the other having the feeling that they are being led.

To do this it's important to have an unconditional stance about the fact that there's always something that people do that works well. And when you have your doubts about this, sit down, take pen and paper and write down all the good stuff that you noticed lately or even in the more distant past.

After all, as Leonard Cohen says in his song *Anthem*:

"*There's a crack in everything, that's how the light gets in*".

References

de Shazer, S. (1986). Minimal elegance. *The Family Therapy Networker*, 11(8), 57-60.
de Shazer, S. (2005). *Don't think but observe: What is the importance of the work of Ludwig Wittgenstein for Solution-Focused Brief Therapy?*
Godat, D. G., & Czerny, E. (2019). *Into the essence of SF*. Retrieved 19 August, 2019, from http://sfio.org/the-journal/interaction-vol-11-no-1-august-2019/page-6/
Gompertz, W. G. (2015). *Think Like an Artist: and Lead a More Creative, Productive Life*. United Kingdom: Penguin Books.
Hankovszky, K. H. (2019). SOL World 2019 – Signs of progress. *InterAction – The Online Journal of Solution Focus in Organisations*, 11(1), 3.
Isebaert, L.I. (2017, Feb. 27). Three questions for a good life. Retrieved from https://www.youtube.com/watch?v=kH6HltdE2sw
McKergow, M., & Bailey, H. (2014). *Host: Six new roles of engagement for teams, organizations, communities, movements*. London: Solutions Books.
Szabó, P. S. (2019). *Less than 0 seconds. The art of re-tuning ... When life does not stick to a plan.*

Author

Wim Sucaet *is quality care coordinator of VCLB Regio Gent, a centre for pupil guidance. Besides that, he has a side activity where he gives therapy, coaching, workshops and trainings in the solution focused (SF) approach. He started his SF adventure in 2009 and has followed several trainings in Solution Focus including the Milwaukee model, London Brief Therapy and the Bruges model at the Korzybski Institute where he obtained his qualification as a master solution-focused practitioner. He is a reviewed contributor & member of the board of SFIO (www.sfio.org), www.otiz.be, wim.sucaet@gmail.com*

27
Introducing the Inviter

Veronika Kotrba and Ralph Miarka (Austria)

Inviting is a crucial step in gaining the participation of others. In this chapter, Veronika and Ralph discuss how they introduce people to the soft power of invitation using a simple framework.

Introduction

A key aspect of our trainings in Host Leadership is to introduce the Inviter role. Thinking invitationally, as Mark McKergow and Helen Bailey put it (McKergow & Bailey, 2014) is a surprisingly powerful stance; it looks rather weak at first glance (after all, surely to think in terms of direct orders would be more powerful). However, it transpires that the kind of relationship which is founded on invitation, choice and acceptance is a very strong start in terms of building engagement and performance.

Introducing the Inviter

To introduce the participants to an emotional invitation, we read the paragraph on the invitations that Nelson Mandela offered, as cited in *Host* (McKergow & Bailey, 2014, p. 105). As a reminder, here it is.

An invitation from the President: should I stay or should I go?

Having been in prison for twenty-seven years, Nelson Mandela was finally elected as the first black president of South Africa on April 27, 1994. The following morning, his first day in office, Mandela arrived at the presidential offices to find the security team packing their bags. Having been hired by the outgoing white President FW de Klerk, they assumed that Mandela would wish to replace them with his own, probably black, staff. John Reinders was in the president's office. Mandela arrived and asked him where he was going. Reinders replied that he would be returning to his previous position in correctional services (the prison system).

"Mandela said, 'I would like you to consider staying here with us'. Reinders was astonished. Mandela continued, 'Yes, I am quite serious. You know this job. I don't. I am from the bush. I am ignorant. Now, if you stay with me, it would be just one term, that is all. Five years. And then, of course, you would be free to leave. Now, please understand me: this is not an order. I would like to have you here only if you wish to stay and share your knowledge and your experience with me. So, what do you say? Will you stay with me?' Reinders did not hesitate.

Then Mandela asked Reinders to gather all the presidential staff – including the cleaners, gardeners, and everyone else, in the Cabinet room for a meeting. He walked among them, shaking hands, exchanging a few words (in Afrikaans where appropriate, having learned it in prison). Then he addressed them. 'Hello, I'm Nelson Mandela. If any of you prefer to take the [severance] package, you are free to leave. Go. There is no problem. But, I beg you, stay! Five years, that is all. You have the knowledge. We need that knowledge, we need that experience of yours.' Every single member of the Presidential staff stayed."

When reading, we take care to articulate well and to speak slowly, so the participants can follow well. Maybe you want to try it before you perform in public. After reading, we give some time for the participants to gather their thoughts and then we ask, "What makes these invitations special? What is different to maybe other invitations the participants received?"

Properties of a good invitation

Through this interaction, we co-create together with the participants the three main properties of an invitation: it needs to be attractive, acknowledging and optional, i.e. possible to reject it. Attractive means that it has an impact which I (the recipient) support, the topic and outcome are relevant to me or others and I care about. Furthermore, all necessary information on the event, like date, time, location, setting, people, expectations, etc are given. Acknowledging means that the person is pleased to be invited and feels better about it. Thus, it is relevant to appreciate the people for previous as well as possible future contributions in the context of the event. It helps to personally invite people, using their names, etc. The acknowledgement builds relationships and rejecting the invitation has to be ok – the relationship should not be damaged by a No.

Creating an invitation

Then we invite the participants to create an invitation for an event, meeting, or other occasion from the perspective of a host leader. This activity takes about 20 to 30 minutes. Sometimes we get asked: What if I cannot choose the team I work with? In such cases, we propose to approach this from a hosting position, still to invite these people to work with you. In our experience, this suffices for people to start writing a compelling invitation.

When finished, we ask the participants to form pairs, to stand up, to reflect on the invitations and to improve them. One person reads their invitation and the other asks coaching questions to support the improvement. For example, on a scale of 0 to 10, where 10 means it is very attractive and 0 the opposite – how do you rate your invitation? What makes it that high already – what is compelling about it? And suppose it were one step better, what would be different? Alternatively and/or additionally, the invitee simply provides feedback on how the invitation resonates with them and helps the inviter to improve their piece of work.

Depending on time in the workshop or training, a second round of improvements can be added. Invite the participants to find a new pairing partner to introduce the improved invitation and then improve it once more.

At the end of this part of the training, offer some volunteers the opportunity to read out their invitations to the whole group. Then acknowledge their contribution and highlight the helpful parts of the invitation to support learning of the others. With practice, writing invitations can become a short and enjoyable task.

References

McKergow, M., & Bailey, H. (2014). *Host: Six new roles of engagement for teams, organisations, communities and movements*. London: Solutions Books. The section about Nelson Mandela's invitation was sourced and adapted from John Carlin's book *Playing The Enemy*, Atlantic Books 2008 pp. 154–155.

Authors

Veronika Kotrba is a solution-focused coach, consultant and trainer. Together with Ralph Miarka, she has been supporting people with management tasks in an agile corporate environment since 2012. In 2015, the two of them founded sinnvollFÜHREN GmbH in Vienna. Veronika is co-author of the book Agile Teams lösungsfokussiert coachen *(dpunkt.verlag), has been training solution-focused coaches since 2018 in her in-house course, together with Ralph and a top-class team of trainers, and tirelessly finds new approaches to facilitate cooperation at eye level in the business and working world.*

Dr. Ralph Miarka lives in Vienna and has worked for many years as a solution-focused agile coach, consultant and trainer. In his work, as a well-read practitioner he constantly incorporates new findings from scientific research. Since 2015 he has been managing director of sinnvollFÜHREN GmbH and co-author of the book Agile Teams lösungsfokussiert coachen *(dpunkt.verlag). He is interested in the effective cooperation of people – both at large and small scales. To this end, he supports all those in companies who make decisions and bear responsibility – from leaders to team members.*

Part Six
Next steps for Host Leadership

28
'Its simplicity belies its depth': Picking up where we left off and deepening into the essence of host

Helen Bailey (UK)

One of the fascinating aspects of Host Leadership is the way the metaphor connects with people so quickly. This is at the same time wonderful and also can be a bit frustrating; there is a great deal to explore both in the metaphor and in the models and frameworks we have created around it. A rapid glance can lead some to move on without taking the time to get full value from the ideas. In this chapter Host co-author Helen Bailey reveals how her own learning and awareness has changed since the book first appeared.

Introduction

Working in the field of leadership development and organisational change for approaching twenty years, I have worked with many leaders and witnessed the effects of leadership in many organisations. At the time of writing *Host* (McKergow & Bailey, 2014), I had a growing dissatisfaction with the prevailing view of leadership and what I was witnessing. I had a strong feeling 'there had to be another way', so much so I stepped away from much of the work I had been doing (and providing me with a level of success and reward).

In the time since, change is beginning to happen in the ways people look at leadership. There is a growing awareness that something different is needed. Something is waking us up to a new way being needed: we are hearing an inner prompting and beginning to look for new ways.

Of course, the metaphor of host offers a new way to respond to the inner prompting for change.

When I first met Host Leadership, I instantly connected with the idea. There was an instant appeal, followed by a sense that 'its simplicity belies its depth'. My sense has always been that the metaphor offers huge richness and possibility AND there is so much more to unpack. Since that time, I have seen many people have the same instant connection with the idea. And then what? How do we help people unpack it and go deeper? What does it really mean/take to become a host leader?

The more Mark McKergow and I have worked with the ideas, the more we have begun to grapple with these questions. It is my hope that this chapter offers a response to this question and a way to go deeper.

I will begin where we left off. The final chapter of the book, Chapter 13, offers an invitation, an invitation to 'open our hearts'.

> *"We think that developing as a host means one thing above all – learning to open our heart"* (p. 212).

Accepting the invitation

The invitation continues:

> *"Go back to the beginning and start again … this time you will be more clued in to the possibilities, more aware of the subtleties"* (p. 213).

It is the possibilities and subtleties that I want to draw attention to in this chapter. We can accept the metaphor at face value, it makes sense, or we can accept the invitation to go deeper. As the maxim goes: 'the best way to learn something is to teach it' and introducing many people to the metaphor of host has awakened in me the need to go deeper, to mine this rich metaphor for the wisdom that it has to offer. I urge you to do the same. I offer here a way into the depth based on my own experience, living and working with Host Leadership through the writing of the book and the years since it was birthed, through a re-reading of the text.

The call to go deeper

Let's begin with the call we were hearing at the outset, in Chapter One – *Time for a new look at Leadership*. In this opening chapter (page 7), we presented a series of leadership dilemmas, mutually conflicting requirements of the modern leader, based on work at Ashridge Business School. Let's look at a few of them:

Loyalties:

Putting your own needs first ...... *while* ...... Serving the organisation

Control:

Letting go .... *while* .... Keeping control

Self-belief:

Showing vulnerability .... *while* .... being strong

Understanding:

Enquiring (not knowing) .... *while* .... Knowing

While the places on the right-hand side of these dilemmas may be places we currently associate with leadership, we may be less comfortable with going to the places on the left: self-care, letting go of control, being vulnerable and being with not-knowing. These may not be the places we automatically think of going as requirements of leadership. Yet we hear or see this list and it makes sense.

There is a palpable sense of relief when we show this slide during a workshop. A sigh of "now I know why it feels so difficult". The question is, what do we do with it? Do we pause with it and begin to ask ourselves where we are and how we experience these dilemmas? Do we ask ourselves what it means to put our own needs first, let go of control, actually be vulnerable and be in the not-knowing? Do we ask how we do it?

And how do we help people go to these less comfortable places, in essence to go deeper? A quote from Galileo Galilei might offer a good starting point: *We cannot teach people anything; we can only help them discover it for themselves.*

It begins with awareness: noticing what's happening within us, our responses to things, our inner promptings, our feelings and emotions, our discomforts, our avoidances. We begin with what I call our 'inner work'. We begin with opening our hearts.

Moving on to Chapter Two: *Hosting: a new yet ancient metaphor.* Let's look again at the piece we introduced when considering leadership metaphors. Discussing the hero metaphor, we refer to the work of Bill Joiner and Stephen Josephs in their book Leadership Agility (Joiner & Josephs, 2006). Their work looks at the development stages as we progress in our leadership. Their research found that relatively few leaders (c10%) have actually progressed beyond hero and they propose three levels of post-heroic leadership: Catalyst, Co-creator, Synergist.

We encounter a similar response when we introduce this idea in workshops: everyone gets it. They've likely met many 'Experts and Achievers' (maybe even some pre-Experts) – the different stages of Joiner and Josephs' heroic leadership levels. At a 'head' level it makes sense. Then here's the thing – what does it mean to get it at a 'heart' level, to move that understanding from a head to a heart connection? This might show us a place where we have to 'open our hearts'.

We turn inwards and ask ourselves questions like: where might I be operating at Expert level? Or Achiever level? What's keeping me in the Hero level? What might be the benefit of me moving towards more post-heroic ways of operating and relating? What would it take? Where might I try something different? Where might I need to brave being vulnerable? And what might be a first step towards that?

Going deeper with the six roles and four positions of a host leader

In further chapters, we introduce our six roles and four positions of a host leader, offering a way into the metaphor of host. We can see them as a framework for thinking like a host. I have come to see that the roles and positions are pointing to something more, something deeper. Using them as a framework, they can act as a kind of scaffold to support us in our exploration, our excavation.

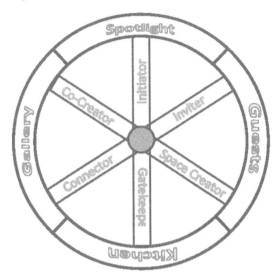

Thirty spokes surround the hub.
It is the empty spaces between them
that drive the cart.
We take clay and form vessels from it.
It is the empty spaces they contain
which make the vessels.
We put doors and windows in walls
to make a room.
It is these empty spaces
that make it a room.
So that which is serves for utility.
That which is not represents the essence.
(Lao Tzu: A translation of the Tao Te Ching 11)

Taking the words of Lao Tzu, "that which is serves for utility, that which is not represents the essence", I am proposing that the four positions, around the rim, and the six roles, the spokes, serve for utility. They offer a framework for us to enter more deeply into the metaphor, consider what it means to lead as a host and access our hearts, our inner wisdom to hear where we are being called to lead differently. It's the *spaces* between the spokes that represents the essence of the metaphor, the essence of what it means to lead as a host.

It is this essence, accessed through the spaces between the spokes to which I will now turn my attention.

The big question that we think host leaders are constantly asking themselves is: "should I step forward, or step back next?" We can see the Ashridge leadership dilemmas as each having a step forward and a step back aspect. Each of the six roles also has a step forward and step back aspect. The four positions contain forward and back aspects. We would naturally associate leadership with stepping forward, making things happen; maybe less so with stepping back. Yet it is in the stepping back that I believe we begin to change the prevailing approach to leadership.

It is worth reminding ourselves at this point of the six roles with their forward and back aspects. In fact, I'm not sure we actually present the roles in this format so specifically in the book, yet we regularly show them in this way in workshops:

Step forward	**Step back**
Initiator	
Getting things started	Listening to what's being called for, then responding
Inviter	
Thinking invitationally	Giving choice & space
Space-Creator	
Creating the space	Freedom to use the space
Gatekeeper	
Defining and excluding	Allowing and including
Connector	
Making connections & intros	Allowing connections
Co-participator	
Initiating and providing	Joining in!

As I look again at the six roles in this way (which I regularly do!), the question I am always drawn to is, "what does it really take to truly be in the stepped back aspect of each of these roles?" I still see many leaders struggling to make this transition. We get in our own way when we aren't able to fully allow ourselves to step back in its true sense. There is a different energy about our interactions when we have fully let go into stepping back. And we begin to get different outcomes from our interactions. We can be surprised and energised by what happens.

At this point let's also bring in the four positions. I want to pick up specifically on two of these positions: 'in the spotlight' and 'in the kitchen'. Essentially 'in the kitchen' is the place of our inner work. 'In the spotlight' represents our outer work. If we think about hosting any event, be it a party, a conference or a meeting of any size, there will likely be times when we just want some down time, some time away from all the action, from the guests, time to re-group or re-charge, even just to take a breath, ready to go on again. Unless we are balancing our outer work with inner work, we won't be as effective as we could be in our outer work. Sustained success in our outer work is dependent on our inner work.

Arianna Huffington in *Thrive* (Huffington, 2014) refers to this as the new third metric for success. She presents four pillars of the third metric: wellbeing, wisdom, wonder, and giving. Thriving begins with attention to our inner work.

It's worth pausing to say something about what I mean by 'inner work'. By inner work I am referring to any activity that helps us drop out of our head and into our heart. That can include meditation, mindfulness, time in nature, exercise, creativity, art, music, prayer. Such activities or practices help us access a different part of ourselves, a part of ourselves that we are increasingly losing touch with but actually offers a much greater spaciousness and therefore a wider range of possibilities. As with our 'in the kitchen' time, inner work may be alone time or it may be time with a coach, mentor or other adviser, someone who is holding space for us to drop deeper in our thinking.

Deepening into the essence of host

As we develop as a host leader, we begin letting go of the framework of the six roles and four positions and begin entering the spaces between, where we find the essence of host and become a host leader.

Continuing my excavation for this chapter, I entered the spaces between the spokes. Each role, with its forward and back aspect, took me deeper, particularly with the step back aspects. There is so much I could write about what I excavated in my deepening into the spaces, several more chapters in fact! I excavated each of the six roles, exploring what the step forward and step back aspects were pointing to, what they mean for the budding host leader in practice. The end of all my exploring led me to a missing piece.

> "The intuitive mind is a sacred gift and the rational mind is a faithful servant. We have created a society that honours the servant and has forgotten the gift." (attributed to Albert Einstein in Jaworski, 1999, p. 197)

Finding the gift: connecting with self

In the book, we proposed three levels of the connector role: connecting with others (understanding people), connecting others (connecting people and ideas) and everything is connected (wise connectedness – which I now call the interconnectedness of all things). I would now add a fourth level: connecting with self.

The role of connector begins with connecting with self. Connecting with self is a theme that's been running right through this chapter. The more we drop out of our heads and into our hearts, the more we connect with self. We come to know ourselves, our habits, fears, values, beliefs, etc, etc.

There is much focus today on wellbeing. Connecting with our heart centres us in our wellbeing, so we more easily recognise when we're 'off centre', when we've been pulled off centre, away from our true self. A regular meditation or mindfulness practice supports our staying centred.

An aspect of wellbeing is resilience: our ability to bounce back. An image I like to use for resilience is a tree. A tree is rooted in the ground, its roots often as deep as its branches are wide. So when the tree is blown around by the wind, sometimes bending far over, it invariably comes back to centre. It rights itself. We are the same. Most of the time we naturally come back to centre, but if we are off centre for a prolonged period, we are less able to naturally come back to centre and problems arise.

This is another important aspect of our in the kitchen time – our self-care, putting our own needs first (as in the Ashridge dilemmas). We may have a tendency to gloss over the idea of self-care, dismissing it, but it's another important aspect of our inner work and I have come to see that we can't be as effective in our outer work unless we our consistently doing our inner work through regular practices. With this right balance, we can be surprised at what begins to happen, seemingly effortlessly, beyond our expectations.

This new first level of connector creates the right foundation for the other three levels of connector. It is at this level that we begin to open our hearts and we become better able to connect with others, their hearts opening in response, creating better understanding and deeper connection, more emergence and co-creation. As we become increasingly able to be connected with ourselves, we are increasingly able to let go of ourselves, creating a new space for others to step forward. Spaces become more about the growth of the other person. They have room to grow into.

From here we naturally connect people and ideas. There is more spaciousness and we see new possibilities and connections. As we connect with self, our leading – and relationships – transform.

Conclusion

As I draw this chapter to a close, I have a sense of beginning the next cycle with host and leadership. Our challenge as we journey forwards is 'remembering the gift', remembering to be out of our heads, the rational mind and be more in the intuitive mind, the heart, accessing the sacred gift.

This chapter points to implications for taking the work forward and being an increasing part of the change that is required.

The more we connect with self, the more we open up the other levels of connector AND the other roles AND the spaces between them. The question is what are the implications for developing host leaders, for supporting people to become host leaders?

Deepening into the essence of host leads to the possibility of a paradigm shift, a new way of thinking and being in the world. It begins with self, connecting with self, then letting go of self. A re-orientation then begins to happen. We come into 'right relationship' with ourselves and others. Our job, and that of host leaders, is one of holding space; holding space for transformation to happen. Step back and watch the magic begin to happen.

I sense there is more significance to the wheel that I have introduced in this chapter. A wheel, a circle, offers us further scope for the change that is required. The organisational structure and operating system implied by both the hero and servant metaphors is a triangle. In contrast, the organisational structure and operating system pointed to by host is a circle. I have been working in and with circle processes, widely seen in the Art of Hosting movement, for some time now and am curious about how our organisations and relationships might change if it were to become a more widely adopted way of working together.

> *"The circle way is a practice of re-establishing social partnerships and creating a world in which the best of collaboration informs and inspires the best of hierarchical leadership" (Baldwin & Linnea, 2010, p.11).*

And finally, it feels apt to end this cycle of excavation in the same way we ended the first cycle, with a poem, a translation of the Tao Te Ching 34 by Witter Bynner (1988):

> *"Bountiful life, letting anyone attend,*
> *Making no distinction between left or right.*
> *Feeding everyone, refusing no one,*
> *Has not provided this bounty to show how much it owns,*
> *Has not fed and clad its guests with any thought of claim;*
> *And, because it lacks the twist*
> *Of mind or body in what it has done,*
> *The guile of head or hands,*
> *Is not always respected by a guest.*
> *Others appreciate welcome from the perfect host*
> *Who, barely appearing to exist,*
> *Exists the most."*

References

Baldwin, C., & Linnea, A. (2010). *The Circle Way: A Leader in Every Chair*. Oakland, CA: Berrett-Koehler.
Bynner, W. (1988). *The Way of Life According to Lao Tzu*. New York: Penguin Putnam.
Huffington, A. S. (2014). *Thrive: The Third Metric to Redefining Success and Creating a Happier Life*. New York NY: Random House.
Jaworski, J. (2011). *Synchronicity: The Inner Path of Leadership* (2nd ed. San Francisco CA: Berrett-Koehler).
Joiner, W. B., & Josephs, S. A. (2006). *Leadership Agility: Five Levels of Mastery for Anticipating and Initiating Change*. San Francisco CA: Jossey Bass.
McKergow, M., & Bailey, H. (2014). *Host: Six new roles of engagement for teams, organisations, communities and movements*. London: Solutions Books.

Author

Helen Bailey *is the co-author of Host: Six New Roles of Engagement for Teams, Organisations, Communities, Movements. She has worked in the field of Leadership Development and Organisational Change for approaching twenty years. Her vast experience is gained with clients in organisations of all sizes in both the public and private sector. Helen continues to work as a coach and facilitator, supporting clients with their inner work and their outer work, increasingly holding space for people to walk into the conversations they need to have which brings about transformation in relationships. She teaches meditation, and leads circles and retreats from her home on the edge of the beautiful English Lake District.*

29

Combining Host Leadership and coaching: Towards a new 'Agile humanware'

Laurent Sarrazin (France)

> In one way Host Leadership is a metaphor and a model for new yet ancient ways of leading and building engagement and connection. In this fascinating chapter, Laurent Sarrazin explores even further. Perhaps reconnecting with hosting is a way to reorient ourselves as human beings? Laurent describes his experiences and the some of the ways he has found to use hosting ideas in many situations.

Introduction

Helen Bailey and Mark McKergow are great geneticists – even though they might not be aware of it. As soon I discovered Host Leadership a few years ago, my DNA started to deeply mutate, changing my everyday personal and professional life. I now realise that Host Leadership, along with some other developments, contributed to seeding in my heart a new technology named "Agile Humanware". This was born in the corporate sphere, but can be used throughout our challenged world. I will let you know more later in the chapter.

As a short introduction, let me quickly introduce the host of this story. I'm Laurent, I'm in my 50s, and my day job is to help corporate organisations to become agile, digital or whatever: just something in sync with our 21st century, meaning an ability to cope with the VUCA world of volatility, uncertainty, complexity and ambiguity. To accomplish this giant task, I run a small company named Rupture(21 (rupture21.com), where we use various competencies, in this priority order:

1) Brief coaching with Solution Focus methods

2) Facilitation, mostly playful and now energised with the tremendous liberating structures

3) Training to pollinate your own job and passion in order to instill changes at scale in the organisation

4) Mentoring as our clients value our hands-on Agile experience.

Host Leadership has changed a great many things in my professional fields. Here, I will share with you how to turn a boss into an exemplary host within a very short time to change the culture of his organisation, how to seed coaching competencies within anyone, and how to leverage the wisdom of the crowd to nurture a new working culture. You will soon see how my competencies have been evolving. I suspect it is just the beginning of my journey. I feel it like an ignition stage, starting by managing myself in a better way, especially coping with my overactive brain which led me to a burn-out. As a gift, I will also offer you three micro-tools that we have developed at Rupture(21 in the form of flash cards, mostly offering a reflective space for you, especially when you are in the kitchen: The Invitation Frame, The ROTI-Keeper and the Speed-Hosting Flash Card.

Chilling my internal volcano: Initiating and inviting

Let's be honest: I have a problem! My brain is highly active, always clicking on new ideas, and starting people on numerous initiatives. So much that ... one day, I crashed. Doctors called this a 'burn out'. Yes, I managed to burn myself, from the inside, without any external pressure. I had to stop everything for two months, while I repaired myself with mindfulness. However, I have also been informed that I'll have to work with the brain I have until my death!

And then, with the Host Leadership and the soft power of the invitation, I discovered another fantastic way to help manage my internal furnace, in a way which doesn't block my creative brain but keeps it under safe-as-possible control.

So, I keep allowing myself to have as many ideas as I want, unleashing my power of being an initiator. I can be anywhere when ideas pop up: in my kitchen, in a gallery, in the spotlight or with my guests. I have learnt that it doesn't make sense to fight against this flow. It's far better to let it flow, assuming I can channel it. For instance, when I feel I will soon reach a flood level, I go into my 'kitchen', and spend time appreciating myself storing everything on beautiful clouds, like digital parking lots (Evernote, Trello or Google Keep for instance). I learnt to sort my ideas, and keep the focus on the most appealing ones. I learnt to celebrate the fact that I will only take very few of them forward, without any sadness at leaving many ideas parked.

This is the first trick to channel my energy, but the real energy-catalyst comes when I need to turn my ideas into action. From standing in the role of the initiator, I need to switch to the inviter role. This step has been a revealing switch for me. Standing in the shoes of an inviter brings a deep change as you start to think invitationally. Still in my kitchen, I see myself enjoying the writing of an appreciative and attractive invitation that will unleash its soft power once it is received by my guests.

The time of writing an invitation has become a delicious moment because I have to carefully explore my guest-list, what makes me think of them, what I appreciate about them, how I will tell them all of that. It is also delicious to find the right words to turn my idea into an attractive 'thing' that they will love. Spending time and appreciating the writing of a great invitation has become a pure pleasure of mindfulness. This is the quintessence of "thinking invitationaly".

To help, I have created the following Invitation Frame. You can also check my Speed-Hosting flash card.

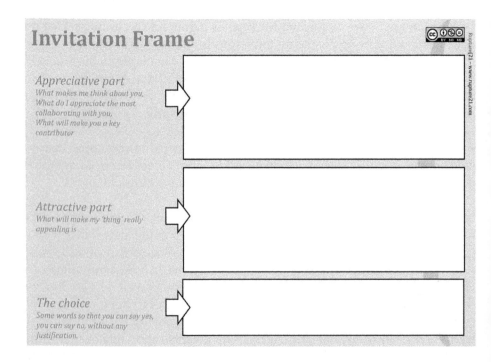

Thriving for effective coaching: concepts to powerful outcomes

In 2014, after many years of being involved in a giant Agile culture transformation, burnt by my passion, I got one of best pieces of advice in my life from the person who helped me to recover. "Laurent, I think it would be highly valuable for you to get professional training in coaching. You do it yourself. You seem to do it well. I feel that after your burn-out, it would be a great opportunity to take some time for you, to structure your learning a bit". As I trusted my adviser, I decided to be trained by one of our three old masters in systemic coaching.

I learned brief and systemic coaching with Alain Cardon. I chose this training because it is short (4 times x 2 days, separated by 6 weeks of self-practice within the group). Alain is straight and strict, with a very ancient way: you are told to do something … you had better follow the instruction as you are a novice. Obviously, in this training, you get some basic tools like the silence, the reformulation, a couple of powerful questions, the in-between focus.

But that's really not the most important thing; Alain taught me the posture of the right coach. If you do not get this point, as I saw with a lot of my comrades, you just apply the tools like processes, resulting in anything from very low effectiveness to actually damaging people. I remember some beautiful insights like "In a coaching conversation, the coach is there to create a wide space for the client, and then allow the client to explore this space. So you can't occupy the space for the client. You need to find a way to invite him, listen to him, just asking some short questions from time to time, to help him to accomplish his journey to the destination clarified before walking in".

For a newbie, the chances of receiving these words as pure concepts are high. Now we train people ourselves to acquire coaching capabilities, I have found that Host Leadership is a terrific weapon to turn this kind of concept into effective outcomes.

Here is a short debriefing discussion I had with a trainee:

– *Tell me Frédéric: How did Host Leadership help you in the evolution of your practice?*
– *Well, I feel I'm enjoying the gallery more and more, now.*

- *How do you see that?*
- *I guess that before I was spending too much time with my guest, meaning asking long questions. Worse: if my client was taking time to answer ... I saw myself filling the silence.*
- *What does it change for you?*
- *Curiously, it is much more relaxing for me to step back, focusing on my presence, and not working at the place of the client. He is there for that until he decides to stop!*
- *Relaxing?*
- *Hmmm, may be it is not the right word, because it is taking a bit of energy to be present in this way, especially without "computing" the next dozen of questions I could ask. Stay being there.*
- *Sounds good! If you spend less time with the guests, what else do you see yourself doing now?*
- *Easy! I shut my mouth and listen. If I'm sitting with my client, I also enjoy observing how he is reacting. Especially his eyes. When I see them disconnected from me, I know he is exploring the space we co-created for him.*
- *What else?*
- *I guess I also use my kitchen a little bit, just to write some notes that are important to me, about my practice. It is minimal as I want to ensure that my client feels I'm still there, but I know. By the way, I guess I'm in between the gallery and the kitchen, not fully disconnected. Today, I feel I need it to grow, so I explain to my client what the purpose of these notes is. I do it when I am the Gatekeeper of the space.*
- *So, how do you share your time in the four different places?*
- *Might be 10-20% with the guests, and the remaining time in the gallery. I've no use of the "Spotlights", except when it is coaching group, when I'm playing the Gatekeeper to share the rules we will follow.*
- *Great. I feel you are touching the essence of coaching.*
- *Thank you! There is also something turning in a loop in my mind with the Host-Leadership.*
- *Ha?*

Combining Host Leadership and coaching   241

- *Yes, coming to the roles, I now understand the essential value of the connector. Some time ago, it was not so clear to me. I remember starting to ask questions without a clear destination shared by the client. Now, I really take care of the connection. I understood I can't go further if I don't have the 'deal' or the 'contract' with my client. You know, with these famous questions like "How would you know that this conversation has been fruitful for you?"*
- *You are perfectly right. I can just encourage you to keep this in mind. Anything else regarding the roles?*
- *Yes, another thing, but we'll dig into it later: sometimes I feel the host is my client, and I'm his guest.*
- *Waouh! I'm already eager to meet you again to explore this interesting point of your.*

The tool that can be used here is the ROTI-Keeper. This helps us to reflect and assess the ways in which the four positions of a host leader are being used, their benefits, and in particular how to adjust the balance to enhance the situation for host and guests alike.

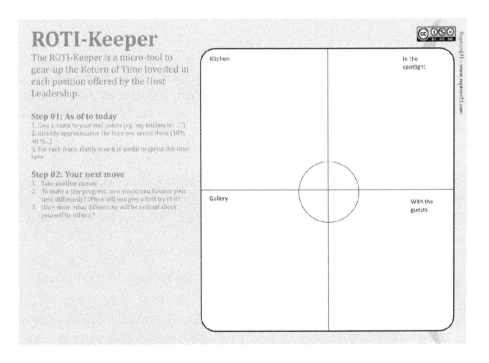

Recoding the managerial routine of "drive": from "give instructions" to "give a direction"

Let's look the confusion between 'drive = give a direction' versus 'drive = giving instructions'. I had some interesting discussions with managers who have been exposed to Servant-Leadership and wanted to leave their 'command & control' habits in favour of a more engaging management style. Servant-Leadership should be helpful. Unfortunately, most of the servant leaders I met might have been a bit extreme in their implementation; they pushed the model to a limit where it became really complicated for them to reconnect their team when things were not going in the right direction.

I am not surprised at this. I felt into this trap when I created a significant Agile competency centre in my previous working life. Day after day, I was privileging the comfort of all 'my' Agile coaches, keeping for myself the tasks that no one really wanted, mainly admin stuff. Progressively, I was letting them do what they wanted. I was quite blind about the misdirection we were steadily taking, till a crisis occurred with some of our internal clients and my top management. The outcomes and the service level provided by the team became disconnected from the global expectations.

I was in a situation where it was absolutely impossible to make a U-turn and get back on track. So I decided it was time to either activate the ejection seat for me, or creat an electroshock to wake up the team. Luckily, as my management helped me to refuse the first option, we considered rebooting the team organisation. I had no choice but to co-participate, so I asked for a mediator to facilitate the remediation. We did it nicely, in a playful way, with the famous Give & Take Matrix game (https://gamestorming.com/give-and-take-matrix/).

Remembering this personal story, I wish I had known about Host Leadership before. You understand why I am eager to spread the metaphor as much as possible for managers to avoid this trap, and to ease their smart postural switch.

- *Laurent, you mean, I should not give instructions anymore?*
- *Look Frank, you understood that leveraging people's autonomy is key to making them feel ok, being also fully engaged. Right?*
- *So, how would you proceed to increase their autonomy if you tell them where to to deliver and how to do it? That's like handcuffing them. In that case, ces do you leave to them?*

- *Hummm. Okay, but that sounds odd, for me, and for us. It is not really the culture there...*
- *And? What are you looking for?*
- *Okay, Okay! We are here to find a way to change things. But if I let them do what they want, what will I do if they don't do what is expected?*
- *That's a good point, but I will put it in a different way: with the help of Host Leadership, what could you try at your best to trust them that they will do the needful, and in exceptional situation tell them that the direction they are heading is not the right one?*

I will keep it short. In summary, this discussion will help the manager to be careful about:

1. Clarifying the expected destination for the team, ie the key outcomes that are the reason for the existence of the team;
2. Spending more time in the gallery, thinking twice before stepping forward in the team;
3. Installing a kitchen (this is often a missing place) and reflecting;
4. Inviting rather than summoning, (a very good opportunity to refresh the famous team weekly meeting where everyone looks at their shoes);
5. Asking rather than telling (for this point, the training journey includes Solution Focus coaching modules).

Turning executives into the hosts of the cultural shift of their own organisation

When we initiate the Agile transformation of an organisation with our 'vehicle' named "Rupture Douce" (Soft Disruption), one of the first steps is the "kick-off seminar" with the executives. The typical outcomes expected at the end of this time are:

- Alignment on a desired destination (the shared perfect future);
- Appreciation of current resources (what is already there, what works well in the company and already contributes to a part of this future);
- Visualisation of the possible outcomes after the first small steps, based on the current resources;

- Identification of the people to be invited in the change management project;
- An invitation written and ready to be communicated – this is the first concrete step made by executives.

To frame this seminar, there is a preamble with the boss. He doesn't know that in less than 15 minutes, he will be turned into a host, experiencing a first contact with Host Leadership.

Here is one little story we had with Ludovic, the head of a nice medium-size company. This example has become a pattern for us that we love to apply each time we touch base with a client.

- *Ludovic, who else is triggering this Rupture Douce initiative in your company?*
- *No one at this time, even if I know that it is expected by many people in the company.*
- *Good, so, let's say that you are the primary initiator. It's fine for me because I do praise for effectiveness, dealing as soon as possible with the relevant initiators. What would be the best way to carry on the next steps? The start?*
- *Obviously, I can't go alone, but with people who will help me, and who will be ok with the destination I have in mind.*
- *Great. Who would you consider as your primary guests to be on-boarded in this journey?*
- *Clearly, I will require the five members of my board. I need them to succeed in this challenge.*
- *Good. What do you value the most within these five members?*
- *Many things: they are loyal, always close to me. They are not afraid to challenge my views, in a constructive way. I also appreciate that they help each other.*
- *Perfect! This is something nice that you should keep in mind to tell them when you invite them. If you widen the circle of your guests a little bit, who would be best placed to bring high value to the success of your ambition?*
- *I ould also invite someone from HR, probably Cécile, the HR Director. nds-on experience of cultural transformations. Also Thierry, the head g. We are very connected.*

- *Anyone else?*
- *Hmm. Hum-hum … (silence). The communication team should be there from the beginning. They are very responsive to communicating in an attractive way. It will also prevent the spread of rumours. I'll ask Stéphane, the head of this team.*
- *OK. So we have you, your five board members, Cécile from HR, Thierry from marketing and Stéphane from HR. Nine people. You will see later if you wish to expand further. Up to a dozen people, we find it's a good size. In your opinion, where do you see these people invited for this launch? Where do you generally appreciate inviting guests?*
- *Easy! For this type of project, we will go outside of Paris, close by, in a green place we know well. What do you need, Laurent, to make us work?*
- *Simple (on a white sheet, I write the shopping list): a flat-floored room (ie no auditorium-like setup), with small tables for 4 people, 3 flipcharts, and free space on the walls to hang the works. Here is the shopping list.*
- *OK. I will also invite my assistant for logistics. In this way, she will visualise your mode of operation and what you need. What else?*
- *God! You are already reversing the game, asking my favourite question! The next step is perhaps more tricky but delicious.*
- *Oh! Tell me.*

Before going further, let's review the tricks I used from Host Leadership to start turning this top manager to a great host. First, I checked that Ludovic is the real Initiator of the initiative. Sometimes, it might be necessary to ensure that we are in front the right host, and not a 'proxy'. Thriving for efficiency, I prefer to deal with the right contact.

Then, I drove Ludovic into the second role proposed by Host Leadership: the Inviter. At the same time, we started to explore some appreciative resources of the guests that will be useful for the invitation. I used a trick learnt with Helen and Mark: expand the circle of guests to help the host to bring the right people onboard.

Next, Ludovic went into the role of Space Creator, offering him a moment to visualise where things will happen in a good way.

At this point, I jumped into the opportunity to dig into the soft power of the invitation. The other roles will be explored later.

- I suggest you send them an invitation, not a summons, but a true invitation which has a certain 'power'... The invitation you are going to send them is in three parts. First, you will begin with some appreciative lines, telling them what made you think of them. You will bring out their qualities, their resources, the value brought by these people in the company and for you.
- Whew! I am not used to that!
- You already answered this point. Just remember what you told me when I asked you "What do you value the most within these five members?"
- And I have to do this for each of them?
- Not necessarily. You can write nominative invitations, as well as a collective invitation. It's up to you to see what form makes you feel comfortable.
- OK. You said it was the first part. I hope that the next one is not of the same order of difficulty for me!
- Hmmm... I will let you judge. The second part of the invitation is an 'attractive' part. With are inviting few lines, you have to make them feel that you invite them to something attractive, in which they will find good motivation, even a certain pleasure.
- Ouch! Not trivial either!
- And finally, the most difficult part is to find a small formula to give them the choice to accept your invitation, or to refuse, without having to justify their response. Remember that it is an invitation rather than instruction. Here is a cheat sheet to guide you. Will it be ok?[I give him my Invitation Frame, shown here a few pages above.]
- Hummm...
- To help you, you could put yourself in the shoes of a guest: what are the last invitations you received with a certain pleasure, to which you said "yes" with no hesitation. Remember what you liked.
- Well... if I understood correctly, the work is now seriously starting for me. I take it and will try to do my best. Can I send you a draft to get your opinion?
- Of co... wanted to offer this option. But you understand that my opinion... ...y be in the form of questions, because I remain coach first and ...g smile)

The various missions that we carried out have shown us that this interview has become a classic and a serious settlement of trust between the client and us, even if the exercise is not obvious to them. On one hand, we have the demonstration of the difficulty of being appreciative. On the other hand, it is complicated when it comes to proposing attractive things, in the form of an invitation rather than a summons.

Each time, our contacts are thankful to be offered this stage of reflection: they perceive very early in the process that they can smartly be the forerunner of the cultural transformation of their organisation, demonstrating visible signs of exemplarity.

To help, I have created the following the Speed-Hosting Flashcard.

Speed-Hosting Flash Card
Get myself ready as a good host

Question	Role	Answer
What outcome would I like to achieve at the end of the experiment? What is my intention?	Initiator	
Who do I have in mind for a first experience? What makes me particularly think of these people? How am I going to invite these people? What will I communicate to them? How do they receive this invitation arrive? What returns do you get?	Inviter	
Where do I want to make my first experience? When? What details do I have to pay attention?	Space Creator	
How will I set the 'rules of the game'? Or how are we going to agree on shared rules?	Gatekeeper	
How am I going to welcome my guests? What words will create a smart context? Where will I stand? How will I connect each other? Who knows who? How will I connect them to the context? What do they already know?	Connector	
During the experiment, what do i do? What do they see me doing?	Co-Participant	

Covering the last mile with Host Leadership: the birth of Agile Humanware

When I was 40, ten years ago, I said to myself:

> "Laurent, you have already been working for 15 years. Ok to go for 15 more years, but then let's be free, so that you can leave the corporate world, give your time to people who cannot afford our 'technology'. Keep also a lot of time for yourself to explore new areas, mainly outdoors as you are delighted by mountain biking, hiking, permaculture, etc..."

For a long time, I have been reflecting and setting down various tiny stepping stones to pave my way to this destination. Year after year, I have been integrating top-notch components experienced in the corporate world to help to deeply (re-)engage people and teams, with purpose, to deliver value, and to nurture a culture of self-improvement. Sometimes, it was even linked to smart entrepreneurship.

During this journey, I also became more and more convinced that this material would be really helpful outside the corporate world, to help people in the challenged world to access a decent life, although they cannot afford our services. I am now also considering helping NGOs, to spread this work.

So was born the idea of Agile Humanware technology. We all know things like software, hardware, process ware, etc... I decided to name my material "Agile Humanware" because we also need great technology when dealing with humans. I now feel an inner pleasure when I introduce myself as a neoCTO (Chief Technology Officer) for any organisation willing to acquire this humanware technology, and impact our planet in a positive way.

Agile Humanware is a system assembling great-practical-powerful signatures:

- A language that will induce appreciative-and-constructive interactions between people: The Solution Focus, after the brief therapy work devised by Steve de Shazer and Insoo Kim Berg, and developed by a tremendous community
- riential and delivery mode fuelled by attractive workshops: cilitation (Innovation Games® by Luke Hohman, by Dave Gray and Sunny Brown), now enhanced by the structures of Henri Lipanowicz and Keith McCandless

(http://www.liberatingstructures.com/) combined with nice flavours of design thinking (Bason & Austin, 2019).

- A smart engine to steer the journey, driven by tiny outcomes, delivered step by step, with a lot of learnings: the Mobius Loop (mobiusloop.com), created by Gabrielle Benefield, illustrated by a marvellous inspiring experience run by Kubair Shirazee in Pakistan (Mobius Loop, 2019).
- A compass to guide the journey, based on Heart of Agile (heartofagile.com), a signature development of Alistair Cockburn, one of the original authors of the Agile manifesto. Heart of Agile is a pure Agile compass with four axes: deliver, collaborate, reflect, improve. Reflect, for me, is the cornerstone.

- *Do I see an objection in your eyes?*
- *Fine Laurent, but your 'package' seems to be a little 'heavy' to digest!*
- *Yes, I can understand that, at first glance, it might be hard. But let me tell you how I help people to jump quickly into it: first, I teach them the basics for this new language, Solution Focus. It is really like learning a new language, so that we start with words, then sentences, and questions. Finally, like learning Spanish or any other language, you have to practise every day to scale up. Surprisingly, they will become fluent in a very short time. Solution Focus is offers such new refreshing openings that people love it. Sometimes, I have shared some nice gifts offered by Marilee Adams in her great book "Change your questions, change your life".*
- *Oooh! This is one more thing you are adding!!*
- *Yes. This is an easy book to read: the first 2/3 is a novel; the last 1/3 is a collection of 12 tools like the Q-Storming or the Choice map. But anyway, I received some good feedback from people who read it, so I recommend reading it.*
- *Fine, fine. What else do you do to carry on with the learning of your humanware?*
- *During the acquisition of the Solution Focus language, I help them to reflect on their progress, using Solution Focus questions. I also use the Mobius Loop without letting them know. Undercover! I will reveal it later, then there will be no debate as they experienced it!*
- *Learning by doing, isn't it?*
- *Yes, pure reverse pedagogy.*

- And then?
- Then I will also start to reveal progressively Heart of Agile, that I also used to locate their progress. We won't go into all the details, but at least looking at the "reflect" and "improve-by-experiment" axes. They easily get it because they have already been into it without knowing this material. Learning by doing, again.
- Finally, you use few things, but always connected
- You got it! That's my way: simple, nudge, or "jugaad" as they say in India.
- And what about the 'attractive workshops'?
- According to the things they have to explore, I teach them relevant workshops. Better than that, I train them, so that they can facilitate by themselves as soon as possible.
- How long does it last?
- For them? My best hope is that it will last the rest of their lives! Life is a never-ending story, until the end. With this loop, the compass, the language, and an initial workshops kit, they have everything to build the next steps. For me, the Agile Humanware is like a fab'lab' to nurture a continuous evolving culture of work, 100% adaptive, regarding the present context, the existing resources.
- I love the fab'lab' analogy. It's true that, according to what you explained, it makes sense that you are installing a set of tools for creation. It is like a homebrew working culture.
- Anything missing?
- Yes! Where is Host Leadership in this story??
- Right!! Host Leadership is indeed fully embedded in this system. It has been an essential ingredient to give birth to this project, being a kind of cement between the different components. Host Leadership is everywhere-so-nowhere. It is in the DNA of the Agile Humanware: to invite people to adopt it, to train them to use it, to help them to gift it to others, toward a never ending pollination.
- Thats sounds incredibly powerful, smart and generous.
- I hope so. What I'm sure of is that Host Leadership helped me a lot to cover a part of the last mile. Now, it's time to invite guests!

References

Bason, C., & Austin, R. D. (2019). *The Right Way to Lead Design Thinking. Harvard Business Review.* March-April 2019, pp. 82–91. Retrieved from https://hbr.org/2019/03/the-right-way-to-lead-design-thinking.

Mobius Loop. (2019). *Mobius for Social Change.* Retrieved from https://www.mobiusloop.com/case_studies/peace-through-prosperity-creating-a-nation-of-micro-entrepreneurs/

Author

*For the last six years, **Laurent Sarrazin** has been helping organisations to become Agile, using a unique blend of Solution Focus coaching, Heart of Agile, Host Leadership, a bit of Management 3.0 and a lot of playful facilitation. In 2013, after 20+ years in the IT Agile field, working for the investment banking sector in France and India, he decided to fill a gap in the Agile market. At this time, we were quite adept at helping IT teams to move toward agility but, unfortunately, people were bouncing into cultural walls "siloing" their organisations, as an IT team is only a 'node' in the global value chain. Laurent created Rupture(21 to initially help executives and the various management levels, beyond IT, to share a common destination enabling a whole alignment, and then invite their teams into an Agile journey, guided by an engine named "Rupture Douce". Laurent is also a writer, teacher and traveller and is now turning his know-how into the "Agile Humanware" project, to help underprivileged people to access a decent life. www.rupture21.com, Laurent.sarrazin@rupture21.com, @bangalaurent*

30

Why were you born?

Martin Rutte (Canada)
Founder, Project Heaven on Earth

> Martin Rutte is engaged in a long term project to help everyone see the world differently. He is not only a host leader to the project, but has also discovered that a balanced combination of long-term vision and short-term action espoused by host leaders in moving forwards in an emerging world offers possibilities for new engagement and hope. Here is Martin's story...

There is a desire, a longing, deep within us, for a world that works. We yearn for the immoral and recurring problems of the planet – war, hunger, disease, and poverty – not simply to get better but once and for all to *end*. We want our soul's dream of a world that inspires hope, engagement and creativity to flourish.

To put it simply, we want Heaven on Earth.

At first that may seem like an unrealistic, utopian fantasy ... but please bear with me. We've already proven that humanity can accomplish the extraordinary. We've returned a human from the moon, we've extended life by transplanting hearts, we're refining nanotechnology, and we're 3D printing human organs.

But our current human story also contains suffering, fear and horror. Their apparent strength contributes to our feelings of powerlessness. We believe that we are unable to make a true, deep and lasting difference in our world. Yet even through these sufferings, times of Heaven on Earth still emerge and flower. We long for more of this, for more Heaven on Earth.

How can we do this?

We can establish a new model, a new story of existence, a new collective human purpose. This new civilization-fuelling vision expands what's possible, focuses on and multiplies what works, and confronts and reduces what doesn't work. We then need to name this new story, this story of what it means to be a human and what it means to be humanity. We name it Heaven on Earth.

The way to begin this new story, like we begin any new story, is by declaration, by giving our word, by saying "Heaven on Earth *is* our new story". I've asked thousands of people to tell me a time when they experienced Heaven on Earth. What they immediately do is answer my question with clarity and certainty. Some share moments of the birth of a child, an appreciation of nature, or a moment of deep communion.

What no one does is ask what I mean by 'Heaven on Earth.' What they do is simply answer the question. How can they do that? It's because there's an "Already Knowing" about what Heaven on Earth is that lives within each of us. You can find out a lot more about how this works in my book Project Heaven On Earth (Rutte, 2018).

Let me ask you the first Heaven on Earth question. (Please answer it now for yourself.)

1) **Recall a time when you experienced Heaven on Earth. What was happening?**

Heaven on Earth, like the desire for love, peace and joy, is hard-wired into us – an eternal, innate truth that we want to extend from a moment to always. And you can begin extending it to always, by answering the second Heaven on Earth question:

2) **Imagine you have a magic wand and with it you can create Heaven on Earth. What is Heaven on Earth for you?**

Sit quietly and let the answer to this second question emerge from within you. Say your answer out loud, write it down.

Now answer the third Heaven on Earth question:

3) **What simple, easy, concrete step will you take in the next 24 hours to make Heaven on Earth real?**

It's important that you take a *simple* step within the next 24 hours. Why? So you begin, so you start to create Heaven on Earth, not in some far-distant future, but now! You begin the new Heaven on Earth story by beginning – by declaring this is the new story and taking your first steps today and tomorrow and the day after that and on and on, building an unstoppable momentum.

Did you know the Oxford English Dictionary defines "heaven" as a noun and, surprisingly, also as a verb? Yes, a verb, "to heaven," so you can go around heavening all day.

Make getting started easy. You can smile at two people today. You can help someone learn to read. You can welcome a new immigrant family into your community. You can buy some new toys for the local children's hospital. You can simply ask two people in the next 24 hours the three Heaven on Earth questions and ask each of them to ask two people the next day, and so on. (If everyone did this simple act, it would take just 32 days to reach the over seven billion people on Earth – small acts, huge impact.)

Your unique contribution to this building process, that only you can make, is vital. Author Frances Hodgson Burnett said:

> "At first people refuse to believe that a strange new thing can be done, and then they begin to hope it can be done, then they see it can be done, then it is done... and all the world wonders why it was not done centuries ago."

I believe the vast majority of the world's people want to participate and play their part in a new global vision, a new human story of hope and momentum. United, we can and will create a grand and global planetary chorus, each person adding their voice, their gift, their inspiration. Through our declaration, our intention, and our actions, more Heaven on Earth will be created and experienced. This truly is the work of humanity. This truly is fulfilling the deep longing we have for the world we want.

Having your dream for the world come true is exactly what your dream is supposed to do. What one simple thing will you do today?

Thank you for playing your part, for being an Agent of Heaven on Earth.

Reference

Rutte, M. (2018). *Project Heaven on Earth: The 3 simple questions that will help you change the world ... easily.* Santa Fe NM: 3 Questions Publishing.

Author

Martin Rutte is an international speaker and management consultant. As President of Livelihood, a management consulting firm in Santa Fe, NM, USA, he explores the deeper meaning of work and its contribution to society. The company's areas of service include: strategic vision, corporate spirit, performance management and creative leadership. Martin has worked with such organisations as The World Bank, Sony Pictures Entertainment, Southern California Edison, Virgin Records, Esso Petroleum and London Life Insurance, helping them expand their outlook and position themselves for the future. He was the first Canadian to address the Corporate Leadership & Ethics Forum of The Harvard Business School, returning for four consecutive years as keynote speaker. Martin is a co-author of the New York Times *business bestseller,* Chicken Soup for the Soul at Work, *with over one million copies sold and translations into 24 languages. He helps people discover what Heaven on Earth is for them and what simple, easy, concrete action they can take in the next 24 hours to begin making that real. He has presented workshops and given talks on Heaven on Earth in: the US, Canada, England, Germany, Brazil, Mexico, Spain, Sweden & Costa Rica. www.projectheavenonearth.com*

Index

A
Acknowledgement, 15, 32, 89, 116–117, 220
Adventure. *See* Outdoor adventure activities
Agile coach, 184
Agile Humanware, 236, 248–250
Ant Country, 207
Appreciative Inquiry, 134, 187
Art of Hosting movement, 233
Assimoco Group. *See* Organizational transformation (Assimoco Group)

B
Beaming, 192–193
  Chameleon Shuffle, 197–198
  Circle of Presence, 193
  integrated routine, devising, 193
  successful, tips for, 193–194
  taking time to take position, 194
  white box approach for purpose and positional tactics, 194
Belonging, sense of, 36
Bonington, Sir Chris, 42
Boundaries, 3, 39, 55, 69, 77
Buffett, Warren, 203, 204
Burnett, Frances Hodgson, 254
Business Planner orientation, 207

C
Certified Agile Coaches (CACs), 103
Certified Scrum Professional (CSP), 103
Certified Team Coaches (CTCs), 103, 106
  special interest group, 104
    Host Leadership model, 104–105
    impact, 106
    rotation of hosts, 105–106
Chaleff, Ira, 203
Challenge by Choice, 47
Chameleon Shuffle, 194–198
Change agents, 69

Check-in technique, in stand-up meetings, 94
Circle of Presence, 193, 194
Circle of Trust, 190–191, 194, 195
Coach, 101, 147, 173–174, 184, 187. *See also* Certified Agile Coaches (CACs); Certified Team Coaches (CTCs)
Coaching, 173–174
  conversations, 92–93, 95, 115, 116, 239
  training, 239–241
  User's Guide To The Future, 207–209
Co-adventurer, 43, 48
Co-creation, 12–13. *See also* Housing strategies, co-creation of
Collaboration, 45, 47
Company-wide process improvements, 128–131
  connector, 129
  co-participator, 130
  declined invitations, handling, 130–131
  gatekeeper, 129
  inviter, 128, 129, 130–131
  private party, 130
  process improvement teams, 129
  questionnaires, 128
  space creator, 129
Confidentiality, 14, 15, 17, 19
Conflicts, 64–65
  'fight or flight' reaction triangle, 66–67
  harmful effects of, 65
  mediator, 72–73
  paradigms, 71–72
  resolution/intervention, 68
    connector, 70
    co-participator, 70
    gatekeeper, 69
    initiator, 69
    inviter, 68
    space creator, 68–69
    stepping back, 71

stepping forward, 71
tough response to, 65–67, 71
Connection, 3. *See also* Connector
connecting with self, 232–233
and dinner party experience, 21, 24, 26
with other host leaders, 7
in outdoor adventure activities, 45, 48
Connector, 3, 147, 232
co-creation of housing strategies, 17–18
company-wide process improvements, 129
conflict resolution, 70
Global Virtual Teams (GVTs) Project, 57–59, 60
hybrid organisations, 77, 78
organizational transformation, 135
outdoor adventure activities, 48
rural development management, 32–33
stand-up meetings, 94–95
trainer as, 111
Container, 69, 92, 93, 94, 125
Conversation partner, 215
Co-participator, 3, 147, 183
co-creation of housing strategies, 18–19
company-wide process improvements, 130
conflict resolution, 70
Global Virtual Teams (GVTs) Project, 57–59, 61
Host Leadership workshop, 157
hybrid organisations, 77, 78
organizational transformation, 136
outdoor adventure activities, 48
self sustaining community, creation of, 105, 106
stand-up meetings, 95–96
trainer as, 107, 111
Co-production, 12
Courage, 37
Courageous Followership model, 203
Cross-cultural teams. *See* Global Virtual Teams (GVTs) Project

D
Desire-lines, 187
Dialogic Organization Development, 122–123
Dialogue cards, in Relationship Retro, 97

content, 99
using, 99–100
Dinner party. *See* School leaders, Host Leadership goals of
Diversity Icebreaker, 12, 13, 15–16
Double linking, 95
Drive, managerial routine of, 242–243

E
Executives, as hosts, 243–247
Expedition, 42–43. *See also* Outdoor adventure activities

F
Facilitation/facilitating
of change process, 213–214
vs. hosting, 125–126
organizational transformation, 133–138
Facilitators, 16, 44, 184
as host leaders, 54–59
Feedback, 22, 23, 25, 77, 89, 134, 221
Focus of attention, being, 4, 59, 62, 95, 105, 106, 136, 216, 231
Follower-leader relationship, 141–143, 201, 202. *See also* Guests
contract, 202
metaphors, 141–143
risk and permission, 203–204
Freedom of association, 36

G
Gallery, host in, 5, 30, 31, 32, 58, 59, 62, 96, 105, 129, 136, 192, 194, 217
Gatekeeper, 3, 147, 190
co-creation of housing strategies, 15–17
company-wide process improvements, 129
conflict resolution, 69
Global Virtual Teams (GVTs) Project, 54–55, 60
Host Leadership workshop, 152–153
hybrid organisations, 77, 78
organizational transformation, 136
outdoor adventure activities, 47–48
rural development management, 31–32
self sustaining community, creation of, 105

Index

stand-up meetings, 92–93
   trainer as, 110–111
Gemba walks, 192
Generative Change Model, 121–123
Generative conversations
   checklist for hosting, 126–127
   facilitating *vs.* hosting, 125–126
   preparation for, 124–125
Give & Take Matrix game, 242
Global Virtual Teams (GVTs) Project, 53–54
   communication tools, 56, 60
   phases of, 57
      adjourning, 58
      forming, 57
      norming, 58
      performing, 58
      storming, 58
   project facilitators as host leaders, 54
      connectors and co-participants, 57–59
      initiation, invitation, and gatekeeping, 54–55
      space, creation of, 55–57
   project hub, 56, 57
   students as host leaders, 59
      call to action, response to, 59–60
      fostering good communication, 60–61
      sharing leadership, 61–62
   video conferences, 57
Gompertz, Will, 213
Greenleaf, Robert, 141
Growth zones, hosts in, 190
Guests, 201
   being with, 4–5, 29, 31, 32, 129, 130, 136, 186, 217
   choices of, 46, 47
   connections and relationships, 45, 48
   co-responsibility of, 46
   as followers, 143
   and hosts, relationship, 201, 202
   invitations declined by, 130–131
   opinion of, 30
   risk and permission, 203–204
   sense of belonging, 36
   in stand-up meetings, 93, 95
   welcoming, 36, 37, 152–153

H
Hero leader, 45, 104, 146, 228
Horizon, 206, 207, 212, 213
   hopes, dreams and intentions, 206
   small next steps, 206
   tiny signs of progress, 207
Host, 201. *See also* Host leaders
   courage of, 37
   essence of, 231–232
   feelings of, 38
   flexible, 3
   in growth zones, 190
   and guests, relationship, 201, 202
   humility of, 38
   as leader, 143, 202
   in performance zones, 189–190
   responsibility for, 38, 40
   rotation, 105–106
   team members as, stand-up meetings, 90–91
   turning executives into, 243–247
   wisdom of, 38
Host leaders
   acknowledgement of, 15
   connecting with other host leaders, 7
   invitational, 25
   noticing. *See* Noticing
   project facilitators as, 54–59
   students as, 59–62
   trainers as, 107–112
Host leaders, positions for, 4, 25, 155–157, 189, 228–231
   beaming. *See* Beaming
   being focus of attention, 4, 59, 62, 95, 105, 106, 136, 216, 231
   Chameleon Shuffle, 194–198
   gallery, 5, 30, 31, 32, 58, 59, 62, 96, 105, 129, 136, 192, 194, 217
   with guests, 4–5, 29, 31, 32, 129, 130, 136, 186, 217
   and noticing, 216–217
   private place, 5, 32, 58, 59, 95, 129, 136, 155, 157, 185, 217, 231, 232, 237, 238
   ROTI-Keeper, 241
Host leaders, roles of, 2, 13–14, 46, 49, 147–148, 155–157, 189, 228–231

Chameleon Shuffle, 194–198
connector. *See* Connector
co-participator. *See* Co-participator
gatekeeper. *See* Gatekeeper
initiator. *See* Initiator
inviter. *See* Inviter
shapeshifting. *See* Shapeshifting
space creator. *See* Space creator
Host Leadership, 44–46, 107, 202, 226, 236, 237
 concept, 67–68
 in conflict resolution and intervention, 68–72
 as dance, 21, 136
 experimentation, 7, 121, 122
 as a feedback tool, 134
 flexibility of, 45–46
 goals with, 21–27
 as integrating metaphor, 147
 introducing to organizations, 145–149
 intuitive style of, 201
 Maasai view of. *See* Maasai view of Host Leadership
 as metaphor. *See* Metaphor, Host Leadership as
 strategies for promoting, 149
 third metric for success, 231
Host Leadership workshop, 150
 benefits from, 153–154
 co-participator, 157
 invitation, 151
 outcomes, 158–159
 physical space, 152
 posters, 161–167
 reflecting teams, 158
 roles and positions, 155–157
  using, 157
 steps, 155–157
 timeliness of metaphor, 154–155
 welcoming guests, 152–153
Housing strategies, co-creation of, 11–12
 connector, 17–18
 co-participator, 18–19
 gatekeeper, 15–17
 ideas of participants, 16

 initiator, 14
 inviter, 14
 in practice, 13
 sharing, 15, 17–18
 space creator, 14–15
 theoretical background, 12–13
Humility, 38
Hybrid organisations. *See* Roskilde Festival

I
Informal leadership, in hybrid organisations, 77
Initiator, 2, 147, 195, 237–238, 245
 co-creation of housing strategies, 14
 conflict resolution, 69
 Global Virtual Teams (GVTs) Project, 54–55
 hybrid organisations, 77, 78
 organizational transformation, 136
 outdoor adventure activities, 47
 rural development management, 29–30
 self sustaining community, creation of, 105
 stand-up meetings, 87–88
 trainer as, 108
Inner work, 228, 231, 232
Invitation
 accepting, 226
 conflict, dealing with, 116–117
 creating, 221
 declined, handling, 130–131
 emotional, 219–220
 good, properties of, 220
 Host Leadership goals of school leaders, 22–23
 Host Leadership workshop, 151
 powerful, aspects of, 89
 writing, 238
Invitation Frame, 238
Inviter, 3, 147, 219, 238, 245
 co-creation of housing strategies, 14
 company-wide process improvements, 128, 129, 130–131
 conflict resolution, 68
 Global Virtual Teams (GVTs) Project, 54–55
 Host Leadership workshop, 151
 hybrid organisations, 77, 78

introducing, 219–220
organizational transformation, 136
outdoor adventure activities, 46
rural development management, 30
self sustaining community, creation of, 105
stand-up meetings, 88–91, 95
trainer as, 108–109

J
Journaling, 185

K
Kanban board, 86–87, 95
Kitchen. *See* Private place

L
Leader
  dilemmas for, 227
  and follower
    contract between, 202
    metaphors, 141–143
    relationship, 141–143, 201, 202
    risk and permission, 203–204
  hero, 45, 104, 146, 228
  as hosts, 53–54, 150
  as problem-solver, 39
  team/organisational, 183–184
Leadership, 225
  as engagement, 44
  informal, 77
  and interaction among people, 146
  post-heroic, 228
  role, 202
  self-leadership, 202
  Servant-Leadership, 44, 141, 242
  sharing, 61–62
  skills, 200
  styles, 200
Leave No Trace, 47

M
Ma (empty space), 194
Maasai view of Host Leadership, 34–37
  boundaries, 39
  courage, 37

humility and wisdom, 38
respect, 38–39
responsibility, 38–39, 40
self-confidence, 40
trust, 39–40
welcoming ceremony, 36
Mandela, Nelson, 219
Mediator, in conflict resolution, 72–73
Metaphor, Host Leadership as, 113, 189, 226
  conflict with invitation, dealing with, 116–117
  flourishing new manager, 115–116
  introducing Host Leadership to organizations, 145–149
  leader-follower metaphors and relationships, 141–143
  newbie project manager, 114–115
  presentation review, 113–114
Mindfulness technique, in stand-up meetings, 94
Motivation, 32, 71, 84
Munger, Charlie, 203

N
Non-compliance, spotting, 187
Noticing, 212–213, 228
  and conversation partner, 215
  facilitation of change process, 213–215
  and host leader positions, 216–217
  muscle, training, 215–216

O
Objectives and Key Results (OKRs), 194
Open Space Technology, 125
Organisational leader, 183–184
Organizational transformation (Assimoco Group), 132–133
  connector, 135
  co-participator, 136
  exercises, 135–136
  gatekeeper, 136
  initiator, 136
  internal leaders, 133–134
  inviter, 136
  positions, 136, 137

roles, 135–136, 137
  space creator, 136
Organizations, introducing Host Leadership to, 145–146
  attitudes, 147
  role model, 146–147, 148
  roles, 147–148
  speaking loudly, 148
  starting straight away, 148
  strategies for promoting Host Leadership, 149
Outdoor adventure activities, 42
  Challenge by Choice, 47
  connector, 48
  co-participator/co-adventurer, 43, 48
  exceptions, 43
  gatekeeper, 47–48
  Host Leadership, 43–44, 45–48
  initiator, 47
  inviter, 46
  Leave No Trace, 47
  risk assessments, 47, 48
  Servant-Leadership, 44
  space creator, 47
Outer work, 231, 232
Outward Bound Process Model, 43
Overtrust, 203

P
Pain points, 186
Paradigms, and conflicts, 71–72
Paradoxes, in hybrid organisations, 77–78
Pasteur, Louis, 6
Performance zones, hosts in, 189–190
Permission, 203–204
Post-heroic leadership, 228
Powerful invitation, aspects of, 89, 220
  acknowledgement, 89, 220
  attraction, 89, 220
  choice, 89, 220
Power of not knowing, 30
Private place, 5, 32, 58, 59, 95, 129, 136, 155, 157, 185, 217, 231, 232, 237, 238
Probes, 7, 121, 122
Problem-solver, leader as, 39

Process improvement. *See* Company-wide process improvements
Project Heaven on Earth, 252–254
Psychological contracts, in Relationship Retro, 97, 98, 101

R
Relationship Retro, 97
  dialogue cards, 97
  content, 99
  using, 99–100
  psychological contracts, 97, 98, 101
  rationale, 100
  results, 100–101
  special qualities of, 101
  timing, 101
Relationships
  building, 4, 44–46
  guest-host, 201, 202
  leader-follower, 141–143
  trainer-participant, 107, 108
Resilience, 232
Respect, 38–39
Retrospective, 97, 101. *See also* Relationship Retro
Risk, 203–204
Roskilde Festival, 74, 79
  complexity, clashes and contradictions, 75–76
  connector, 77, 78
  co-participator, 77, 78
  gatekeeper, 77, 78
  initiator, 77, 78
  inviter, 77, 78
  leadership development, 76
    diversity in volunteer team, 76–77
    informal leadership, 77
    limited time, 78
    organisational paradoxes, 77–78
  operation of, 74–75
  space creator, 77, 78
ROTI-Keeper, 241
Rural development management, 28–29
  connector, 32–33
  gatekeeper, 31–32

initiator, 29–30
inviter, 30
space creator, 30–31

S
Scharmer, Otto, 12
School leaders, Host Leadership goals of, 21
   connection, 24, 26
   dinner party, 21, 23
   invitation, 22–23
   menus, 23
   reflections, 23–25
Scrum Alliance Certified Team Coach (CTC) certification, 103
Scrum master, 184
Self, connecting with, 232–233
Self-care, 232
Self-confidence, 39, 40
Self sustaining community, creation of, 103–104
   Certified Team Coach special interest group
      impact, 106
      starting, 104
   co-participator, 105, 106
   gatekeeper, 105
   initiator, 105
   inviter, 105
   launching with Host Leadership, 104–105
   rotation of hosts, 105–106
   use of new technology, 105
Sensemaker, 187
Servant-Leadership, 43, 44, 141, 242
Shackleton, Sir Ernest, 42
Shapeshifting, 190
   Chameleon Shuffle, 195–196
   Circle of Trust, 190–191
   learning and teaching, 191–192
   performance, praising, 192
   successful, tips for, 191–192
   verbs, host roles as, 191
Small next steps, 206
Small talk, before stand-up meetings, 94
Social housing. *See* Housing strategies, co-creation of
Social innovation, 12

Software company, creation of, 168–172, 178–179
   afternoon tea, 176
   coaching, 173–174
   hotels, 172
   innovation, 175
   key customer facing, 174
   measurement, 176
   member surveys, 176
   new business development, 173
   office design, 176
   project guidance, 174
   projects, 175
   Q-cell structure, 170–171, 177
   quorum, 172
   recruitment, 174–175
   results, 175–176
   showroom, 174
   vision and values, 171
   who does what?, 172–173
   workshops, 169
Solution Focused practice, 43, 46, 215–216
Solution Focused Reflecting Teams model, 158
Space
   for change, 69
   functions of, 47
   influence on thinking, 91
   interactional, 154
   ma (empty space), 194
   physical, 91, 95, 152
Space creator, 3, 147, 233, 245
   co-creation of housing strategies, 14–15
   company-wide process improvements, 129
   conflict resolution, 68–69
   Global Virtual Teams (GVTs) Project, 55–57
   Host Leadership workshop, 152
   hybrid organisations, 77, 78
   organizational transformation, 136
   outdoor adventure activities, 47
   rural development management, 30–31
   stand-up meetings, 91–92
   trainer as, 109–110
Speed-Hosting Smartcard, 247
Spotlight. *See* Focus of attention, being
Stakeholders, hosting, 121

attendance at engagement events, 124
diversity of participants, 125
Generative Change Model, 121–123
generative conversations
  checklist for hosting, 126–127
  facilitating vs. hosting, 125–126
  preparation for, 124–125
  purpose, 124
Stand-up meetings, 83
  characteristics of, 84–85
  check-in technique, 94
  coaching conversations, 92–93, 95
  connections with other teams, 95
  connector, 94–95
  co-participator, 95–96
  definition of, 83
  efficiency of, 84
  formats, 85
    Kanban wall, 86–87
    Three Question format, 86, 90
    4-Part Game Structure, 89–90
  gatekeeper, 92–93
  goals of, 95
  hypothesis template, 88
  initiator, 87–88
  inviter, 88–91, 95
  inviting team members to host, 90–91
  large mobile white board, 91
  mindfulness technique, 94
  powerful invitation, aspects of, 89, 220
  purpose of, 83, 95
  signals, 93, 95
  small talk before, 94
  space
    comfortableness of, 91
    customisation of, 91, 92
    space creator, 91–92
  structure of, 85
  timing, 85, 93
  virtual, 92, 94, 95
Stepping back, 2, 21, 67, 217, 229–230, 231
  company-wide process improvements, 128, 129, 130–131
  conflict resolution, 71
  dinner party, 24, 25
  facilitation of change process, 213, 214
  Global Virtual Teams (GVTs) Project, 58, 59, 62
  organizational transformation, 134, 137
  rural development management, 30, 31, 32, 33
  stand-up meetings, 90, 92, 95
Stepping forward, 2, 21, 147, 216, 229–230, 231
  co-creation of housing strategies, 15
  company-wide process improvements, 129, 130–131
  conflict resolution, 71
  dinner party, 23, 25
  facilitation of change process, 213
  Global Virtual Teams (GVTs) Project, 59, 60, 62
  organizational transformation, 134, 137
  rural development management, 30
Stories, 186–187

T
Team leader, 183–184
Theory U, 12, 13, 15, 16, 134
Therapeutic alliance, 44, 45, 47, 49
Third metric for success, 231
Topics for initiation, identification of, 183
  contexts as sources for, 183–184
  desire-lines, 187
  developing habits/rhythms for checking in with yourself, 184
  feelings/sensations, noticing, 185
  non-compliance, spotting, 187
  pain points, 186
  Problem To Solution framework, 186
  stories, building, 186–187
  things that make your life/work easier and better, 185–186
  verbal/written descriptions, building, 185
Trainer, as host leader, 107–108
  connector, 111
  co-participator, 107, 111
  gatekeeper, 110–111
  initiator, 108
  inviter, 108–109

space creator, 109–110
trainer-participant relationship, 107, 108
Trust, 39–40, 47, 53, 55, 61, 71, 190, 191, 202, 203

U
U-curve. *See* Theory U
User's Guide To The Future, 205–207, 212
   Ant Country, 207
   as coaching tool, 207–209
      reaction from coachees, 210
   hopes, dreams and intentions, 206
   horizon, 206
   precursors/building blocks, 206
   small next steps, 206
   tiny signs of progress, 207

V
Volunteers. *See* Roskilde Festival

W
Wellbeing, 232
Wisdom, 38, 204
Working agreements, in retrospective, 97
Workshop. *See* Host Leadership workshop